That Tuesday
in November

That Tuesday in November

How Presidential Elections Changed History

Mike Henry

ROWMAN & LITTLEFIELD
Lanham • Boulder • New York • London

Published by Rowman & Littlefield
A wholly owned subsidiary of The Rowman & Littlefield Publishing Group, Inc.
4501 Forbes Boulevard, Suite 200, Lanham, Maryland 20706
www.rowman.com

6 Tinworth Street, London SE11 5AL, United Kingdom

British Library Cataloguing in Publication Information Available

Library of Congress Control Number: 2020943414

ISBN: 978-1-4758-5823-5 (cloth)
ISBN: 978-1-4758-5824-2 (pbk.)
ISBN: 978-1-4758-5825-9 (electronic)

Contents

Preface   vii

Chapter 1. The Election of 1788–1789: George Washington   1

Chapter 2. The Election of 1800: John Adams, Incumbent (Federalist) vs. Thomas Jefferson (Democratic-Republican)   7

Chapter 3. The Election of 1820: James Monroe, Incumbent (Democratic-Republican)   13

Chapter 4. The Election of 1824: John Quincy Adams (Democratic-Republican) vs. Andrew Jackson (Democratic-Republican)   17

Chapter 5. The Election of 1852: Franklin Pierce (Democrat) vs. Winfield Scott (Whig)   25

Chapter 6. The Election of 1860: Stephen Douglas (Democrat), John C. Breckenridge (Southern Democrats), John Bell (Constitutional Union) vs. Abraham Lincoln (Republican)   31

Chapter 7. The Election of 1864: Abraham Lincoln, Incumbent (Republican) vs. George B. McClellan (Democrat)   37

Chapter 8. The Election of 1876: Rutherford B. Hayes (Republican) vs. Samuel J. Tilden (Democrat)   47

Chapter 9. The Election of 1892: Benjamin Harrison, Incumbent (Republican) vs. Grover Cleveland (Democrat)   55

Chapter 10. The Election of 1896: William McKinley (Republican) vs. William Jennings Bryan (Democrat)   59

Chapter 11. The Election of 1900: William McKinley, Incumbent
(Republican) vs. William Jennings Bryan (Democrat)   65

Chapter 12. The Election of 1912: William Howard Taft (Republican)
vs. Woodrow Wilson (Democrat) and Theodore Roosevelt
(Bull Moose)   73

Chapter 13. The Election of 1916: Woodrow Wilson, Incumbent
(Democrat) vs. Charles Evans Hughes (Republican)   81

Chapter 14. The Election of 1932: Herbert Hoover, Incumbent
(Republican) vs. Franklin D. Roosevelt (Democrat)   89

Chapter 15. The Election of 1944: Franklin D. Roosevelt, Incumbent
(Democrat) vs. Thomas Dewey (Republican)   99

Chapter 16. The Election of 1948: Harry S. Truman, Incumbent
(Democrat) vs. Thomas Dewey (Republican)   111

Chapter 17. The Election of 1960: John F. Kennedy (Democrat)
vs. Richard Nixon (Republican)   121

Chapter 18. The Election of 1968: Richard Nixon (Republican)
vs. Hubert Humphrey (Democrat)   133

Chapter 19. The Election of 1972: Richard Nixon, Incumbent
(Republican) vs. George McGovern (Democrat)   145

Chapter 20. The Election of 1980: Jimmy Carter, Incumbent
(Democrat) vs. Ronald Reagan (Republican)   155

Chapter 21. The Election of 1992: George H. W. Bush, Incumbent
(Republican) vs. Bill Clinton (Democrat) and Ross Perot
(Independent)   165

Chapter 22. The Election of 2000: George W. Bush (Republican)
vs. Al Gore (Democrat)   175

Chapter 23. The Election of 2008: Barack Obama (Democrat)
vs. John McCain (Republican)   185

Chapter 24. The Election of 2012: Barack Obama, Incumbent
(Democrat) vs. Mitt Romney (Republican)   191

Chapter 25. The Election of 2016: Hillary Rodham Clinton
(Democrat) vs. Donald J. Trump (Republican)   197

Bibliography   207

About the Author   227

Preface

Greetings once again. Every four years adult Americans have the opportunity to express their views about the direction of the country by voting for its leader. Since 1788, the citizenry has gone forth in an orderly and dignified manner to decide who the person will be that will have the responsibility of wearing the moniker, the World's Most Powerful Person.

While everything in the nation doesn't work perfectly, the election system has been pretty close. Voters don't have to worry about showing up at their polling place with weapons drawn in their direction and orders of whom they will vote. Subsequently, the exercise is usually noneventful although many times the end result is unexpected.

That's not to say that every election or president was memorable. In fact, many were not, but like other events, there are those elections and individuals that stand out.

As an example, George Washington wasn't just the first president, but the first war hero to be elevated by the people to become the nation's chief executive. That paved the way for other battlefield stalwarts like Grant and Eisenhower, each of whom had never held a political office, to make their way to 1600 Pennsylvania Avenue. It's a trend that shows that the United States loves its military heroes and rewards them with command of the nation.

While the Founding Fathers could only hope that they had covered all the possibilities when it came to elections, new challenges, such as television, presented obstacles that were unimaginable at the time that they were trying to hammer out the Constitution.

The reality is that presidential elections are now and will continue to be a work in progress. With all of technology's advances, there will always be a few missteps along the way. However, the people and stories that compose US election history have made it an aspect of the country's past that provides a fair share of examination from both the inside and out.

1

The Election of 1788–1789

George Washington

"George Washington is the only president who didn't blame the previous administration for his troubles."

—Anonymous

It can be argued that America's first presidential election is the most unique. That's because there were no political parties, incumbents, or records to run on. In essence, the practice of electing a leader for the world's newest country was an exercise that was starting from scratch.

On September 13, 1788, the Confederation Congress passed an election ordinance, which set the date for choosing electors (January 7, 1789); electing the president (February 4, 1789); and beginning the new government under the Constitution (March 4, 1789). There were no political conventions as there were no parties to host them and those considering running did no campaigning on the level that would take place in later years. The only thing that was for sure was that the Framers wanted nothing more to do with any type of monarchy.

The Treaty of Paris had gone into effect five years earlier turning the British American colonies into the United States of America but converting the one-time underling into a real country was still a work in progress. Among the items that needed to be addressed was the election of the first president, and while many potential candidates were important individuals who would carve out their niche in history, there was one who stood above the crowd.

At the conclusion of the Revolutionary War, George Washington became the most famous person in the fledgling country marking the beginning of America's love affair with their war heroes. From that time forward, many of those who had excelled on the field of battle were either elected president or, at the least, mentioned as a potential candidate.

Washington's credentials were the definition of that feeling as he had taken a group of inexperienced individuals from various corners of society, organized and turned them into a fighting force that went on to defeat the most powerful military in the world. Early on, after a series of losses, he had suffered the wrath of his fellow officers and certain members of Congress, but in the end, the veteran of the French and Indian War overcame the skeptics and became the people's choice.

However, when he was approached about becoming the new nation's first president, he had doubts of his own. In fact, there were six items that he saw as potential obstacles to running for office.

OLD AGE

By 1789, Washington had made it to the ripe old age of fifty-seven in an era when the average life expectancy among white males was thirty-six. He had survived smallpox as a teen and made it through two wars without so much as a bullet wound. In retrospect, there have been eleven presidents who have been older than the Father of Our Country including Ronald Reagan who started his second term at age sixty-nine.

"ENCREASING FONDNESS FOR AGRICULTURAL AMUSEMENTS"

After the war, the victorious general went home to Mount Vernon, his grand estate on the banks of the Potomac in Virginia. At the farm he not only grew crops but worked on methods to improve their output, such as their rotation. He also maintained a profitable distillery.

"MY GROWING LOVE OF RETIREMENT."

Washington was away from his beloved Mount Vernon for six years (1775–1781) during the American Revolution. Upon his return he worked, fished, and lived the life of a country gentleman. The general also enjoyed riding one of the selections from his prime stock of fine horses and could usually be found in the saddle on most mornings.

BELIEF THAT THE ANTI-FEDERALISTS
MAY OPPOSE HIS SELECTION

The Anti-Federalists had their own group of power brokers like James Winthrop of Massachusetts and Melancton Smith in New York along with Patrick Henry and George Mason in Washington's home state of Virginia. But it didn't prevent the Federalists and other constitutional supporters from attempting to install Washington into the presidency. After having already retired in 1783, the general feared that he would be looked upon as inconsistent, rash, and ambitious if he returned to office.

Washington had a brief political career from 1758–1761 as a member of the House of Burgesses. However, he had dealt with a number power hungry subordinates when he was commanding during the revolution and didn't want to be identified with them. But the fact that he was held in such high esteem by the public placed him at a different level of respect.

BELIEF THAT "SOME OTHER PERSON . . . COULD EXECUTE
ALL THE DUTIES FULL AS SATISFACTORILY AS MYSELF"

This was the age of the Founding Fathers, many of whom could have served the office and performed adequately. But it was recognized that America's first president would be the standard bearer that all others would be measured, making it critical that a proven leader be in the position if the experiment was to succeed.

One of the most emphatic proponents was one of Washington's former Revolutionary War officers, Alexander Hamilton, who wrote to the general in September 1788 stating, "First—In a matter so essential to the well being of society as the prosperity of a newly instituted government a citizen of so much consequence as yourself to its success has no option but to lend his services if called for."

The election got underway on Monday, December 15, 1788, and concluded on Saturday, January 10, 1789. There was no actual campaigning as it was presumed that Washington would win the office and he did so, amassing 43,782 popular votes that became 69 votes in the electoral college. Overall, about 1.8 percent of the population cast ballots out of a population of around three million. Some states did not use a popular vote while others restricted their participants to white male landowners over the age of twenty-one.

Prior to 1804, each elector cast two votes for president. All of them selected Washington with one of their ballots, effectively making him the unanimous choice as chief executive. Two of the thirteen original colonies (North Carolina and Rhode Island) had not ratified the Constitution and did not participate. Because the New York state legislature deadlocked over its choice of electors, they did not cast an electoral vote in that year's election.

For the only time in history, the real race of the US presidential election was for second place because it made that person the country's first vice president. That honor went to John Adams of Massachusetts, the former minister to France who garnered thirty-four electors. The remainder of the field followed in order: John Jay of New York, secretary of foreign affairs (nine); Robert H. Harrison of Maryland, former member of the Maryland House of Delegates (six); John Rutledge of South Carolina and its former governor (six); George Clinton of New York and its former governor (three); Samuel Huntington, governor of Connecticut (two); John Milton, one of the Founding Fathers of Georgia (two); James Armstrong, member of the Georgia House of Representatives (one); Benjamin Lincoln who served as the first continental states secretary of war (one); and Edward Telfair, former governor of Georgia (one).

Table 1.1   The Election of 1789

Presidential Nominee	Electoral College
George Washington	69
John Adams	34
John Jay	9
Robert H. Harrison	6
John Rutledge	6
John Hancock	4
George Clinton	3
Samuel Huntington	2
John Milton	2
James Armstrong	1
Benjamin Lincoln	1
Edward Telfair	1

Vice President Elect: John Adams, former minister to France

The Aftermath

George Washington was recognized as one of the wealthiest, if not the wealthiest, persons in the United States. But like a number of rich citizens, most of his funds were tied up in assets like his house and other property. When he set out for his inauguration in New York City, he stopped in Alexandria, Virginia, where he borrowed £600 from his friend and fellow businessman Richard Conway to complete the journey. Conway had served as a captain in Washington's army during the Revolutionary War.

On April 30, 1789, Washington took the oath of office on the balcony of Federal Hall in New York City as the United States' first president. As thousands of onlookers gathered on Wall Street to witness the historic event, they could only wonder if the former general could have as much success as the nation's chief executive as he did on the battlefield.

It was the beginning of a tradition for American citizens of promoting battle tested soldiers to the country's highest office after displaying their gallantry in combat. Among those who followed Washington in this practice were James Monroe, Andrew Jackson, Zachary Taylor, Ulysses S. Grant, Theodore Roosevelt, Dwight Eisenhower, and John F. Kennedy to name a few.

But not many outside the Washington family realized that the odds of him surviving to be sworn in on that day had been 50-50 at best. He was a man who had experienced more than his share of sickness before he ever faced the enemy in warfare. The assembled throng of witnesses who listened to his inaugural address had no idea that their newly affirmed leader had struggled with health issues for most of his fifty-seven years.

Before the age of twenty, young George had already suffered with bouts of diphtheria, malaria, smallpox, and tuberculosis. In 1751, his half-brother Lawrence had contracted tuberculosis and traveled to the island of Barbados in hopes that the tropical climate would aid in his recovery. George accompanied him on the journey where they spent four months. During this time, the younger Washington developed a severe case of smallpox that left him with lifetime scarring.

George returned to Virginia before Lawrence who followed later but was still quite ill. As opposed to his later contemporaries, Barbados was the only foreign country ever visited by Washington. In July 1752, Lawrence died at Mount Vernon. That same year, twenty year old George battled through his second bout of malaria. The disease was common in Virginia due to the numerous breeding areas for mosquitos.

His military career began in 1753 as a colonel in the provincial militia of the Virginia Regiment during the French and Indian War. In 1755, Washington, serving as an aide to British general Edmond Braddock, was ordered to remain behind in Virginia as the army moved into the Ohio Valley because he suffered from severe dysentery. On July 8, still ill with a fever, he rode in a wagon and caught up with his unit near Fort Duquesne (present day Pittsburgh).

The British regulars found themselves in battle against the French and Indians the following day. The enemy didn't resort to the open field attacks used on European battlefields but countered with guerilla warfare tactics that had long been employed by the natives. Braddock was killed and Washington had two horses shot out from underneath him while several bullets pierced his military jacket. He was later struck with another round of dysentery and tuberculosis before the war's end.

With the conclusion of hostilities in 1758, Washington returned home to run the estate at Mount Vernon and its huge tobacco plantation. It was during this period until he departed for battle in 1774 that he remained relatively healthy even though his beloved stepdaughter Patsy had died of a seizure a year earlier.

With the exception of a 1779 bout with quinsy, a complication of tonsillitis, Washington's health remained steady throughout the American Revolution. His biggest obstacle was keeping himself away from the British army that pursued him.

Washington's war record is littered with close calls and narrow escapes as he constantly dodged death while constantly moving his troops. He was one of the redcoat's prime targets among a select group of the Founding Fathers whom, had he been captured, would have been taken to London for trial and probable execution. The British yearned for nothing more than to use the American commander as an example to frighten any colonist away from the rebellion.

It began on August 29–30, 1776, as Washington masterminded the nighttime escape of his troops from Long Island to Manhattan. But even with that success, the general was still in the role of the hunted.

On September 11, 1777, while on a march through Pennsylvania, Captain Patrick Ferguson, a Scottish marksman, had Washington in his sights as he rode through the countryside but passed up an opportunity to fire on him explaining, "It was not pleasant to fire at the back of an unoffending individual, who was acquitting himself very coolly of his duty—so I let him alone."

American forces were not as philosophical, and Ferguson was shot dead by Continental troops three years later at the Battle of King's Mountain (South Carolina).

As opposed to other presidents who served in battle and faced death during their military days, Washington holds a distinction among his successors of having two of his own soldiers attempt to harm him. In the spring of 1776, one of the commander's bodyguards Thomas Hickey tried to poison him at Fraunces Tavern but was unmasked in the plot and hanged a few weeks later before a crowd of twenty thousand in New York City.

Following his treason in 1779, Benedict Arnold attempted to have Washington kidnapped on the road leading to West Point. The general's decision to take an alternate route proved to be fortuitous. After almost seven years of the stress of running a war, when he accepted the British surrender in October 1781, the forty-nine year old Washington was in better health than he had been as a young man.

In 1784, prior to becoming president, Washington went through his fourth episode with malaria. He suffered a fifth bout in 1798.

As the crowd began to dissipate from the inaugural festivities at Federal Hall, none of those who were departing would ever know the valleys that their new president had endured to arrive at the mountain top. Any one of which could have changed the course of history.

THE FOLLOWING ELECTIONS

1792: George Washington was unanimously reelected (all 132 electoral votes) without campaigning.

1796: Even though Washington had announced that he would not seek a third term, there were those who refused to let him go as Alexander Hamilton and Thomas Jefferson attempted to get the incumbent to run for one more term of which he refused. John Adams became the nation's second president by winning all the New England states over Thomas Jefferson.

2

The Election of 1800

John Adams, Incumbent (Federalist) vs. Thomas Jefferson (Democratic-Republican)

"Murder, robbery, rape, adultery, and incest will be openly taught and practiced, the air will be rent with the cries of the distressed, the soil will be soaked with blood, and the nation black with crimes."

—The *Connecticut Courant* newspaper warning its readers against the possible election of Thomas Jefferson during the campaign of 1800

Thomas Jefferson approached the election of 1800 well organized for victory and determined to win. One factor that elevated his chances of becoming president was the general mood of the country. During John Adams's administration, public discontent had risen due to the Alien and Sedition Acts, a direct tax in 1798, Federalist military preparations, and the use of federal troops to crush the minor Fries Rebellion in Pennsylvania.

As the Federalist candidate and incumbent, Adams led a split party. Many of its members opposed his candidacy because of his refusal to declare war on France and when a naval war did occur, Adams used diplomacy to end it when many Federalists would have preferred the dispute to continue. Jefferson understood that to win he would have to carry New York, thus his running mate, the state's former senator Aaron Burr was brought onto the ticket. When the New York legislature turned out its Federalist majority in 1799, prospects looked good for Jefferson.

Given the intense rivalry and conflict, it was not surprising that the election of 1800 reached a level of personal animosity seldom equaled in colonial politics. The Federalists attacked the fifty-seven-year-old Jefferson "as a Godless Jacobin who would unleash the forces of bloody terror upon the land." Others criticized the challenger's deist beliefs as the views of an infidel who "writes aghast the truths of God's words; who makes not even a profession of Christianity; who is without Sabbaths;

without the sanctuary, and without so much as a decent external respect for the faith and worship of Christians."

Meanwhile, the luckless Adams was ridiculed from two directions: by the Hamiltonians within his own party and by the Jeffersonian-Republicans from the outside. For example, a private letter in which Hamilton depicted Adams as having "great and intrinsic defects in his character" was obtained by Aaron Burr and leaked to the national press. It fueled the Republican attack on Adams as a hypocritical fool and tyrant. His opponents also spread the story that the second president had planned to create an American dynasty by the marriage of one of his sons to a daughter of King George III. According to the unsubstantiated story, only the intervention of George Washington, dressed in his revolutionary military uniform, and threatening to use his sword against his former vice president had stopped Adams's scheme.

In reality, Adams had made a similar mistake that as so many others in various walks of life, he followed a legend. In short, he was not a victorious general or the Father of the Country, the new nation's capital wasn't named for him and he wasn't a national hero. Simply, he wasn't George Washington.

Even though he had retired more than three years earlier, there were those who were dissatisfied with Adams's performance as president and clamored for the good old days with Washington back in office.

On June 22, 1799, Connecticut governor Jonathan Trumbull Jr., who also served as his military secretary during the war, conveyed those thoughts in a letter to the former chief executive stating, "Election of a President is near at hand, and I have confidence in believing, that, should your Name again be brort [*sic*] up."

But Adams's predecessor wasn't as concerned, as the nation's first president was ensconced at Mount Vernon tending to his crops and riding the countryside. Even though he had been appointed commander in chief of the Continental Army in 1798, it turned out to be more of a ceremonial honor as he had no intention of returning to the daily grind of a political office. However, Washington never saw the results of the upcoming election as he died on December 14, 1799.

Voting in the election of 1800 began on October 31 and concluded on December 3. For the first and last time in US history, a president found himself running against his vice president. Jefferson easily won the popular vote with more than 61 percent.

Although, when the electoral ballots came in, Jefferson and Burr each won seventy-three. Adams and his running mate, Charles C. Pinckney, the brother of Thomas Pinckney who ran in 1796, won sixty-five and sixty-four votes, respectively.

No one had expected those results, although the possibility was perfectly plausible—if all of the Democratic-Republican electors cast their votes in unison for the party's two candidates, which they did in this case, the result would be a tie. In those days, the US Constitution contained no means for electors to differentiate between their choices for president and vice president, yet in 1804 the nation ratified the Twelfth Amendment, which required electors to vote separately for the two offices.

Table 2.1   The Election of 1800

Presidential Candidate	Party	Home State	Popular Count	Pop Vote (%)	Electoral Count
Thomas Jefferson	D-R	Virginia	41,330	61.4%	73
Aaron Burr	D-R	New York	—	—	73
John Adams (Inc.)	Fed.	Massachusetts	25,952	—	65
Charles Pinckney	Fed.	South Carolina	—	—	64
John Jay	Fed.	New York	—	—	1
	Total		67,282	100%	
	Needed to Win				70

Vice President Elect, Aaron Burr, former US Senator (DR-NY)

The Framers had anticipated that there might be an electoral situation that would need to be addressed but probably not so soon in the process. For that reason, they created Article II, Section 1 of the Constitution, which stated that if two candidates each received a majority of the electoral votes but were tied, the House of Representatives would determine which one would be president. That left the decision with the lame duck, Federalist-controlled House.

Thirty-five ballots were cast over five days but neither candidate received a majority. Many Federalists saw Jefferson as their principal foe, whose election was to be avoided at all cost. But Alexander Hamilton, the well-respected party leader, who opposed Burr, advised Federalists in Congress that Jefferson was the safer choice. Finally, on February 17, 1801, on the thirty-sixth ballot, the House elected Jefferson to be the next president by a 10–4 margin. Two states, South Carolina and Delaware, did not vote for either candidate.

Had Hamilton's efforts failed and Burr had become president in 1800, it's most likely the pair would have never fought their historic duel four years later and perhaps Burr would have emerged as a two-term White House resident while Jefferson would have stayed busy remodeling Monticello and building the campus at the University of Virginia.

THE AFTERMATH

Thomas Jefferson was sworn in for his first term as president on March 4, 1801, succeeding his former friend John Adams. The outgoing chief executive, who had become the nation's first single-term president, was still upset over his electoral loss. He resented that, unlike his predecessor George Washington, the voters had cast him aside without an opportunity to serve a second term.

It was a difficult transition period for the nation's second president. One month after Adams lost the election, his son Charles, only thirty years old, died from the ravages of alcoholism. In mid-February 1801, First Lady Abigail Adams made an early departure for the family home in Quincy, Massachusetts. The angry spouse believed that God had punished the United States "for our sins and transgressions" by allowing Jefferson to defeat her husband in the election.

The outgoing president feared possible violence between Federalists and Democratic-Republicans and considered resigning several days earlier in order to avoid such conflict at the inauguration. He did not do so, but still chose not to attend the ceremony.

In the early morning hours of March 4, 1801, before he left the White House for the last time, Adams final act in office was to submit his nomination to the Senate for John Marshall to become chief justice of the Supreme Court. At 4:00 a.m. on inauguration day, the president's carriage quietly pulled away from the Executive Mansion and into the darkness toward his Massachusetts home.

Thomas Jefferson was sworn in without his predecessor being present at the ceremony. But his inauguration didn't assemble the pageantry that would be displayed in later events. The newly elected leader walked from the nearby Conrad and McMunn's boarding house to the still-unfinished Capitol Building for the noon proceedings. After that, he strolled back to the lodging establishment in time for an unceremonious inaugural lunch, which he partook with his fellow boarders. When he arrived, the victorious candidate's usual seat was already taken by a guest, so the new commander in chief stood and waited patiently until a female diner volunteered her chair.

When Jefferson retired from the presidency in 1809 Dr. Benjamin Rush, a signer of the Declaration of Independence, set forth on renewing the friendship between the two chief executives. With his help, Adams and Jefferson, who had not spoken to one another in years, began a correspondence that provided some of history's most interesting and important letters.

After fifteen years of resumed friendship, albeit by long distance, on July 4, 1826, Jefferson and Adams died within hours of each other. Ironically, their deaths occurred on the fiftieth anniversary of the signing of the Declaration of Independence. Adams did not know that his friend had died hours earlier when he spoke his final words, "Thomas Jefferson survives."

In 2004, Richard Burr, a distant relative of the former vice president, was elected as a US senator from North Carolina.

THE FOLLOWING ELECTIONS

1804: Prior to the election of 1804, a bill became law that would change the way all future elections would be conducted. On December 9, 1803, Congress passed the Twelfth Amendment to the Constitution "requiring electors to vote for President and vice president separately."

Jefferson's opponent for reelection in 1804 was the former minister to France, Charles C. Pinckney of South Carolina. The incumbent won an easy reelection in November, but the big news took place just a few months earlier.

He had been forced to select a new running mate, which he did in the form of New York governor George Clinton who replaced Aaron Burr. On July 11, 1804, the sitting vice president mortally wounded former Secretary of the Treasury Alexander Hamilton in a duel over negative personal comments made by the former cabinet member of George Washington. The two men had served together as officers in the Continental Army during the Revolutionary War.

1808: The election of 1808 set the record for individual defections as six New York electors from the Democratic-Republican Party refused to vote for James Madison and, instead, cast their ballots for the party's vice presidential candidate, George Clinton. However, it didn't matter as Madison won in a landslide.

1812: Madison won reelection with an electoral margin of 128 to 89, but those numbers didn't tell the entire story. For the first time, America's presidential election came down to the results of one state—Pennsylvania. Although Madison captured nearly 63 percent of the popular vote, had his opponent, New York City mayor DeWitt Clinton, been able to secure the Keystone State with its twenty-five electoral ballots, along with those that he'd already won, the incumbent would have been beaten.

1816: James Monroe (DR-VA) easily defeated Rufus King (F-NY), a foreign diplomat. But the new president was fortunate just to be in his current position. On Christmas night 1776, Lieutenant Monroe was among the soldiers who crossed the frozen Delaware River with the commander in chief (George Washington) as they moved toward Trenton. Also included in those boats were fellow colonials who would later gain fame for their roles in the new government like Alexander Hamilton, John Marshall, and Aaron Burr. When the troops reached their destination, they were engaged by the Hessians.

During the battle, a bullet grazed the left side of Monroe's chest, hit his shoulder, and injured the major artery in his arm. Bleeding profusely, the eighteen year old's life was saved by a local doctor who stopped the bleeding by sticking his index finger into the wound and applying pressure to the damaged artery.

"I would have bled to death," he later admitted. "If this doctor had not been near and promptly taken up the artery."

As the Continentals marched through the snow, Monroe met Dr. John B. Riker on the road to Trenton where the physician saw the Americans preparing for battle and elected to join them. He was always held in high esteem by the future president who searched for Riker or one of his descendants to honor the doctor's duty, but neither were ever found. Surgeons later attempted to remove the bullet but could never find it. Monroe recovered from the wound in just eleven weeks and carried the projectile in his shoulder the rest of his life.

3

The Election of 1820

James Monroe, Incumbent (Democratic-Republican)

"It is by a thorough knowledge of the whole subject that [people] are enabled to judge correctly of the past and to give a proper direction to the future."

—James Monroe, 1821

Imagine being the president of the United States and when it came time to run for reelection, you had no opponent. It sounds like a story concocted as the plot for a political novel or as Mark Twain once wrote, "Truth is stranger than fiction, but it is because fiction is obliged to stick to possibilities, truth isn't."

James Monroe ushered the country through the period referred to as the "Era of Good Feelings" (1817–1825) when partisan rancor was reduced to a whisper rather than a shout. As the nation's highest elected official prepared for his reelection campaign, there was just one thing missing—an opponent. Things were going so well in the young republic that no one lined up to take on the incumbent.

The "Era of Good Feelings" was such that Monroe ran unopposed for reelection in 1820 and was just one vote short of an unanimous electoral college victory. The only blemish on a possible Monroe sweep was the vote of independent elector William Plumer, the former US senator and governor from New Hampshire, who cast a single ballot for John Quincy Adams because he felt that Monroe had been an ineffective president and did not deserve a second term.

George Washington was virtually unopposed in his two elections for the nation's highest office and remains the only unanimously elected candidate by the electoral college for both elections.

The biggest decision for voters was their choice of a vice president. There were four separate tickets featuring Monroe with a different running mate on each. In the end, the public went with the incumbent: Daniel Tompkins.

Table 3.1   The Presidential Election of 1820

Presidential candidate	Party	Home state	Popular vote Count	Percentage	Electoral vote
James Monroe (incumbent)	Democratic-Republican	Virginia	87,343	80.61%	231
No candidate	Federalist	N/A	17,465	16.12%	0
DeWitt Clinton	Democratic-Republican	New York	1,893	1.75%	0
J. Q. Adams	Democratic-Republican	Massachusetts			1
Unpledged Electors	None	N/A	1,658	1.53%	0
Total			108,359	100.0%	232
Needed to win					117

Vice President Elect: Daniel Tompkins, incumbent

However, while most of the country was at ease, not everyone inside the White House could say the same. Some bad feelings had erupted between the president and one of his top cabinet members.

In the winter of 1824, treasury secretary William H. Crawford had been seen as one of the top contenders to replace the outgoing Monroe, but he suffered a stroke a year earlier, which greatly diminished his chances. During the transition, the fifty-two-year-old Crawford, who was ready to retire to his home in Georgia, called on Monroe at the White House to discuss potential appointments of custom officers at ports in the northeastern United States. At some point, the discussion evolved into a quarrel between the men

The president was a wounded Revolutionary War veteran who was about to face off against the younger Crawford, who had killed a man in a duel years earlier. When the treasury secretary suddenly shook his cane, Monroe called him a "damned infernal old scoundrel" and grabbed two red hot tongs from one of the fireplaces for self-defense. But before Monroe could ask him to leave, Crawford departed the mansion on his own and the two men never spoke again.

The incident marked an official end to the "Era of Good Feelings" between Monroe and Crawford.

THE AFTERMATH

James Monroe had been a war hero and is highly rated among America's presidents. On many fronts, his notable achievements had followed the path of his predecessors Thomas Jefferson and James Madison, which included his postpresidency as he became the third consecutive chief executive to personally leave the office in debt.

After two terms, Monroe owed $75,000 (equal to $1.955 million today!) to his creditors forcing him to sell his properties and go live with his daughter's family in New York City. His wife had died in 1830. The fifth US president became a virtual pauper by the time he died on July 4, 1831.

4

The Election of 1824

John Quincy Adams (Democratic-Republican) vs. Andrew Jackson (Democratic-Republican)

"The four most miserable years of my life were my four years in the presidency."

—John Quincy Adams

Young boys often want to grow up and work in the same profession as their fathers. Since his dad was the former president of the United States, that task was a bit more challenging for John Quincy Adams than for the average youth.

John Adams had set a high bar of achievement for his oldest son as, in addition to being the nation's second chief executive, he had served as minister to the Court of St. James and minister to the Netherlands; was one of the country's Founding Fathers; was a delegate to the First and Second Continental Congress as well as the nation's first vice president. He was also a graduate of Harvard University.

The pair went on to become the first father and son to each be elected president although that almost didn't happen.

On February 18, 1778, Adams was aboard the ship the *Boston* bound for Paris on a diplomatic mission. Joining him on the journey was ten year old John Quincy who would be a firsthand witness to the techniques of international diplomacy, although there would be difficulties along the way.

Two days out of port, they were chased by an enemy vessel before eluding its pursuit. That provided time to gather themselves from the incident, the ship was then battered by a hurricane that killed four crew members, injured twenty others, and blew them two hundred miles off course.

When it finally appeared that it would be smooth sailing for the remainder of the journey, the *Boston* ended up in a skirmish with the British merchant ship the *Martha*. Several shots were exchanged without major damage or casualties as the elder

Adams patrolled the deck armed with a musket. On March 30, the *Boston* arrived in Bordeaux, France, safely delivering the two future presidents to their destination.

Months later, the pair returned home but were off again in November 1779. They departed Boston aboard the French frigate *Sensible,* but it didn't take long for trouble to take its place among the passengers and crew. After just two days at sea, the ship began taking on water. Once again, the two travelers found themselves in peril aboard a ship crossing the Atlantic.

With the aid of two pumps, the vessel struggled across the sea and on December 8, limped into harbor at El Ferrol, Spain, to address its much needed repairs.

Over time, Quincy earned a master's degree from Harvard in 1790 and, without attending law school, completed his legal education as an apprentice to the future chief justice of the Massachusetts Supreme Court Theophilus Parsons.

Like his father, Quincy began his career in public service as a diplomat serving in several different countries before his election to the Senate in 1803 and eventually becoming secretary of state (1817). He became a candidate for president in 1824 but, even though he hailed from a famous family, his election to the office was far from a sure thing.

James Monroe had followed the trend of Jefferson and Madison and chose not to run for a third term. His declining health was a major factor in his decision.

Treasury Secretary William H. Crawford had been an early front-runner to replace Monroe, but a stroke in 1823 ruined those chances. He had been serving in the cabinet since 1816 and continued on throughout Monroe's presidency. But by 1824 he was tired, frustrated, and eventually retired to his home in Georgia,

From early on, American voters have had a fascination with war heroes as evidenced by the landslide election victories of George Washington and Monroe. But they were from the revolutionary era where, by 1824, many of the better known individuals were either dead or too old to run for the office. However, since then, there had been another war with a new group of heroes.

The War of 1812 provided a platform for candidates who the public believed could better serve as president because of their military background. It provided no shortage of available names for the voters to evaluate.

Among them was fifty-seven-year-old Andrew Jackson, a US senator from Tennessee. Even though he was already an elected official, he was better known as the major general who led his troops to victory during the decisive Battle of New Orleans at the conclusion of the conflict. Additionally, in his teens, he served as a courier during the American Revolution for Washington's army before being taken as a prisoner of war.

Jackson's exploits were the stuff that many Americans believed were the qualities that their president should possess. In contrast, Quincy's time during those periods was spent as a Harvard professor and politician with no military service. Also in the field was the indomitable speaker of the house Henry Clay, which made all four of the major candidates Democratic-Republicans.

Early on, there was doubt that Quincy would be able to fill the high standard that his father's accomplishments had set for him. He did not possess a gift for public speaking and had lost his first bid for the US House of Representatives. But he had gone on to serve in several ambassadorships, the Senate, and as secretary of state in the Monroe administration.

As the campaign of 1824 got underway, Crawford, who had been endorsed by Thomas Jefferson, suffered a second stroke in May prompting Clay, who wasn't a doctor, to write in correspondence to a friend that he expected the big man from Georgia would soon die. But that prediction was short-sided as Crawford not only recovered, he remained in the race.

What has often been lost in the story of the 1824 contest was that it was the first campaign that saw a straw poll employed. It was conducted by the *Harrisburg Pennsylvanian* newspaper with the survey being done in Wilmington, Delaware. That July, participants chose Jackson by a commanding 70 percent margin (335 votes) over Adams (23 percent), Clay (4 percent), and Crawford (2 percent).

Since that time, the business of political polls and surveys has grown into a multimillion dollar enterprise. As an example, one needs to look no further than 2016 when the Democratic Party nominee Hillary Clinton spent nearly $45 million on polling for her campaign.

As summer turned to fall, on October 26, 1824, the citizens of the twenty-four states began the task of choosing the country's new leader. Going into the contest there was no clear-cut favorite as each candidate had their own regional strongholds where they could depend on a successful gathering of support from its voters. The election concluded on December 2 as the states submitted their counts to Washington, DC, for tabulation.

When the results of the popular vote were released, Jackson had easily outdistanced the others with 153,544; Adams 108,740; Clay 47,136; and Crawford 46,618. But in the all-important electoral count, 131 ballots were needed to secure a victory and "Old Hickory" had only accumulated 99 even though he had soundly beaten Adams, with 84.

The inconclusive results meant that for the second time in twenty-four years, the US House of Representatives would break the stalemate. Under the provisions set forth in the Twelfth Amendment of the Constitution, Congress would decide from the three top finishers meaning that Clay, who finished last in the electoral count, was out.

Crawford had won twenty-four electors in Virginia along with nine more from his home state of Georgia. A sprinkling of others gave him a total of forty-one. Four other states, including Ohio, combined to provide thirty-seven for Clay. Had Jackson been able to take some combination of thirty-two from those seventy-eight combined ballots, he would have won the contest outright but his challenge came from the fact that, like himself, Crawford and Clay were southerners so they were taking votes away from each other in their home territory.

Meanwhile, Adams had used the New England states as a firewall to keep himself viable and in the hunt. The results left no doubt that, as opposed to most of the past elections, voters had cast their preferences on a regional basis.

Table 4.1   The Election of 1824

Presidential candidate	Party	Home state	Popular vote Count	Popular vote Percentage	Electoral vote
Andrew Jackson	Democratic-Republican	Tennessee	151,271	41.36%	99
John Quincy Adams	Democratic-Republican	Massachusetts	113,122	30.92%	84
William Harris Crawford	Democratic-Republican	Georgia	40,856	11.21%	41
Henry Clay	Democratic-Republican	Kentucky	47,531	12.99%	37
Unpledged electors	None	Massachusetts	6,616	1.81%	0
Other			6,437	1.71%	0
Total			365,833	100.0%	261
Needed to win					131

Vice President Elect, John C. Calhoun, Secretary of War

Clay may have been out of the running, but he was determined to play a role in determining the winner. During December, there were a series of meetings that took place where some well positioned politicians made their way between Adams and Clay. They made it clear that the Speaker would support the candidate from Massachusetts in exchange for a position in the new administration.

On January 9, 1825, Clay called on Adams at the latter's home, to work out the details of what became known as "The Corrupt Bargain." While he was no fan of the son of the former president, the Speaker's disdain for Jackson ran much deeper and he was determined to use his influence to keep him out of the White House.

The friction between the two began in 1818 when Clay publicly criticized the general for his unauthorized invasion of Spanish West Florida. He viewed Jackson as an irresponsible opportunist who was a political outsider that hadn't earned a place among the hierarchy in the nation's capital. Clay once said of the former war hero, "I cannot believe that killing 2,500 Englishmen at New Orleans qualifies for the various, difficult, and complicated duties of the Chief Magistracy."

On February 9, 1825, the House of Representatives convened to make the final decision. The candidate who received the largest number of House votes would become president. Everything seemed to be set to make John Quincy Adams the next chief executive but, as is the case with many plans, the unexpected began to take place.

Even with all of the political maneuvering, the deciding vote in the House was cast by Representative Stephen Van Rensselaer of New York. He was originally undecided between Jackson and Crawford. Each state was entitled to a single vote, and New York's delegation seemed deadlocked between Adams and Crawford. Adams needed

New York to win the election, which required Van Rensselaer's vote to carry the Empire State.

But the congressman roomed at the same boarding house with loyal Crawford supporters, Martin Van Buren and Louis McLane, and was thought to be leaning toward their candidate. On the morning of the vote, Van Rensselaer assured his friends that he would never vote for Adams over Crawford. But when he arrived at the Capitol, the New York representative was intercepted by the powerful duo of Daniel Webster and Clay, who whisked him into the Speaker's office for an arm twisting session in support of Adams.

The meeting unnerved Van Rensselaer to the point that he forgot to bring a ballot when he entered the House chambers. Still undecided, he bowed his head to pray and then opened his eyes to see an Adams ballot on the floor at his feet. Van Rensselaer dropped it in the box, giving New York's vote and the presidency to John Quincy Adams.

Table 4.2   Results by State in the House of Representatives

	Delegation winner	Adams vote	Jackson vote	Crawford vote
Maine	Adams	7	0	0
New Hampshire	Adams	6	0	0
Vermont	Adams	5	0	0
Massachusetts	Adams	12	1	0
Rhode Island	Adams	2	0	0
Connecticut	Adams	6	0	0
New York	Adams	18	2	14
New Jersey	Jackson	1	5	0
Pennsylvania	Jackson	1	25	0
Delaware	Crawford	0	0	1
Maryland	Adams	5	3	1
Virginia	Crawford	1	1	19
North Carolina	Crawford	1	2	10
South Carolina	Jackson	0	9	0
Georgia	Crawford	0	0	7
Alabama	Jackson	0	3	0
Mississippi	Jackson	0	1	0
Louisiana	Adams	2	1	0
Kentucky	Adams	8	4	0
Tennessee	Jackson	0	9	0
Missouri	Adams	1	0	0
Ohio	Adams	10	2	2
Indiana	Jackson	0	3	0
Illinois	Adams	1	0	0
Total votes	Adams	87 (41%)	71 (33%)	54 (25%)
Votes by state	Adams	13 (54%)	7 (29%)	4 (17%)

Crawford finished third in both the general election as well as in the House vote. However, a total of 25 percent of the congressmen cast their ballot for him. He netted fifty-four House votes which hurt Jackson's effort as he needed just seventeen to win the election. In the end, the third candidate didn't capture this contest, but his mere presence decided who did.

Following the House vote, with the conclusion of the election, it was time to make good on the "The Corrupt Bargain" as Adams appointed Clay to the highest position in the cabinet—secretary of state. When the arrangement was exposed, Jackson and his followers immediately declared that the election for 1828 was already underway.

THE AFTERMATH

Adams near-death experience at sea as a boy wasn't the only act that almost cost him his life. Just four months after taking office, he nearly became the first president to die on the job and, once again, it involved water.

On June 13, 1825, the nation's leader and his manservant, Antoine Michel Giusta, decided to paddle a canoe across Tiber Creek, a tributary of the Potomac that now flows through an underground tunnel. His son John was with them and warned the pair that the boat was dangerous.

The canoe sprang a leak and the wind kicked up. Adams and Antoine jumped overboard and swam to the opposite shore. Adams took off his waterlogged clothes and gave them to Antoine, then lay gasping on the bank of the river. Adams recounted the near-tragedy in his diary on June 13, 1825:

> *I attempted to cross the river with Antoine in a small canoe, with a view to swim across it to come back. He took a boat in which we had crossed it last summer without accident. The boat was at the shore near Van Ness's poplars; but in crossing the Tiber to the point, my son John, who was with us, thought the boat dangerous, and, instead of going with us, went and undressed at the rock, to swim and meet us in midway of the river as we should be returning.*
>
> *I thought the boat safe enough, or rather persisted carelessly in going without paying due attention to its condition; gave my watch to my son; made a bundle of my coat and waist-coat to take in the boat with me; put off my shoes, and was paddled by Antoine, who had stripped himself entirely naked. Before we had got half across the river, the boat had leaked itself half full, and then we found there was nothing on board to scoop up the water and throw it over.*
>
> *Just at that critical moment a fresh breeze from the northwest blew down the river as from the nose of a bellows. In five minutes' time it made a little tempest, and set the boat to dancing till the river came in at the sides. I jumped overboard, and Antoine did the same, and lost hold of the boat, which filled with water and drifted away. We were as near as possible to the middle of the river, and swam to the opposite shore. Antoine, who was naked, reached it with little difficulty. I had much more, and, while struggling for life and gasping for breath, had ample leisure to reflect upon my own indiscretion. My principal difficulty was in the loose sleeves of my shirt, which filled with water and hung like two fifty-six pound weights upon my arms. I had also my hat, which I soon gave, however, to Antoine.*
>
> *After reaching the shore, I took off my shirt and pantaloons, wrung them out, and gave them to Antoine to go and look out for our clothes, or for a person to send to the house for others, and for the carriage to come and fetch me. Soon after he had gone, my son John joined me, having swum wholly across the river, expecting to meet us returning with the boat.*

Antoine crossed the bridge, sent a man to my house for the carriage, made some search for the drifted boat and bundles, and found his own hat with his shirt and braces in it, and one of my shoes. He also brought over the bridge my son's clothes with my watch and umbrella, which I had left with him.

While Antoine was gone, John and I were wading and swimming up and down on the other shore, or sitting naked basking on the bank at the margin of the river. John walked over the bridge home. The carriage came, and took me and Antoine home, half dressed. I lost an old summer coat, white waistcoat, two napkins, two white handkerchiefs, and one shoe. Antoine lost his watch, jacket, waistcoat, pantaloons, and shoes. The boat was also lost. By the mercy of God our lives were spared, and no injury befell our persons.

THE FOLLOWING ELECTIONS

1828: In a move that would stun modern day politicians, Adams refused to campaign for reelection because he felt that public service should not be likened to a popularity contest. He stated that, "If the country wants my services, she must ask for them." In turn, the remark made him appear elitist and was the beginning of the end of his time in the White House.

For a person who had relied on the Twelfth Amendment of the Constitution and the vote of the House to secure the office, Adams could ill-afford not to campaign, so he allowed his friends and surrogates to do the dirty work. In the end, Jackson (D-TN) won by a decisive 178–83 electoral margin.

1832: The popular Jackson was easily reelected over Senator Henry Clay (NR-KY), 219–49.

1836: When it came time for the Democrats to choose Jackson's replacement as the party's nominee, they unanimously selected the vice president, Martin Van Buren. However, the choice of Kentucky congressman Richard M. Johnson as vice president wasn't without controversy as it was discovered that he had been involved in a long-term relationship with Julia Chinn, a slave with whom he had fathered two daughters. Even without the support of the Virginia delegation, who were taken back by the news, Johnson was able to gain the nomination.

Their opponent came from the two-year-old Whig Party. It was a loose blend of non-Democrats consisting of disenfranchised Federalists, National Republicans, and Jacksonians who lacked a national voice and organizational structure. The group didn't hold a convention, instead opting for a process that was conducted at the state levels through the legislatures and rallies.

The strategy produced, not just one, but four candidates consisting of William Henry Harrison, a former war hero and US senator from Ohio; Senator Daniel Webster of Massachusetts; Senator Hugh L. White of Tennessee; and Senator Willie Person Magnum of North Carolina. White and Mangum represented states that were heavily dependent on slavery which, for the first time, moved to the forefront as a major campaign issue.

Whatever possibility of victory that the Whigs hoped to achieve by employing such an unconventional plan was rejected by the voters. Van Buren easily reached 170 electors while needing just 148 to win. On the other side, the quartet of Whig candidates further divided an already fractured electorate by splitting the ballots four ways: Harrison (73), White (26), Webster (14), and Mangum (11).

The young party had learned a difficult lesson that would pay off as they prepared to go forward in future contests.

1840: William Henry Harrison had been a hero during the War of 1812, won by a landslide (234–60) but his presidency, just thirty-two days, was the shortest in history. On April 4, 1841, at 12:35 a.m., Harrison became the first commander in chief to die in office. His official cause of death was listed as pleurisy and pneumonia.

1844: James K. Polk (D-TN) defeated Henry Clay, 170–105. He made five campaign promises: (1) Reestablishment of an independent Treasury system. (2) Reduced tariffs. (3) Settlement of the Oregon boundary dispute in order to acquire more land. (4) The acquisition of California, New Mexico, and the rest of the interior West. (5) He pledged to retire from office after only one term and became the first president to voluntarily serve just four years.

Amazingly, he became one of the rare politicians to keep all his promises.

1848: Zachary Taylor (W-LA) was a lifelong soldier who took part in four wars. When he voted for himself in 1848, it was the first time that he had participated in a national election. He was victorious, but on July 9, 1850, the commander in chief succumbed to a bout of gastroenteritis (severe stomach flu). He became the second president during the decade of the 1840s to die in office, but as time passed, there were persistent questions regarding his death. Many believed that the sixty-five-year-old military veteran had been assassinated.

After more than a century of debate over the matter, on June 17, 1991, the former president's remains were exhumed from the Taylor Mausoleum in Louisville, Kentucky. One week later, George Nichols, the state's chief medical examiner, reported that Taylor's death was a result of any of "a myriad of natural diseases which could have produced the symptoms of gastroenteritis."

In short, he had not been murdered.

5

The Election of 1852

Franklin Pierce (Democrat) vs. Winfield Scott (Whig)

"I hope he won't be elected for I should not like to be at Washington and I know you would not either."

—Franklin Pierce's son Bennie's words to his mother about the election of 1852

Throughout society there are many examples of people who appear, in the material sense, to have everything that money can buy except for one thing–happiness. The stories of those who have attained wealth and fame without self-satisfaction could fill volumes. This chapter is about one such individual.

Two hundred and thirty years after William Shakespeare's death, Franklin Pierce was elected president of the United States. If anyone resembled a tragic character from one of the Englishman's masterpieces, it was the man from New Hampshire who outwardly appeared to have everything one could want in life but was wrestling with inner demons away from the public eye.

Pierce's resume going into the election of 1852 was quite impressive. He was an 1824 graduate of Bowdoin College in Brunswick, Maine, where two of his closest friends were the famed authors Nathaniel Hawthorne and Pierce's cousin Henry Wadsworth Longfellow. After a rocky start as an undergraduate, he went on to study law and in 1827 was admitted to the bar.

In 1834, the young attorney married Jane Appleton, a protemperance teetotaler and daughter of the former president of Bowdoin. They had three sons, all of whom died as children.

Pierce began his political ascension serving two terms in the US House of Representatives (1833–1837) and one as a US senator (1837–1842). He resigned his Senate seat prior to the end of his term in order to return to New Hampshire where he resumed practicing law but remained active in politics at the state level.

When the Mexican-American War broke out in the spring of 1846, Pierce enlisted for duty turning down President James K. Polk's offer to make him attorney general. The handsome former senator in his dashing military uniform looked the part of a war hero and was involved in several battles. He eventually rose to the rank of brigadier general but suffered several painful injuries during the conflict, most of them resulting by being thrown from horses. Physically battered from his service, Pierce left the military in March 1848.

He again went home to New Hampshire and headed the state's Democratic Party while Millard Fillmore moved into the White House following the death of President Zachary Taylor. But Fillmore's audition to secure the Whig Party's nomination in 1852 failed having been pushed aside in favor of Pierce's former battlefield commander Winfield Scott. The snub meant that Fillmore became a member of an unenviable fraternity of incumbent presidents who were unable to win their party's nomination for the next election.

In June 1852, after thirty-four ballots at the Democratic National Convention in Baltimore, the lead position was constantly changing between prospects Stephen Douglas, James Buchanan, Lewis Cass, and William Marcy. On the thirty-fifth ballot Pierce's name was added to the mix in the jumbled field as a dark horse candidate with no clear-cut favorite. He was able to secure his party's candidacy on the forty-ninth ballot.

During the campaign the nominee kept a relatively low profile as there were questions about some of his so-called heroics in combat. Among those being his conspicuous absence from his brigade at the Battle of Chapultepec, where he was reportedly in the sick ward with a bout of diarrhea.

In addition, the nomination also brought Pierce's biggest impairment to the forefront. Although the people who were close to him had known about it for years, the politician/soldier had struggled with a problem to help mask his insecurities. He was an alcoholic.

Pierce's addiction manifested during his years as a congressman in Washington, DC. Many political figures in the nation's capital were known to tip a few drinks at the end of a day, but boredom and loneliness became the instigators that turned Pierce's obsession with the bottle from recreational to compulsive. His drunken escapades were not a secret among those on Capitol Hill.

Seeking to take advantage of the situation, the Whigs mocked their opposing candidate as the "Hero of Many a Well-Fought Bottle." A counterstrategy by the Democrats of limiting public access to Pierce during the campaign worked, as on November 2, 1852, he was elected the fourteenth president of the United States. The former military officer with a questionable war record and a drinking problem was on his way to becoming the nation's commander in chief.

Table 5.1   The Election of 1852

Presidential candidate	Party	Home state	Popular vote		Electoral vote
			Count	Percentage	
Franklin Pierce	Democratic	New Hampshire	1,607,510	50.84%	254
Winfield Scott	Whig	New Jersey	1,386,942	43.87%	42
John P. Hale	Free Soil	New Hampshire	155,210	4.91%	0
Daniel Webster	Union	Massachusetts	6,994	0.22%	0
Jacob Broom	Native American	Pennsylvania	2,566	0.08%	0
George Troup	Southern Rights	Georgia	2,331	0.07%	0
Other			277	0.01%	
Total			3,161,830	100%	296
Needed to win					149

Vice President Elect, Rufus King, former US Senator (F-NY)

To the public Pierce had become the political world's big winner. But two months before taking office, any hopes that he might climb aboard the sobriety wagon disappeared on January 6, 1853. Franklin, Jane, and their eleven-year-old son Bennie boarded a train in Andover, Massachusetts, where they had spent the Christmas holiday with the family of Mary Aiken, the future First Lady's sister. They departed from Shawsheen Village Station for the forty-eight mile journey to their home in Concord, New Hampshire.

Bennie had been the lone survivor among the trio of Pierce offspring. In February 1836, the family's first son, Franklin Jr., died just three days after his birth. The baby's death took place in an era when high rates of infant mortality were common. Three years later, Jane gave birth to Frank Robert Pierce who succumbed in 1843 to typhoid fever.

But by all appearances, Bennie, who had been born in 1841, was a healthy and happy child who would probably be following in his father's footsteps and enrolling at the exclusive Phillips Exeter Academy.

It was a bitterly cold New England winter day as the Pierces took their seats in the passenger car just before the train departed for Concord. About a mile north of the Andover station, the departing locomotive broke an axle and jumped the track going over a fifteen-foot embankment causing several cars to derail. Amazingly, only one person on board was killed but for the Pierce family, tragedy had intervened in the lives of their children once again.

Franklin and Jane received minor injuries but watched as Bennie, who was standing near a window, was nearly decapitated. A few days later when the boy's remains were returned to Concord for burial, his mother was so overcome with grief that she was unable to make the journey. Jane had struggled with depression for many years and the horrific manner in which she witnessed her youngest son's death stayed with her for the remainder of her life.

THE AFTERMATH

When February arrived it was time for the president-elect to begin his trek to the nation's capital to organize his administration and prepare for the inauguration. But by this time Jane's sorrow for her son had manifested as anger toward her husband, believing that Bennie's death was God's punishment for Franklin's political ambition. She had kept a note that Bennie had written to her during the campaign which said, "I hope he won't be elected for I should not like to be at Washington and I know you would not either."

As a way of displaying her anguish, Jane refused to attend the inauguration causing Franklin to leave without her.

Pierce's ceremony was unique on several fronts. First, when he took the oath, he replaced the word "swear" with "affirm," placing his hand on a law book rather than on a Bible, emulating the same procedure as John Quincy Adams. He then used his outstanding oratorical skills to deliver his 3,319 word speech from memory without the use of notes. In one line he discussed his vision for the country but may have been reflecting on Bennie as he said, "From that radiant constellation which both illumines our own way and points out to struggling nations their course, let but a single star be lost, and, if these be not utter darkness, the luster of the whole is dimmed."

In memory of his departed son, all the inaugural balls were canceled. That evening, when he went upstairs to go to sleep on his first night in the White House, the mansion's newly elected resident discovered something strange. None of the beds had been made. Four years later he moved out of the palace a day early so his successor could get a head start.

In his first year in office, Pierce was arrested for running over a woman with his horse. He never received jail time though, likely because of insufficient evidence. The case was dropped in 1853.

At the end of March Jane joined her husband in Washington, DC, but was far from being a traditional First Lady. She remained upstairs in the mansion for more than a year continuing to mourn Bennie's loss by writing letters to him on a consistent basis. Continuously adorned in widow's weeds for the remainder of her life, the grieving parent was referred to as the "shadow in the White House" by the press corps as she attempted to contact her boys through séances. A family friend, Abigail Kent Means, served as White House hostess during her absence.

Jane made her first formal appearance after her husband had been in office almost two years.

Twenty days following the inauguration, death knocked at the White House doors as Vice President William R. King died of tuberculosis. He was so ill that Congress had passed a special act allowing him to take the oath in Cuba where he was convalescing. Following King's death, the new president chose to leave the office vacant for the remainder of his term.

Although there were high points during Pierce's tenure like the Gadsden Purchase and the Treaty of Kanagawa allowing trade with Japan, there were not enough of them. Slavery continued to be a troublesome issue for the administration as northern abolitionists felt slighted by laws such as the Fugitive Slave Act that favored southern slave owners. But those who were close to the situation concluded that Bennie's death had demoralized the president to a point that it had crippled his ability to govern.

The Democrats felt the incumbent was unelectable and their campaign slogan for the 1856 presidential race became "Anyone But Pierce!" In June 1856, unhappy with the president's performance, the Democratic National Convention nominated James Buchanan of Pennsylvania to head the ticket. After being passed over for the nomination, Pierce reportedly told an acquaintance, "There is nothing left to do but get drunk."

He had become the only elected president to have been rejected by his own political affiliates. In March 1857, Pierce left office spending much of his time tending to Jane who was dying of tuberculosis. From 1857–1859, the couple toured Europe enjoying trips in the Portuguese islands of Madeira along with Switzerland, Italy, Paris, and London. Jane died on December 2, 1863, at age fifty-seven and the former president followed six years later from illnesses related to his years of alcohol abuse.

Franklin Pierce is often ranked among the nation's worst presidents. While his alcoholism began long before Bennie's death, one can only surmise if the events of that day had not occurred in the manner that took place, how the lives of Franklin and Jane Pierce, along with his presidency, might have been different.

In 2001, Pierce's fourth cousin, five times removed, assumed his former job as the country's chief executive. George W. Bush, who was related to the ex-president on his mother's side of the family, was sworn into office. Ironically, he, **too**, at one time, had battled with a severe drinking problem, but unlike his bygone relative, was able to overcome its ravages.

THE FOLLOWING ELECTION

1856: The sixty-five-year-old Democratic candidate James Buchanan of Pennsylvania was known as "Old Buck." He had served in both the House and the Senate in addition to secretary of state with stints as minister to the United Kingdom and Russia. He defeated the well-known frontiersman John C. Fremont from California, but it was close.

In fact, the final results showed that a change of fewer than eight thousand votes in Louisiana, Kentucky, and Tennessee would have thrown this election into the House of Representatives, where a three-man race, which would have included former president Millard Fillmore, may have produced a completely different outcome.

6

The Election of 1860

Stephen Douglas (Democrat), John C. Breckenridge (Southern Democrats), John Bell (Constitutional Union) vs. Abraham Lincoln (Republican)

"Honestly, if I were two-faced, would I be showing you this one?"

—Abraham Lincoln's response to Stephen Douglas during their
historic debate when he was accused of being two faced

A rematch is when two or more entities that have met previously in competition meet again. In sports it's a pretty common occurrence. As an example, from 1962 to 1969, the Boston Celtics played the Los Angeles Lakers on six different occasions for the championship of the National Basketball Association. Those were good times for Boston as they won all six titles.

Rematches in sports are common but not so much in politics. There have been a few noted exceptions, such as the presidential elections of 1888 and 1892 when Grover Cleveland (Democrat) and Benjamin Harrison (Republican) split their contests against each other. But as time has moved on and campaigning has gotten more demanding and expensive, second opportunities have become a rarity.

Perhaps the most unusual of repeated face-offs between candidates came within a period of less than twenty-four months when two contenders from the same state competed for a US Senate seat and then squared off once more to become the next president of the United States. To make this political tale even more extraordinary was the fact that each man won one of the elections, they eventually became friends, and one of them died a few weeks after their second encounter.

Stephen Douglas and Abraham Lincoln were from Illinois and they were not strangers. In fact, there were many aspects of their lives that traveled a parallel path. In the early 1830s, each passed the bar and became a lawyer. However, the first bout between the two rivals had nothing to do with politics but rather winning the charms of a well-known female. In 1839, Mary Todd moved from the family home in Lexington, Kentucky, to her sister's residence in Springfield, Illinois, where she didn't long for suitors. The young woman attracted many of the community's most eligible bachelors including the two young attorneys.

When Lincoln was reelected to his seat in the Illinois State House of Representatives in 1836, Douglas joined him as a first-time member. The freshman legislator began courting Mary and eventually proposed to her twice only to be rejected each time. She eventually chose Lincoln, a fellow Kentucky native, to begin her new life as a wife and mother.

Each man eventually worked his way from Illinois to the halls of the US Capitol Building where they served together in the 30th Congress (1847–1849). But it was there that their political futures began going in separate directions.

By the 1850s, with three terms as a member of the House of Representatives and two in the Senate on his resume, Douglas had made a national name for himself. With his profile becoming more eminent across the country, there were those who were mentioning his name as a future presidential candidate. By 1856, he was one of the Democrats' final four contenders for the White House nomination.

Meanwhile, Lincoln had returned to Illinois where he resumed the practice of law. His career was far less than impressive from those who had built their names to eventually make a run for national office. His personal history included:

- He ran for the Illinois state legislature in 1832, finishing eighth in a field of thirteen.
- He was unable to attend law school although he eventually passed the bar by borrowing books and studying on his own.
- In 1833, Lincoln's business, a general store in Springfield, Illinois, went bankrupt. He spent several years repaying the debt from the loan that he had recieved.
- By the time of the 1838–1839 legislative session, Lincoln had twice been an unsuccessful Whig candidate for the position of speaker of the Illinois House of Representatives.
- In 1849, Lincoln sought the job of federal land officer in Illinois but was passed over for another candidate. That same year, he declined an appointment as governor of the Oregon Territory.
- In 1854, he withdrew from the US Senate race in Illinois.
- He finished second in the 1856 Republican nomination for vice president.

Then came 1858 and what many believe was the most famous Senate race of all-time as the Republican made a make or break career decision choosing to run against the popular incumbent. This proved to be a different campaign than any of those previously held in Illinois, for rather than debating topics such as agriculture and foreign trade, the nominees followed a similar script that was playing out in many other states where the hot button issue was slavery. On June 16, 1858, shortly after accepting the party's nomination, Lincoln delivered his "House Divided" speech which catapulted him into the national spotlight.

The campaign was off to a rousing start although some in his own party believed that the address was too radical and ill-timed.

The candidates then agreed to a series of debates that were held in seven of the state's nine congressional districts. From August 21 until October 15, Douglas and Lincoln verbally jousted before large and enthusiastic crowds. Douglas advocated popular sovereignty while Lincoln drove home the point that slavery was morally wrong. Equally important was the fact that the series of meetings set the standard of how candidates should present their views on the issues that concerned voters. The events bore no resemblance to today's made for television parleys that often leave the viewing public with more questions than answers.

Senate elections during that era were held in the Illinois General Assembly, and when the ballots were tabulated Douglas had held on to his legislative seat with a 54–46 victory. Lincoln enthusiasts could only wonder about the outcome had the election been held by popular vote. That practice took effect in 1913 with the passage of the Seventeenth Amendment to the United States Constitution.

Douglas returned to Washington, DC, to begin his third six-year stint in the Senate. However, those duties were interrupted on May 3, 1860, when the Democratic Convention concluded with the political stalwart from the Prairie State being chosen as the party's presidential nominee. Ironically, the event had been held that year in Charleston, South Carolina, a state that was at the center of the storm over slavery. Four years earlier, Douglas had lost a close battle with James Buchanan for the party's top spot on the ticket.

A few months later, Buchanan indicated in his 1857 inaugural address that he would be a one-term president and did not detour from that pledge. He became the eighth consecutive chief executive who did not serve a second term.

Two weeks after the Democrats gathered, Lincoln joined his fellow Republicans as they convened in Chicago. On the second night of the assemblage, the play *Our American Cousin* opened at the McVicker's Theater a few blocks from the convention hall. It was the same production that Lincoln was watching at Ford's Theater when he was assassinated some five years later.

He was selected as the party's nominee on the third ballot setting up a rematch between the two men from Illinois who had battled for the Senate seat less than two years earlier. But if voters were expecting a set of history-making debates like those of 1858, they were quickly disappointed. Lincoln changed his strategy and remained in Illinois, ignoring the southern region, greeting supporters and dignitaries while Douglas became the first candidate to take part in a national tour making appearances in twenty-three of the existing thirty-three states. However, the power of Lincoln's words from the earlier campaign continued to resonate with many voters who searched for the differences among their options for the White House.

But Douglas had another problem that followed him on the campaign road in conjunction with slavery. There was a fracturing within his own party as sitting vice president John C. Breckenridge ran as the candidate representing southern Democrats along with former US Senator John Bell of Tennessee representing the Constitutional Union Party.

Lincoln captured eighteen states that included all of the northern area, sans Delaware and Maryland, plus the West Coast duo of California and Oregon. He had close calls in California (0.6%), Illinois (3.5%), New Jersey (3.8%), and Oregon (1.7%), but lost his birth state of Kentucky. Nonetheless, Lincoln garnered 180 electoral ballots over Breckinridge (72), Bell (39), and Douglas (12). The challenge of running against three candidates with southern roots proved problematic for the Illinois senator who eventually finished in a disappointing last place among the four-man field.

Table 6.1   The Election of 1860

Presidential candidate	Party	Home state	Popular vote Count	Percentage	Electoral vote
Abraham Lincoln	Republican	Illinois	1,865,908	39.82%	180
John C. Breckinridge	Southern Democratic	Kentucky	848,019	18.10%	72
John Bell	Constitutional Union/Whig	Tennessee	590,901	12.61%	39
Stephen A. Douglas	Northern Democratic	Illinois	1,380,202	29.46%	12
Other			531	0.01%	—
Total			4,685,561	100%	303
Needed to win					152

Vice President Elect, Hannibal Hamlin, US Senator (R-ME)

THE AFTERMATH

Lincoln's challenge to become the nation's sixteenth president of the United States didn't end with the election. It then became a matter of safely getting him from his home in Springfield, Illinois, to Washington, DC, to be sworn in. His train departed for the nation's capital on February 11, 1861, after seven states had already seceded and amid a flurry of assassination rumors. He was accompanied by his wife Mary and their sons Robert (seventeen), Willie (ten), and Tad (seven).

The Secret Service had yet to be created so government officials were responsible for their own security details. For Lincoln, a resident of Illinois, that meant hiring Chicago's most famous bodyguards headed by the well-known private investigator Allen Pinkerton. As he prepared to move the president-elect and his family to their new residence, the native of Scotland had also heard the rumblings about an attempt on Lincoln's life and that many of those threats were connected to Baltimore, a city heavily divided over slavery.

To counter the threat, Pinkerton changed Lincoln's travel plan having him skip an address originally scheduled to be delivered to Pennsylvania state legislature in Harrisburg. On the evening of February 22, the group boarded a sleeper car in Harrisburg and arrived in Baltimore later that night. From there, they slipped undetected from the Calvert Street station to Camden station across town boarding another train and arriving unscathed at the famed Willard Hotel in Washington, DC.

"I did not then, nor do I now believe I should have been assassinated had I gone through Baltimore" commented Lincoln about the covert operation.

That year's inauguration wasn't just the usual ceremony but featured the reemergence of former rivals Lincoln and Douglas appearing together. The two men had last shared a stage for their seventh and final senatorial debate on October 15, 1858, in Alton, Illinois. On Inauguration Day, March 4, 1861, any difficult feelings that may have lingered after the pair of hard fought campaigns were gone, as Douglas was one of the invited few to sit among the honored guests on the platform.

Although the time had been chronologically brief, a great deal of change had taken place in the young nation from 1858 to 1861. As the new president rose to give his inaugural address, the senator offered to hold his famous stovetop hat in a gesture of cooperation. That evening at the Inaugural Ball being held inside a temporary structure near City Hall, Mary Todd Lincoln danced the quadrille with her former beau Stephen Douglas one last time. It was twenty-two years after he had proposed to her.

It was also one of his final appearances as on June 3, 1861, Senator Douglas died at his Chicago home of typhoid fever. Had he won the election of 1860 his death would have had him serve the second shortest term in the nation's history. It also meant that his vice presidential running mate Herschel V. Johnson would have become the new commander in chief. He was the former governor of Georgia and ironically would later serve as a Confederate senator during the Civil War.

Buchanan escorted Lincoln to the ceremonies and then accompanied him to the Executive Mansion. He began the tradition of the outgoing president leaving a letter behind to his successor. His departing words were, "If you are as happy, my dear sir, on entering this house as I am in leaving it and returning home, you are the happiest man in this country."

After more than a century, Ronald Reagan resurrected the practice of a farewell note to the successor George H. W. Bush in 1989, which has continued with every chief executive since then.

In 1866, Buchanan wrote the memoir, *Mr. Buchanan's Administration on the Eve of Rebellion*, where he attempted to explain the events of his presidency. It was the first such work by a former living president.

7

The Election of 1864

Abraham Lincoln, Incumbent (Republican) vs. George B. McClellan (Democrat)

"Elections belong to the people. It's their decision. If they decide to turn their back on the fire and burn their behinds, then they will just have to sit on their blisters."

—Abraham Lincoln

The English philosopher Francis Bacon (1561–1626) once said, "A man that studieth revenge keeps his own wounds green." By the time the American Civil War was underway, Sir Francis was just a memory in British history, but his words could have been applied to one of the Union's most prominent figures.

Major General George B. McClellan was a West Point graduate who became the commander of the US Army. He was a veteran of the Mexican-American War where he was confined to a hospital for a month with malaria. In the ensuing years, the native of Pennsylvania gained the respect of his fellow officers as he used his skills as a trained engineer to improve passages and open areas for railroad lines.

In 1857, McClellan resigned his commission to become vice president of the Illinois Central Railroad followed by president of the Ohio and Mississippi line three years later. In 1861, with the outbreak of the War Between the States, he returned to the army as a major general joining numerous other ex-soldiers who had reenlisted for the cause.

McClellan's reputation as a military leader with great potential was built on the publicity that he received during two skirmishes in the summer of 1861 at Philippi and Rich Mountain, both in Virginia. The *New York Herald* billed him as, "the Napoleon of the Present War" and even though the victories were minor as the Federals vastly outnumbered the Confederacy, they were important in keeping the public morale supportive of the Union.

Lincoln and McClellan met at command headquarters following the Battle of Antietam on October 3, 1862. Credit: Library of Congress

Conversely, the shine on the star of commander Irvin McDowell's career had quickly tarnished on July 21, 1861, with the disaster suffered by the Union at the First Battle of Bull Run. Four days later, President Abraham Lincoln replaced McDowell with the thirty-four-year-old "Young Napoleon" who was placed in command of the new Army of the Potomac. While neither man realized it at the time, the initial step toward the election of 1864 had just been taken.

McClellan's first task was to reinforce the defenses surrounding Washington, DC. Not unlike George Washington, the new commander found his army composed of disorganized, poorly trained rabble with no resemblance of a fighting force. The general used his experience from West Point and the Mexican-American War to transform the disorderly mob into faithful soldiers who were combat ready.

But McClellan had another target in addition to the Confederate Army. Winfield Scott was the commanding general of the Feds, a position that he had held since 1841. He had been a general since before McClellan was born and was a candidate for the Whig Party's presidential nomination in 1840, 1844, and 1848, before finally becoming their nominee in 1852. The longtime military veteran had also been one of the American heroes of the Mexican-American War.

However, those accomplishments meant little to the ambitious McClellan who only saw his superior officer as a tired seventy-four year old in poor health and well past his prime. By November, Scott had announced his retirement and Lincoln offered McClellan the post making him the youngest commanding general in

America's history. Unfortunately, the burgeoning general had reached his pinnacle after just a few months following his return.

As commander, McClellan's task greatly differed from those at the battles at Philippi and Rich Mountain. He would face better trained troops under the leadership of some of best military minds in the field. Among them were Robert E. Lee who had once been offered command of the Union Army and Thomas "Stonewall" Jackson, a master strategist who was beloved by his men and struck terror into the souls of the enemy. The South continued with a string of impressive victories that had begun at Bull Run.

While McClellan's engineering skills were unquestioned, the same couldn't be said for his political tact. He referred to Lincoln, his commander in chief, disrespectfully in discussions with others calling him "the original gorilla." He also had little use for other members of the administration with no military background such as Secretary of State William Seward.

History portrays Lincoln as a kindly gentleman long known by the moniker "Honest Abe." He was a doting father to his young sons and immensely patient with his temperamental wife, Mary, who was known to public displays of anger. However, when it came to generals in battle, he had little tolerance for their lack of aggression. The president had served as a captain during the Black Hawk War some thirty years earlier but saw no action. Among his men was James Reed who, in 1846–1847, was part of the tragic Donner Party. During the devastating journey, he carried the unit's muster rolls, which had been handwritten by Lincoln.

Even though he hadn't been in a battle, Lincoln had seen the successful results of leaders who pushed the enemy as opposed to those who relied on delaying tactics, which is what he perceived had happened to McClellan. It was the summer of 1862, a year after Bull Run, and the commander had yet to launch a retaliatory strike on the Confederacy. Lincoln had had enough and ordered McClellan to invade Richmond.

It began on June 26, 1862, with the Battle of Mechanicsville in Virginia, which marked the initial conflict of the Seven Days' Campaign. The Rebels suffered about 1,400 casualties compared to Union losses that numbered less than half that figure, but Lee's aggression had forced McClellan to withdraw his troops rather than press the attack providing an opportunity for the Southerners the next day. The fighting had just begun but it had already put McClellan's inexperience as a battlefield leader on full display to all including President Lincoln.

Frequently, the chief executive could be seen walking across the street (Jackson Place NW) from the White House to the Telegraph Office located in the War Department building (site of the present-day Eisenhower Executive Office Building) where he read the discouraging updates by wire transmission. Even in battles where he had a troop size advantage, the losses continued to mount for McClellan.

The "Young Napoleon's" own version of his namesake's Waterloo came on September17,1862, at Sharpsburg, Maryland, with the Battle of Antietam. While casualties were massive on both sides (almost twenty-three thousand combined) in the single bloodiest day of fighting in the nation's history, Lincoln felt that McClellan's strategy was overly cautious and didn't put his charges in the proper position for victory.

From September 17 to October 26, the president and Secretary of War Edwin Stanton became even more frustrated with their hesitant general when McClellan failed to pursue Lee while he was in retreat from Antietam as he blamed shortages of equipment and the fear of overextending his forces for the delay. On October 4, Lincoln and McClellan met at the battlefield headquarters at Sharpsburg (see above photo). General in Chief Henry W. Halleck wrote in his official report, "The long inactivity of so large an army in the face of a defeated foe, and during the most favorable season for rapid movements and a vigorous campaign, was a matter of great disappointment and regret."

The even tempered president had seen enough and on November 5 he relieved McClellan of his command and with that, he effectively put an end to the general's military career. Four days later, he was replaced by General Ambrose Burnside but the business between Lincoln and McClellan wasn't over.

The Union started 1863 on a lopsided note with another costly "victory" at the Battle of Stones River in Murfreesboro, Tennessee. While the Confederate Army was forced to retreat on January 2, the Union suffered more than a thousand additional casualties than did their enemy. Ulysses S. Grant summed up his difference of opinion of the battle's outcome with Lincoln who viewed it as a win for the Feds, "Stones River was certainly no victory, and he [Lincoln] knew of no great results which followed from it."

McClellan had no background in politics and no real interest in attaining office once he left the military. He was still popular and made a few appearances in 1863, such as one in New York City to raise funds for the relief of the poor of Ireland. But while he insisted that he was not in attendance for political gain, during a lengthy greeting he stated, "Although, as I said before, we have come here to-night for no political purpose, yet no true friend of his country, in the present crisis, can repress altogether the thoughts that will crowd upon his brain."

McClellan may have been out of a job, but he wasn't out of the public's eye. As the year moved along, he became more comfortable among crowds and drew interest from Ohio to run for governor on the state's Democratic ticket. Republicans feared McClellan's popularity and wanted to placate him even talking about a cabinet post but Lincoln and his inner circle would have nothing of it. In October 1863, the former general took the next step toward seeking public office by declaring himself a member of the Democratic Party.

The bloody battles at Fredericksburg, Chancellorsville, and Gettysburg spawned intense rumors of a McClellan comeback to command. However, Lincoln squelched the talk on March 1, 1864, by nominating Grant for the newly revived rank of lieutenant general, which carried with it the supreme command of the Union forces. That news was followed a few months later in August when the Democrats nominated McClellan for president. The selection set up the ultimate confrontation between the displaced general and his former commander in chief who had already been renominated by the Republicans.

McClellan believed that he had a realistic chance at victory based on the results of the midterm elections of 1862. The Republicans lost 22 seats in Congress, while the Democrats picked up 28, for a net swing of 50 seats (or 27%) out of a total House membership of 185. Also, many blamed Lincoln for the war, which meant that a certain number of voters would favor his opponent, no matter who it might be.

While McClellan was well-educated, he didn't possess Lincoln's political savvy. The man from Illinois hardly had the persona of an intellectual, but he could read people and, over the years, had developed sharp instincts when it came to maneuvering around the political landscape. In an effort to retain his presidency, he made two important moves in 1864.

In June, Vice President Hannibal Hamlin traveled to the Republican National Convention in Baltimore assuming he would be renominated. However, on the first roll call, he won only 150 votes as opposed to 200 for Andrew Johnson. Before the second roll call, enough delegates switched their ballots to give Johnson the second spot on the ticket.

Hamlin was a strong antislavery New Englander who was born in Massachusetts and later relocated to Maine. In an effort to gain some favor with Southern voters, Lincoln chose Johnson who, at the time, was the military governor of Tennessee but firmly believed in the Union. He was also a former slave owner who had successfully lobbied the president to exclude Tennessee from the Emancipation Proclamation. In order to gain some support with those undecideds who lived below the Mason-Dixon Line, Lincoln elected to play both sides against the middle.

His other strategy was to expand the Union by bringing Nevada into the Union by October 31, 1864. Lincoln was the primary force behind the plan but because of the uncertain prospects of his reelection, he believed that making Nevada a state might provide some electoral insurance. The truth of the matter was that the area was not actually eligible for statehood in 1864.

Under the Northwest Ordinance, one of the first requirements before a territory could petition for statehood was a population of 60,000, but in 1860 the census of Nevada was recorded at just 6,857. Although small in numbers, Lincoln's political advisers thought the addition of another Northern state would boost the Union's morale and add support for the president's reelection bid.

Although the territory had been pursuing statehood for quite some time, they held a referendum that overwhelmingly passed in 1863 and led to a state constitutional convention that same year. On October 31, just nine days before the election on November 8, 1864, Nevada became the thirty-sixth state. State officials had already telegraphed the new Constitution of Nevada to the US Congress on October 26 and 27. The 175-page transcription contained 16,543 words at a cost of $4,313.27 ($59,229 in today's dollars) to communicate. It was the largest and costliest transmission ever by telegraph.

America's newest group of citizens participated in the election the following week with more than sixteen thousand voters going to the polls. Lincoln captured the contest and its two electoral votes. Even though in the final outcome the new state wasn't needed to secure a win, it was a harsh lesson in hardball politics for McClellan who was swarmed under in the electoral college 212 to 21.

For the second time in two years, "Young Napoleon" had been cast aside by a president who wouldn't tolerate the practice of nonaggression and, just as before, became an afterthought not just in war but also at the ballot box.

But all the bad news wasn't on McClellan's side when Lincoln ran for reelection in 1864, he was $27,000 in debt (that would be more than $400,000 today!). Almost all was due to his wife's habit of compulsive shopping from the merchants of the nation's capital.

Table 7.1   The Election of 1864

Presidential candidate	Party	Home state	Popular vote Count	Percentage	Electoral vote
Abraham Lincoln (Incumbent)	National Union	Illinois	2,218,388	55.03%	212
George Brinton McClellan	Democratic	New Jersey	1,812,807	44.95%	21
Ellsworth Cheeseborough	Independent	Kansas	543	0.01%	0
Other			112	<0.01%	
Total			4031887	100%	233
Needed to win					117

Vice President Elect, Andrew Johnson, former Governor (D-TN)

THE AFTERMATH

Among the more well-known individuals fighting for the Confederacy was John C. Breckenridge, a major general who was later appointed as secretary of war for the Southerners by Jefferson Davis. He had previously served as James Buchanan's vice president from 1857–1861 and returned to the United States following the conflict in 1868.

Breckenridge had been the candidate of the Southern Democrats in 1860. He died in 1875 at the age of fifty-four having never returned to political office.

On March 4, 1865, the actor John Wilkes Booth, along with several of his followers (Lewis Powell, George Atzerodt, John Surratt, Mary Surratt, David Herold, Michael O'Laughlin, Ned Spangler, and Samuel Arnold), attended Abraham Lincoln's inaugural address on the steps of the Capitol Building. It was there that he became engaged in a confrontation with a police officer along with Benjamin Brown French, the clerk of the US House of Representatives, who later stated, "My theory is that he meant to rush up behind the president and assassinate him, and in the confusion escaped into the crowd again and got away. But, by stopping him as we did, the president got out of his reach."

A month later, Booth told a confidant, "What a splendid chance I had to kill the president on the fourth of March [at the inauguration]."

But that attempted assassination wasn't Lincoln's first close call. From 1862 to 1864, the president and First Lady spent June through November living in the cottage on the grounds of the nearby Soldiers' Home where he continued to oversee the war. He enjoyed the country setting and the open areas where he could ride his trusted horse "Old Abe."

On a warm night in August 1864, an unaccompanied Lincoln was returning to the cottage aboard his steed when he heard a nearby gunshot. The round startled his horse and it galloped away, but when they returned home, Lincoln saw a bullet hole through the crown of his silk plug hat. The president ordered the matter to be kept quiet and on future trips he traveled by carriage.

Booth changed his mind about killing Lincoln and put together a plot to kidnap the president figuring that he might be of more value to the Confederacy as a hostage. On March 17, 1865, the commander in chief was scheduled to go to the Campbell General Hospital, north of Washington, DC, to attend the play *Still Waters Run Deep*, written by Tom Taylor who also wrote *Our American Cousin*. The plan was to abduct the chief executive at the hospital site and move him to Richmond. But the scheme was foiled when Lincoln changed his mind opting to go to the National Hotel on Pennsylvania Avenue for a presentation where he was given a Confederate battle flag by the governor of Indiana that had been captured by the 140th Indiana Volunteer Infantry at Fort Anderson, North Carolina.

The National Hotel was Booth's preferred lodging establishment whenever he stayed in the nation's capital. Had he remained at the location rather than going to the hospital area, Lincoln would have walked right into the plot.

On Sunday April 9, 1865, Confederate commander Robert E. Lee formally surrendered to his counterpart Ulysses S. Grant at Appomattox Court House, Virginia, thus ending the War Between the States. The news further infuriated Booth who continued to believe that a Southern victory was possible as other battles continued to take place until word of the surrender became known.

While the twenty-seven-year-old stage actor prepared his next move, there were others who were already attempting to instigate their own plots. The day following the surrender, the 8th Illinois Cavalry captured and arrested Thomas F. Harney, an explosives expert with the Confederate Torpedo Bureau. He had been given the assignment by the Confederate Secret Service to blow up a wing of the White House but was seized near Burke, Virginia, before he could carry out the order.

On Friday, April 14, General Grant met with cabinet members at the White House to discuss the surrender terms. Throughout the city, the locals were eagerly anticipating the evening's festivities as it had been announced that Lincoln and Grant, along with their wives, would be attending the popular play *Our American*

Cousin at Ford's Theater. But the general was tired from his time battling the enemy and wanted to see his children rather than attend the production. The meeting concluded about 2:00 p.m., and shortly afterward, the Grants departed for the station where they took a 6:00 p.m. train to New Jersey.

Meanwhile, Booth had elected not only to kill Lincoln but also vice president Andrew Johnson and Secretary of State William Seward. The plan was to murder the trio at three separate locations at the approximately the same time (10:15 p.m.), which he contended would throw the government into disarray allowing the Confederacy to mount its resurrection.

Among the plans being made for the evening were selecting the members from the 150 man Metropolitan Police Force who would be assigned to the security detail. They were responsible for the president's safety in the days prior to the Secret Service. In a stroke of irony, Lincoln had signed into law a piece of legislation that created the Secret Service just a few hours earlier that same day. In its beginning, the organization's primary function was to root out counterfeiters.

In one of the most unusual decisions in the history of the presidency, officer John F. Parker was selected as part of the four man detail to guard Lincoln at Ford's. The fact that the thirty-four year old was still with the department was a mystery in itself. Since joining the force in 1861 when it was created by Lincoln, Parker had faced the Police Board at various times on charges of conduct unbecoming an officer, visiting a house of prostitution, firing a pistol through a window, being drunk on duty, being asleep on duty, and using abusive language. Even with multiple reprimands in his file, the former carpenter had been allowed to keep his badge.

Parker was ordered to report for duty at the White House at 4:00 p.m. but was three hours late. He was then sent to the theater where he was assigned the critical task of guarding the presidential box from the outer hallway. He was armed with a revolver with orders to prevent any unauthorized person(s) from entering the small room. The officer was authorized to use deadly force if necessary.

The play had already begun when the president and his party arrived at 8:30 p.m. Accompanying him were his wife Mary, US Army major Henry Rathbone and Clara Harris, the daughter of US senator Ira Harris of New York. Rathbone and Harris were last minute substitutes for the Grants. The two couples made their way up the stairs where they were greeted by Parker. They took their seats and the box door was closed but not locked.

As the play progressed, the guard left his post in the hallway that led to the box. At intermission, he joined the footman and coachman of Lincoln's carriage for drinks at Taltavull's Star Saloon next door to the theater. Neither the president nor anyone else in his group were aware of Parker's absence. Later, having quenched his thirst, the on-duty policeman returned to the playhouse electing to take a seat in the balcony far away from his designated station.

Booth arrived at Ford's Theatre at about 9:30 p.m. with a .44 caliber derringer pistol and a hunting knife concealed in his coat. Since the popular actor was known to attend plays when he wasn't performing, those who saw him had no reason to suspect anything was amiss. He made his way to the same saloon where Parker had been drinking just moments earlier and ordered whiskey and water.

Booth left the establishment and entered Ford's at around 10:00 p.m. He began to climb the stairwell leading to the box expecting to find a guard looming in the area.

He was surprised to see a clear path to the upper tier as Parker was still relaxing in the audience. With the unanticipated opening at hand, Booth quietly entered the room and walked toward Lincoln's back, aiming the single shot weapon at his head. The sound of gunfire coupled with Mary Lincoln's screams sent the crowd into pandemonium. After slashing Rathbone's arm with his knife, Booth leaped from the box landing awkwardly on the stage breaking his ankle in the process. He was able to limp to the stage door where he had left his horse and rode away into the night. Fortunately, the other conspirators had not been as lucky as Booth as their attempts on the lives of Johnson and Seward had failed.

Anarchy reigned through the auditorium as doctors rushed to the box to treat the fallen leader, but Officer Parker was nowhere to be found. A short time later, the nonresponsive president was carried across the street and placed in a bed at the Petersen Boarding House where onlookers awaited the inevitable. The manhunt for Booth began immediately under the direction of Secretary of War Edwin Stanton.

As soldiers and civilians began scouring the countryside around the nation's capital for the assassin, Parker surprisingly reemerged at police headquarters at 6:00 a.m. the following day. With him was a woman named Lizzie Williams whom he had arrested for prostitution, but the high command was in no mood to deal with such matters at that moment and immediately released her. Perhaps Parker thought that an arrest might cause his bosses to overlook his egregious mistake.

On April 26, Booth was ambushed in a barn and killed by Union troops at Port Royal, Virginia. Most of the other conspirators were hanged in public before a large crowd in Washington, DC, on July 7.

But once again, John F. Parker escaped any major disciplinary action. On May 1, he was charged with neglect of duty during the assassination even though he was still able to retain his job. The incompetent officer remained on the Metropolitan Police Force for three more years, but was finally fired on August 13, 1868, for once again sleeping on duty. He drifted back into his former profession of carpentry and died in Washington, DC, in 1890.

After more than a century after the fact, two critical questions remain unanswered. Did the Metropolitan Police Force sweep Parker's behavior, on the night of the assassination, under the rug in order to save face? Additionally, where was he from the time Lincoln was shot until he reappeared at 6:00 a.m.?

One thing was certain, had a capable police officer been on duty that evening in place of Parker, Abraham Lincoln may have left Ford's Theater and returned to the White House to begin the Reconstruction Era.

THE FOLLOWING ELECTIONS

1868: Andrew Johnson, who had succeeded Lincoln as president, was in the wrong place at the wrong time in 1868. Even though he had served in a Republican administration as a Democrat, neither party wanted him as its candidate for the next election cycle.

Part of the reason was the stain on his record from his impeachment. But the biggest obstacle was for someone that he, nor anyone else, could beat—the winning general of the Civil War, Ulysses S. Grant. He became the latest hero to take up residence at the mansion.

In post–Civil War America, the victorious battlefield commander was recruited by both major parties before settling on the GOP. He was an overwhelming choice over former New York governor Horatio Seymour for president.

1872: While Grant's effectiveness as chief executive was questionable, the admiration of the public for him was solid. He was easily reelected to a second term over the challenge of former senator Thomas Hendricks (D-IN), 286–42.

8

The Election of 1876

Rutherford B. Hayes (Republican) vs. Samuel J. Tilden (Democrat)

"Every expert was once a beginner."

—Rutherford B. Hayes

"What if?"

Perhaps no phrase congers up memories of individuals throughout history who, for one reason or another, had their destiny altered by events beyond their control. Some of the best known examples include:

What if Queen Isabella had denied Christopher Columbus the funds that he needed to make his first voyage?

What if the colonists decided not to take on the British and fight for their independence?

What if Lincoln had elected not to go to the theater on that final evening?

On March 2, 1877, former governor Samuel J. Tilden of New York was one of those who could only wonder, "What if?" as Rutherford B. Hayes was officially declared the nineteenth president of the United States. That's because after an unprecedented long, drawn out process, he had lost the nation's most important election by the slimmest of margins.

Tilden was a native New Yorker and a protégé of former president Martin Van Buren. He had played key roles in the campaigns of others and was instrumental in taking down William "Boss" Tweed of the corrupt political machine, Tammany Hall. With that, in 1872, he was elected to the State Assembly followed by a term as governor some three years later.

Tilden served eight years (1866–1874) as the chairman of New York's Democratic Party. His personal profile continued to grow as one of the political elites in the nation's most populous state, which started rumors about a possible 1876 presidential run. At the Democratic National Convention in St. Louis, where no African American delegates were seated, the sixty-two-year-old Tilden easily won the nomination on the second ballot capturing 738 votes to the runner up, Indiana governor Thomas A. Hendricks. In order to build a stronger ticket, the party chose to make Hendricks, a racist who voted against the Thirteenth, Fourteenth, and Fifteenth Amendments, the vice presidential running mate.

The Republicans had met two weeks earlier (June 14–16) in Cincinnati, Ohio, and after the first ballot, it appeared that US Senator James G. Blaine of Maine was destined to become the nominee over eight other contenders. Following the opening address by former slave turned abolition spokesperson Frederick Douglass and the first round of voting, Blaine had secured 285 of the 378 delegates needed to guarantee the top spot on the ticket.

The first six ballots proceeded with little movement among the nine candidates although Blaine was edging ever closer with 308 delegates. The only other candidate who was continuing to move up in the count was Ohio governor Rutherford B. Hayes, who finished the round with 113 votes.

He was a former Civil War officer who had served in the 23rd Ohio Volunteer Infantry eventually attaining the rank of general. Among those who served under him was an eighteen year old private from Niles, Ohio, named William McKinley. A true hero, Hayes and his men took part in more than fifty battles including those at Lynchburg, Winchester, Berryville, Opequan, Fisher's Hill, and Cedar Creek. He was wounded in battle seven times and had four horses shot out from under him. Both Hayes and McKinley concluded their military service in 1865 when the war ended.

At the end of the conflict, Hayes served in the US House of Representatives from 1865 to 1867 when he resigned to run for governor. He was elected to two (four year) terms as Ohio's top official (1868–1872 and 1876–1877) before being placed in nomination for president at the convention in 1876. He did not complete his second gubernatorial term.

For those who longed for a candidate that reminded them of Ulysses S. Grant, Hayes filled many of those qualities. Both men were Republicans from Ohio, Union generals, had seen action in several important Civil War battles, and each wore a fashionable beard.

As the seventh ballot got underway, anxious delegates were shifting their votes, some away from Blaine as others caucused in an effort to promote Hayes.

One of the reasons that Blaine's potentially assured nomination had slowed to a crawl was that he suffered from the same affliction that burdened so many other politicians of his day—he was linked to a railroad scandal. In 1869, the Speaker used his influence to leverage the passage of a land grant for the Little Rock & Fort Smith

Railroad. Warren Fisher, one of the company's contractors, allowed Blaine to sell securities in the railroad company and pocket an ample commission in the process.

However, when the business started to have financial trouble, the value of the bonds decreased. Tom Scott, one of the company's wealthiest supporters, bought back the shares from Blaine and his friends for a price well above market value. In one deal he was paid $64,000 (around $1.5 million today) and, in return, Blaine supported legislation that benefited Scott's railroad.

The senator's problems were no secret to those who had convened in Cincinnati to select a candidate. A collection of letters that had been exchanged between Blaine and Fisher were previously revealed by a company clerk, James Mulligan. The scandal took on a life of its own becoming known as the "Mulligan Letters," resulting in an investigation by the House of Representatives.

However, in July 1876, when President Grant selected US senator Lot M. Morrill of Maine to fill the vacancy of secretary of the treasury, the state's governor appointed Blaine to take on Morrill's former Senate seat. With that, the inquiry was discontinued as Blaine moved from the House to his new position in the Senate.

The scheme was the latest episode of corruption tied to the ever growing railroads. With the expansion of lines in the west, those looking for a short cut to riches believed that they had found their personal pot of gold.

At the convention there had been serious movement on the fifth ballot as the Michigan delegation, which had previously been split three ways, unified for Hayes. That pushed the Ohio governor's total over the 100 mark (104 exactly) for the first time as he was also the only candidate during that round to produce a net gain in delegates.

Entering the seventh ballot, Blaine led the race 308–113 needing just 70 votes to finalize the nomination. But there were still those in the anti-Blaine group, especially the party's liberal wing known as the "Mugwumps," who wouldn't support the favorite. Party officials mingled with state chairmen trying to find a resolution to the problem. Indiana provided a boost to Hayes's chances as twenty-five of the thirty Hoosier faithfuls voted for the Ohioan and other states, like New Jersey, New York, and Pennsylvania followed after that.

As the count took place, it was evident that seven had become Blaine's unlucky number as on that ballot, he was defeated 384–351. Fortunately, the vice presidential vote ended quickly as Congressman William A. Wheeler of New York was nominated in a landslide on the first ballot.

Hayes had narrowly cleared the first hurdle. It was now on to the general election.

Tilden had done the math. He knew that it would take 185 electoral votes to win and that he could count on his home state of New York to come through for him. That would put 35 votes in his column with just 150 more needed to cinch a victory.

Neither Tilden nor Hayes actively campaigned, which was considered improper for a party's candidate during the era. Surrogates spread the word and held nothing back while the mud- slinging was hot and heavy as proxies carried on a war of words between the two sides. Democrats spread a rumor that Hayes had once shot his own mother "in a fit of insanity" after a night of drinking in Ohio.

The Republicans stayed busy declaring that Tilden was guilty of tax evasion. Among the celebrities of the day endorsing Hayes was the well-known author Mark Twain, but there was no proof that the accusations being hurled from either side contained any degree of truth. While the banter ensued, there were other matters connected to the upcoming election that could be critical.

On August 1, 1876, Colorado became the nation's thirty-eighth state, but there was a problem. With just three months until voting was to commence, there wasn't enough time to organize a presidential election in the new state so Colorado's legislature chose its electors, who gave their three votes to Hayes, which was the last election where a state chose electors through its legislature.

However, during the campaign, in a move reminiscent of James K. Polk, Hayes promised that if elected, he'd only serve one term. After months of trash-talking by the party faithful, on November 7, the public made their own voices heard at the voting booth.

The following morning, *The New York Times* reported that Tilden was on the brink of victory with 184 of the needed 185 electoral votes secured as compared to Hayes's 166. But there were problems with the vote counts in Oregon (one), Florida (four), South Carolina (seven), and Louisiana (eight) leaving twenty electoral ballots in dispute. Each situation was different and no amount of planning by the Founding Fathers could have predicted four such bizarre cases.

Oregon: Hayes won the statewide popular vote by about 3.5 percent, but Governor La Fayette Grover claimed that former postmaster John Watts was constitutionally ineligible to serve as an elector since he was a "person holding an office of trust or profit under the United States."

The governor attempted to substitute a Democrat elector in his place but the two other Republicans bypassed Grover's action and filed all three votes for Hayes with the electoral college. Two of the ballots were valid but it was Watts's vote that was suspect under the law.

Louisiana: Tilden unofficially carried the state by more than six thousand votes. But the Returning Board, which was controlled by Republicans, threw out more than fifteen thousand ballots (more than thirteen thousand for Tilden). The law required that the board have five members with both parties represented, but only one Democrat was seated, and he resigned prior to the election.

Hayes was declared the winner by 4,807 votes and awarded Louisiana's eight electoral votes, but the Democratic Party instituted its own state government and, in turn, certified that Tilden had won, thus signifying an impasse in the bayou.

South Carolina: The Palmetto State followed nearly an exact script as Louisiana when Hayes was initially seen as the winner. Once again, the Democrats organized a rival state government and declared Tilden the victor. In South Carolina, where the election was marred by racial violence, the voter turnout was 101 percent of the total male voting population resulting in the courts holding members of the board in contempt, serving them with fines, and incarcerating them in the county jail.

More than one thousand ballots for Tilden were tossed out pushing Hayes into the lead by just 974 votes.

Florida: The initial count showed Hayes ahead by forty-three votes, but after a correction was made, Tilden took the lead by ninety-four votes. Subsequently, the election board disallowed numerous ballots, delivering the election to Hayes by nearly a thousand votes out of nearly fifty thousand cast.

But the confusion didn't stop there. The board declared that in the coinciding gubernatorial election, the Republican candidate (incumbent Marcellus Lovejoy Stearns) had also won his election, although the Florida Supreme Court overruled them following a mandated recount and awarded the victory to Democrat George Franklin Drew. In turn, the state's new governor announced that Tilden, not Hayes, had carried Florida.

On top of all of the ballot-counting confusion, the day after the election, a train derailed that was carrying votes that were bound for the state's capital city of Tallahassee. Persistent stories circulated that the Ku Klux Klan had played a part in the accident.

There was no novelist alive during that era, not even Mark Twain, who could have conceived of such a series of events taking place that could throw the presidential election into such chaos. Hayes won the popular vote in all four of the states that were in question, but the margins were close enough that both parties claimed victory. Overall, the Ohioan won the popular vote in five states by a spread of 2 percent or less. Tilden also had a close call in Indiana winning by just 1.14 percent.

Congress was now in possession of two sets of competing election certificates from Florida, Louisiana, and South Carolina. Each party controlled one set of ballots giving their candidate nineteen electoral votes. Additionally, there was that one vote from Oregon that was in dispute.

In the midst of an electoral sea of confusion, negotiations soon began in an attempt to reach a solution to the dilemma. On January 29, 1877, Congress formed the Joint Committee on Electoral Count. Its fifteen members were comprised of five Republicans and five Democrats from Congress with five of the nine members of the Supreme Court. One of the GOP members was a man who would know the feeling of being a presidential candidate four years later, Congressman James Garfield.

Among the court's justices that were chosen was David Davis who was viewed as one of its most independent jurists. However, as the presidential contest had been taking place, Davis was elected US senator from Illinois and was removed from consideration. Replacing him on the committee was Joseph P. Bradley, a Republican who had been appointed to the court by Ulysses S. Grant, a well-known Hayes supporter. The selection gave the Republicans a one seat advantage on the fifteen person panel.

The group held its meetings in the Supreme Court Building but those gatherings made little progress. Like most political quandaries, the search for answers often took place in a secret room at a clandestine location, and the election of 1876 was no different. An agreement was hammered out during a series of gatherings that took place at Washington, DC's Wormley Hotel, where in exchange for putting Hayes in the White House, the Republicans conceded the following items:

- Federal troops would be removed from the states in the South (the erstwhile Confederate States).
- At least one Democrat would be included in Hayes's cabinet.
- A second Transcontinental Railroad would be constructed in the South using the Texas and Pacific Railway.
- Legislation would be passed aimed at helping to industrialize the Southern states.

To no surprise, the voting went along party lines with an eight to seven GOP count that had Bradley casting the deciding ballot. With that, Hayes was awarded all of the twenty disputed electoral votes.

On March 2, 1877, the commission concluded its work at 4:10 a.m. just three days before the inauguration. The Republican Rutherford B. Hayes was declared the winner of the 1876 presidential election defeating the Democrat Samuel J. Tilden in the most controversial outcome in American history. When the final numbers were submitted, Hayes won the contest by a single electoral vote count of 185 to 184.

Table 8.1   The Election of 1876

Presidential candidate	Party	Home state	Popular vote Count	Percentage	Electoral vote
Rutherford B. Hayes	Republican	Ohio	4,034,142	47.92%	185
Samuel J. Tilden	Democratic	New York	4,286,808	50.92%	184
Peter Cooper	Greenback	New York	83,726	0.99%	0
Green Clay Smith	Prohibition	Kentucky	6,945	0.08%	0
James Walker	American National Party	Illinois	463	0.01%	0
Other			6,575	0.08%	—
Total			8,418,659	100%	369
Needed to win					185

Vice President Elect, William A. Wheeler, US Congressman (R-NY)

THE AFTERMATH

While the forming of the electoral commission and the confusion in the four disputed states has dominated the history of the election of 1876, there was another important aspect that has, more or less, been forgotten by many. The voter turnout of 81.8 percent is the highest ever and more than a ten-point increase over the previous contest just four years earlier.

Even though the participation was high, turnout among African Americans was low. It was only the second presidential election since passage of the 15th Amendment allowing the black vote. Tilden carried thirteen of the sixteen states in the Deep South where Confederate sympathizers and the Klan still practiced racism despite the latest laws.

However, the final choice of a new leader did nothing to subdue the continuing confusion. In 1877, Inauguration Day fell on a Sunday, so Hayes was sworn in a day early on Saturday. Outgoing president Ulysses S. Grant recommended not waiting until Monday because there were rumors that supporters of the defeated James G. Blaine might take to the streets and try to prevent Hayes's swearing-in. Grant did not want there to be a day when the nation didn't have a president, thus his successor took the oath at a private ceremony.

Even though the country officially had a new president, there was no grand inaugural parade because due to all of the problems with the election, there simply hadn't been time to organize one.

For Tilden, he was philosophical in defeat stating with a note of humor, "I can retire to public life with the consciousness that I shall receive from posterity the credit of having been elected to the highest position in the gift of the people, without any of the cares and responsibilities of the office."

Not everyone was enthralled about Rutherford B. Hayes's election as president in 1876. The decision that was handed down by the fifteen-man commission didn't sit well with a number of citizens. Some of those were in his home state of Ohio, where a disgruntled individual fired shots into the outgoing governor's residence, hitting the dining room. No one in the Hayes family was harmed and they proceeded on to their new home in Washington, DC.

Unlike many politicians of the past and present, the chief executive stuck by his word and served only one term although with just a few months remaining before departing the office, he made presidential history by embarking on a western tour of the United States.

It began on September 2, 1880, in Burlington, Iowa, and continued to Illinois, Wyoming, Utah, Nevada, California, Oregon, and Washington. While in California, he delivered speeches at eleven different stops.

Hayes returned to Washington, DC, after two months on the road and the conclusion of the 1880 election.

THE FOLLOWING ELECTIONS

1880: On November 2, 1880, James Garfield became the only person in American history to be a US representative, a US senator-elect, and a president-elect all at the same time. As a hedge of protection, he had kept his name on the ballot for senator just in case he lost the presidency. Having won both, he immediately resigned from the Senate. It was one of those rare occasions where citizens could legally vote for the same candidate twice during the same election day.

On July 2, the president was at Washington's Baltimore and Potomac Railroad station where he was scheduled to travel to his alma mater Williams College in Massachusetts to deliver a speech. He had no security detail but was accompanied by his secretary of war Robert Todd Lincoln, the son of the sixteenth president. Two days earlier, the two men had a meeting where most of their discussion revolved around the assassination of the secretary's father.

Before he could board the train, the chief executive was shot by a mentally imbalanced government job seeker Charles Guiteau in front of several witnesses. On September 19, Garfield died from his wound and Guiteau was tried, found guilty, and hanged on June 30, 1882.

1884: New York governor Grover Cleveland overcame a scandal that alleged that he had fathered an out-of-wedlock son a decade earlier and had been paying hush money to the mother for years.

The Democrats' nominee won the electoral count, 219–182 over former Maine senator James G. Blaine. The election came down to the votes of one state. Cleveland picked up thirty electors by winning his home territory of New York but only by 1,047 popular votes out of more than 1.16 million cast. His winning margin in the national popular vote was scant 0.57 percent.

1888: On November 6, 11.38 million citizens went to the polls and for the third time in the nation's brief history, the potential winner came up short. President Grover Cleveland won the popular vote with 48.63 percent but was soundly defeated 233 to 168 in the electoral college. It was once again top heavy New York, with its thirty-six ballots, that was the difference maker just as it had been four years prior.

Former Indiana senator Benjamin Harrison, the grandson of President William Henry Harrison, won Cleveland's home state by just 1.09 percent, which provided the margin of victory. Had the incumbent been able to defend New York, he would have been reelected, 204 to 197 (201 was needed for victory). Instead, he became the fifth president seeking reelection to lose after being renominated by their party or a third party.

9

The Election of 1892

Benjamin Harrison, Incumbent (Republican) vs. Grover Cleveland (Democrat)

"Sensible and responsible women do not want to vote."

—Former president Grover Cleveland, 1905, on the subject of women's suffrage

On May 25, 1965, Sonny Liston squared off against Muhammad Ali for the World Heavyweight Boxing Championship. It was a rematch of their first bout that took place a year earlier, which was won by Ali in a stunning upset.

What made the second match unique was that Liston was the former champion while Ali was the reigning titleholder. It is rare whenever two individuals or teams meet in competition where both have been at the pinnacle of their profession. In this case, Ali retained the championship scoring a first round knockout over the former titlist.

There was another famous rematch some seventy-three years before Ali's right hand sent Liston to the canvas, but there were no fisticuffs involved between those individuals of the Gilded Age. In 1888, two men had squared off for the biggest prize in politics where the champion went down in a narrow defeat, and four years later they found themselves matched against each other once again.

One of the last times that Grover Cleveland and Benjamin Harrison were seen together in public prior to 1892 was on Inauguration Day, March 4, 1889. In a peaceful transition of power during a pouring rainstorm, the outgoing president held an umbrella over his successor as he took the oath of office. Cleveland then returned to being a private citizen in New York while Harrison moved into the White House inheriting all of the nation's woes.

Time passed and the new president got down to the business of governing. Meanwhile, the burly fifty-five year old ex-commander in chief was planning how to eliminate the mistakes of 1888 and make his wife's prognostication of another term a reality. The nation's last two chief executives were already moving onto a collision course.

On June 7, 1892, the Republican National Convention began in Minneapolis. Harrison won an easy first ballot renomination. But due to his shaky relationship with Vice President Levi Morton, he was replaced on the ticket's second rung by Whitelaw Reid, a wealthy newspaper publisher who had previously served as minister to France.

Two weeks afterward, Cleveland was repositioned as the candidate for the Democrats on the first ballot at their gathering in Chicago. Allen G. Thurman, Cleveland's former vice president, was replaced by former congressman Adlai E. Stevenson of Illinois. It was the third consecutive presidential election where the New Yorker had been the party's choice as the two conventions had served as formalities to set up the rematch.

The election became the only one in which the nominees of both major parties had previously served as president, but the roles were reversed from what they had been in 1888 when Cleveland was the incumbent. Since then, Harrison had four years on the record, which meant that he would be held accountable by the voters for his actions.

There were four issues that drew particular attention:

1. The Sherman Silver Purchase Act of 1890: The law was passed by Congress to replace the Bland-Allison Act (1878). It required the US government to purchase nearly twice as much silver as in the past to prevent undermining of the Treasury's gold reserves.
2. The McKinley Tariff of 1890: The act was sponsored by Ohio representative William McKinley and became law on October 1, 1890. It raised the average duty on imports to almost 50 percent as a protectionist tool against foreign competition. Condemned by Democrats, it was replaced with the Wilson–Gorman Tariff Act in 1894, which lowered rates.
3. The USS *Baltimore* Incident: On October 16, 1891, a mob attacked a group of sailors on shore leave from the cruiser USS *Baltimore* at the Chilean port of Valparaíso. One of the American sailors was accused of spitting on a picture of Arturo Prat, a national hero of Chile. Two sailors were killed, seventeen injured, and forty-eight were arrested in the brawl.
4. The Homestead Strike of 1892: Multimillionaire businessman Andrew Carnegie reduced wages at his steel mill in Homestead, Pennsylvania, and the union workers, refusing to accept the pay cut, went on strike. The company locked out the union workers and hired Pinkerton agents to defend the property and nonunion labor.

On July 6, violence erupted resulting in the deaths of seven workers and three Pinkertons. The strike carried into October, which didn't help Harrison's reelection chances even though he had nothing directly to do with the situation. However, he did take a public relations hit during the same summer when he dispatched federal troops to the mines in Coeur d'Alene, Idaho, at the governor's request. That strike was crushed, as union workers retreated into the mountains.

However, Harrison had a difficult time keeping his focus on the campaign. His wife, Caroline, had been diagnosed with pulmonary tuberculosis and her condition continued to deteriorate through the summer months. She died just days before the election on October 25, becoming the second First Lady to pass away while holding that distinction. She and the president had been married for thirty-nine years.

The election was a landslide for Cleveland as he won 277–145 although he once again lost his home state of New York. Even third party candidate James B. Weaver secured twenty-two electoral ballots. With the loss, Harrison became the eighth US president to that point in history to serve just one complete term in office while Grover Cleveland remains the only president ever to win two nonconsecutive terms.

Table 9.1 The Election of 1892

Presidential candidate	Party	Home state	Popular vote Count	Percentage	Electoral vote
Grover Cleveland	Democratic	New York	5,553,898	46.02%	277
Benjamin Harrison (Incumbent)	Republican	Indiana	5,190,819	43.01%	145
James B. Weaver	Populist	Iowa	1,026,595	8.51%	22
John Bidwell	Prohibition	California	270,879	2.24%	0
Simon Wing	Socialist Labor	Massachusetts	21,173	0.18%	0
Other			4,673	0.04%	
Total			12,068,037	100%	444
Needed to win					223

Vice President Elect: Adlai Stevenson I, former US Congressman (D-IL)

THE AFTERMATH

After completing his term, Harrison returned home to Indiana where he practiced law, gave speeches, and traveled extensively. In 1896, at age sixty-two, he married Mary Scott Lord Dimmick, the widowed thirty-seven-year-old niece of his deceased wife. The nuptials touched off a family feud as his two adult children, who were both older than their new stepmother, refused to attend the wedding. The couple had one child together before Harrison's death in 1901.

Grover Cleveland's two terms as president fell between the Civil War and the Spanish-American War, thus he was not forced to send soldiers into a major military offensive. But in 1894, because of the Chicago rail strike (also known as the Pullman strike), the commander in chief was forced to dispatch federal troops to halt the violence. By the end of the work stoppage, thirty-four strikers had been killed, including thirteen in Chicago. There had also been federal and/or state troops called out in Illinois, Indiana, Nebraska, Iowa, Oklahoma (Indian Territory), Colorado, and California.

There were other problems in the second term as the administration featured a severe depression, the railroad strike, and an army of jobless workers demonstrating in Washington for relief. In the 1894 midterms, the Democrats lost 116 seats in the House—the biggest wipeout on record—and 5 in the Senate. The result prepared the populace for the elections of Republicans William McKinley and Theodore Roosevelt to the White House.

With no hopes of a third term, in 1897, the sixty year old Cleveland retired to his home in Princeton, New Jersey, where he served as a trustee of the Ivy League university. He fathered four more children before his death in 1908.

10

The Election of 1896

William McKinley (Republican) vs. William Jennings Bryan (Democrat)

"Well, Judge Day, every change so far in the office of Secretary of State has been an improvement!"

—William McKinley to his outgoing secretary William R. Day.

In the annals of presidential contests, the election of 1896 normally doesn't rate among the most well-known. There was no incumbent, there wasn't a famous battle-field hero in the mix, there was no disciple of the Founding Fathers, or any of the other variables that are often part of the campaign process.

In the end, this election, like the others, would be about the candidates and how the people voted for them, but, as opposed to prior contests, this face-off would feature an element that had only played a minor role in the past but in 1896 became a major factor. In fact, as the years passed, it has grown into the key element for all candidates.

Although, before that happened, there was the business of each party finding a candidate. For the Republicans, it was back to the same successful formula that had worked for them in the past—nominating a Civil War officer from Ohio. Grant, Hayes, Garfield, and Harrison (although he was from Indiana, he was born in Ohio) had provided a long line of White House winners for the GOP and the heir apparent was waiting in the wings.

In 1896, William McKinley was completing a term as governor after serving in the US House of Representatives. During the Civil War, he was part of the 23rd Ohio and saw action at the Battle of South Mountain, Antietam, and the Shenandoah Valley campaigns. A short while before the conclusion of the conflict, McKinley received a promotion to brevet major.

On June 16, delegates and officials arrived in St. Louis for the eleventh Republican National Convention. While former vice president Levi Morton appeared to be a strong contender in the beginning, McKinley swept to an easy first ballot nomination. Garret A. Hobart, a local and state politician from New Jersey, was also voted in as the ticket's running mate on the first ballot.

It was amazing that the convention ever took place in St. Louis. On May 27, just three weeks prior to the event, a major tornado ripped through the city killing 255 people, injuring more than 1,000, and leaving numerous families homeless. An intense cleanup effort got underway immediately, including the construction of a temporary facility after severe damage to the St. Louis Exposition and Music Hall made it impossible for that building to host the proceedings. Modern day scientists have estimated that the tornado that struck the Gateway City measured as an EF-4 and remains the third deadliest in US history.

The Democrats were scheduled to gather in Chicago on July 7, but this convention was different than any that had taken place in several years. That was because for the first time in more than a decade, the incumbent president Grover Cleveland, would not have a major role. Any thoughts of a possible third term for the Buffaloian disappeared during his disastrous second round in the White House.

Among the problems that plagued the final Cleveland administration were gold reserves that fell below $100 million for the first time (1893); The Panic of 1893 that was triggered by a sharp decline in the New York stock market the day after the Philadelphia and Reading railroads went bankrupt; the Wilson-Gorman Tariff Bill (1894) included an income tax of 2 percent on all personal income greater than $4,000 and on all corporate income above operating expenses; and four bond sales between 1894 and 1896 that created $262 million in federal debt.

On top of the country's dilemmas, the president was also dealing with his own issues. In the summer of 1893, he disappeared for four days to have a secret surgery on a yacht. The procedure was kept so secret that it remained unknown to most of the public for years.

At the start of his second term, Cleveland noticed a little bump on the roof of his mouth that grew larger over the following weeks. A doctor's diagnosis confirmed it was cancerous and recommended that it promptly be removed. The president felt that it was critical that his condition be kept from the public so not to have a negative effect on Wall Street.

It was decided that the operation would take place aboard a friend's yacht by a team of six surgeons. The procedure took about ninety minutes, removing the tumor along with the president's upper left jawbone. The surgery was unprecedented for its time but successful. The public was told that the leader of their country was away on a four-day fishing trip.

When certain journalists attempted to go forward with the real story, they were stonewalled by the White House. The truth was kept hidden for the next twenty-four years until one of the doctors, William Williams Keen, finally came forward with the facts. With his health in question, along with a difficult second term, it meant that Cleveland wasn't a factor in 1896.

The Democrats' favorite at the start of the convention was Richard P. Bland, a twenty-two-year member of the House of Representatives from Missouri. He was a supporter of bimetallism where gold and silver are used as legal tender. After the first ballot, Bland had 235 delegate votes over a field of 13 other contenders.

In second place was William Jennings Bryan, a former US congressman from Nebraska. On the third day of the convention, the skillful orator won over the audience with his "Cross of Gold" speech that criticized the gold standard and advocated inflating the currency by the free coinage of silver. It is considered one of history's greatest political speeches and helped wrap up the nomination for Bryan who was just sixteen months over the legal age of thirty-five to run for president.

He was also the nominee of the Populist Party, which was known as the People's Party. While the two political bodies shared a presidential candidate, they nominated different candidates for vice president. The Democrats selected Arthur Sewall and the People's Party chose Thomas Watson.

McKinley and Bryan may have been their party's nominees, but perhaps the most important person involved in the race was Mark Hanna, the chairman of the Republicans. He was also McKinley's chief fundraiser compiling a staggering $3.5 million (more than $90 million today) war chest as compared to Bryan's $500,000.

It was the initial concept of trying to outspend an opponent in order to get to the White House, a strategy that still plays a prominent role in every election at almost all levels.

In 1896, Hanna raised more money than any previous US presidential campaign. From there, he launched a massive ground campaign hiring a throng of 1,400 workers who busily distributed buttons, leaflets, pamphlets, and posters. He was reputed to have poured more than $100,000 of his own money into the effort.

The McKinley campaign focused its message on two key geographic areas—New York and Chicago—because of their wealth in money and electoral votes.

But Bryan had his own innovation with a whistle-stop train tour where he hoped to reach more voters than the practice of front porch campaigning that had been done by his predecessors. The plan worked, as between September 11 and November 1 the Democratic candidate made it to twenty-seven of forty-five states, traveling eighteen thousand miles, and giving an estimated six hundred speeches to some five million spectators.

Bryan's road trip set the standard for all future campaigns as front porch speeches went the way of the dinosaurs.

Hanna had suggested a similar plan to McKinley, but the Republican chose to remain in his hometown of Canton, Ohio. His wife Ida's fragile health was a major concern as she had broken down over the loss of their two young daughters within two years of each other. In 1875, three year old Katie died of typhoid fever while her sister, also named Ida, passed away in 1873 just four months after her birth. In her weakened condition, the First Lady developed epilepsy—once having a seizure at McKinley's inaugural ball as governor of Ohio.

Since McKinley wasn't willing to go on the road, Hanna followed Bryan like a bloodhound to every whistle-stop of his campaign train. At each town, the Democrat was greeted by a continual barrage of posters and propaganda attempting to turn voters away from the man from Nebraska.

Fake news is not a recent development and was alive and well in 1896. *The New York Times* endorsed McKinley and also published an article about his opponent with the headline: *"Is Mr. Bryan Crazy?"* The piece interviewed so-called experts from the psychiatric field who concluded that he suffered from megalomania, delusions of grandeur, and quarrulent logorrhea, which is basically complaining too much. One of those who was questioned said, "I should like to examine him as a degenerate."

The public trekked to the polls on November 3 as the two candidates began the wait to see who would reach 224 electoral votes. When the state count came in, it appeared to be a tight race with McKinley opening with a 23–22 edge. But that statistic was misleading as the Ohioan won the electoral college (271–176) and the popular vote (by 4.3%) in comfortable fashion. That included sweeping all four states that carried twenty or more electoral ballots.

It was also the first presidential election for the new state of Utah, which joined the Union that same year, and gave its three electoral votes to Bryan.

Table 10.1   The Election of 1896

Presidential candidate	Party	Home state	Popular vote Count	Percentage	Electoral vote
William McKinley	Republican	Ohio	7,111,607	51.03%	271
William Jennings Bryan	Democratic–People's	Nebraska	6,509,052(a)	46.70%	176
John M. Palmer	National Democratic	Illinois	134,645	0.97%	0
Joshua Levering	Prohibition	Maryland	131,312	0.94%	0
Charles Matchett	Socialist Labor	New York	36,373	0.26%	0
Charles Eugene Bentley	National Prohibition	Nebraska	13,968	0.10%	0
Other			1,570	0.01%	
Total			13,936,957	100%	447
Needed to win					224

Vice President Elect, Garret Hobart, former President of the New Jersey Senate (R-NJ)

Note: The People's Party won thirty-one electoral ballets but four of those electors voted with the Democratic ticket, supporting Bryan for president.

THE AFTERMATH

In the presidential election of 1896, William McKinley defeated William Jennings Bryan, but the real winner may have been businessman and financier "Diamond"

Jim Brady. He won nearly $180,000 (about $ 4.7 million today) by making crooked bets on the outcome of the contest. Then, he put some of those winnings into a pump-and-dump scheme involving stock in the Reading Railroad, which had just emerged from receivership. Brady sold out in time to enrich himself by $1.25 million (or about $33 million today).

While Mark Hanna earned a great deal of credit for his fundraising efforts for the McKinley campaign, he was also doing double duty as the political guru was simultaneously running for the US Senate seat in Ohio, which he won.

Every four years, the presidential inauguration is viewed by millions on television. That trend began with William McKinley's 1897 inaugural, which was the first to be filmed. It was recorded by, what else, Thomas Edison's motion picture camera and phonograph equipment. This was also the first inaugural at which Congress hosted a luncheon for the president and vice president, a tradition that remains intact.

McKinley's wife, Ida, was frail and an epileptic. Whenever she suffered a seizure in public, he would cover her face with a napkin. The president ignored protocol at official dinners by seating the First Lady at his right so he could help her if necessary. At the 1897 inaugural ball, Ida fainted on the steps of the Pension Building where the celebration was being held.

When the Clevelands occupied the mansion, they had the bedroom painted yellow for themselves. But Ida McKinley hated the color and demanded that it be changed to pale pink. In fact, the new First Lady disliked it so much that she had all things yellow removed from the White House, including the yellow flowers in the garden.

On November 21, 1899, Garret Hobart became the sixth American vice president to die in office after suffering with a heart condition for several years. He was so respected by President McKinley that he became the first vice president. to attend cabinet meetings.

Hobart was instrumental in convincing the commander in chief in going to war with Spain in 1898. His suggestions helped persuade McKinley to annex the Philippines for the good of both the former Spanish colony and the security of the United States.

He died just a few months before the 1900 Republican Convention opening the door for the Republicans to nominate Spanish-American War hero Theodore Roosevelt as McKinley's next running mate.

When the president was shot in 1901, it was Hobart's widow, Jennie, who rushed to Buffalo to offer support to the family who had become her close friends.

During the Spanish American War, Bryan headed a two thousand-man regiment of the Nebraska National Guard. They remained in Florida during the conflict and were never deployed to Cuba. He also continued to be a popular speaker at events following his electoral defeat.

In 1899, McKinley became the first president to take a ride in a car. It was a steam-powered "Locomobile" driven through the streets of Washington, DC, by its creator, Freeland O. Stanley.

In November 1896, the twenty-eighth US presidential election took place. Seven months earlier (April 6–15), the first Summer Olympic Games of the modern era was held in Athens, Greece. Fourteen nations participated with the United States winning the most gold medals (eleven).

Since then, the Summer Olympics and the presidential election have been held during the same year. The Games were not conducted during wartime in 1916, 1940, and 1944 but the elections went on as scheduled.

11

The Election of 1900

William McKinley, Incumbent (Republican) vs. William Jennings Bryan (Democrat)

"Why should I? No one would wish to hurt me."

—President McKinley's response that he should cancel a reception
line at the Pan-American Exposition's Temple of Music
due to security concerns, September 4, 1901

With the start of a new century, William McKinley had to be the most satisfied individual in Washington, DC. He was in a comfortable position for reelection as his campaign was about to get underway and had just joined an exclusive club of wartime presidents who had led the country to victory in battle. For the man from Ohio, it was a good time to be him.

While McKinley basked in the glory of victory, he kept one eye peeled on the Democrats who were looking for a candidate, and with the start of a new millennium, they believed that they had found their man.

Seven of the eight presidents that were in office following the Civil War had been officers during the conflict. That group included Andrew Johnson, Ulysses S. Grant, Rutherford B. Hayes, James Garfield, Chester A. Arthur, Benjamin Harrison, and McKinley. The only one who hadn't was Grover Cleveland.

Many Democrats were enthralled with sixty-two-year-old Admiral George Dewey, a veteran of the Civil War and a hero of the recently concluded Spanish-American conflict. He had returned from the Philippines in the spring of 1899 to a raucous reception that included parades, honorary dinners, and products bearing his name like "Dewey Chewies" chewing gum. Several months later, he was given a house in Washington, DC, which had been purchased with the donations from thousands of grateful Americans.

On October 29, 1899, Dewey, a widower, became engaged to a prominent Washington socialite, Mildred McLean Hazen, who was the widow of Civil War general William B. Hazen. The town of McLean, Virginia, carries her family name. The couple secretly married two weeks later although there was a public outcry when it was revealed that Dewey had given the dwelling to his wife as a wedding gift.

She was considered a social climber but underlying much of the criticism was the fact that the new Mrs. Dewey was a Roman Catholic, which was tantamount to political suicide during the era! The situation tarnished the admiral's reputation and remained a popular editorial subject for political cartoonists when he announced his presidential candidacy in April 1900.

However, Dewey was the victim of the same affliction that so often plagued politicians—their own unscripted comments. One of those that came back to haunt him was when he stated, "I am convinced that the office of the president is not such a very difficult one to fill."

At that point, the admiral's quest for the White House had pretty much ended before it ever got started. It wasn't long before he withdrew from the race, but rather than remaining loyal to his own political party, he gave his endorsement to his former commander in chief, the Republican William McKinley.

Although the incumbent was a "sure thing" to be renominated by the GOP, there was business that needed tending to when the party's convention got underway on June19 in Philadelphia. When Vice President Garret Hobart died in 1899, McKinley had opted not to immediately replace him, but with the delegates arriving in the historic city, the party bosses realized that the time had come to get a number two man on the ticket.

Mark Hanna, now a US Senator, was still the chairman of the party and believed that either Navy secretary John D. Long of Massachusetts or Iowa representative Jonathan P. Dolliver would be a good fit for vice president. However, other Republican elites had their eye on another possibility, New York governor Theodore Roosevelt.

A familiar face to delegates, Roosevelt brought two major assets to the table. First, he could deliver New York to the GOP. with its thirty-six electoral votes, the most of any other state. Secondly, he had fought in Cuba during the Spanish-American War and had returned home to as many accolades as Dewey. The fact that the Republicans were attempting to couple together a ticket made up of a pair of battle-tested veterans from America's last two wars didn't get lost in the campaign hoopla by any political observers.

However, there was a problem. The ambitious Roosevelt wasn't particularly interested in the job and preferred to remain governor as so to use the time to set up his own presidential run in 1904. But as a party loyalist, when he was nominated, the governor answered the call and accepted the position.

The Democrats began their process on July 4 in Kansas City, which was the farthest western site to ever host a major party convention. The community's new convention hall had opened about a year earlier but was destroyed by a fire on April 4, 1900. It was rebuilt in only ninety days, just in time for the convention to begin where a sixteen year old from Independence, Missouri, had the opportunity to serve as a page. His name was Harry Truman.

With Dewey out of the running, the party reached back to its past to couple together a ticket. For president, they once again went with William Jennings Bryan who had been soundly defeated by McKinley just four years earlier. On the vice presidential side, delegates nominated a familiar face in Adlai Stevenson who served in the same office from 1893–1897 under Grover Cleveland.

For the first time, the convention featured a woman serving as a delegate to a major party. Elizabeth M. Cohen of Salt Lake City was a member of the Utah delegation and seconded the Bryan nomination. It was also the first time that a member of a royal family attended a US nominating convention as a delegate, as David Kawananakoa, heir to the throne of the Kingdom of Hawaii, represented America's newest territory.

The campaign issues were widespread and included women's suffrage, direct election of US senators, the tariff policy, America's role in world peacekeeping, direct income tax, civil, and worker's rights.

While some of the issues changed, the campaign strategy bore a close resemblance to 1896. Hanna was back as the team's manager and, once again, was out raising the Democrats in the cash department. The Republicans put its money to good use spending large sums on 125 million campaign documents such as 21 million postcards and 2 million written inserts that were distributed to more than five thousand newspapers weekly. They also employed six hundred speakers and poll watchers. It was quite an output considering that the entire population of the United States at that time was slightly more than seventy-six million.

McKinley spent most of his time at the White House attempting to put a strong finish on his first term. Meanwhile, Bryan returned to the rails as he had done four years prior by touring the country, delivering some six hundred speeches to millions of onlookers. But this effort was different than his previous strategy.

While Hobart had been used in running the northeastern campaign from the New York office in 1896, it was evident that Roosevelt's strengths would be better utilized on the road challenging Bryan in a match of dueling train cars. Partisans flocked to see and hear the hero of the "Rough Riders" who had led the charge on Kettle Hill. The bespectacled former New York police commissioner's "whistle-stop" campaign covered twenty-one thousand miles, that included 673 speeches in twenty-four states to an estimated three million people. His standard stump speech attacked Bryan for wanting to "paralyze our whole industrial life" and for appealing to "every foul and evil passion of mankind."

But it wasn't just Roosevelt who was haunting Bryan like a ghost, his old nemesis Hanna was also in play. Between the two McKinley surrogates, they slowly stifled the challenger's campaign into a slow demise from which there was no return.

Just as the campaign tactics resembled the same as 1896, the final numbers four years later were also quite similar. McKinley increased his popular vote count by more than 117,000 and tacked on an additional twenty-one electoral ballots from his past victory. His electoral vote was the largest in the previous ten elections, showing a count of 292–155. Perhaps the most telling aspect of Bryan's defeat was the loss of his home state of Nebraska, which he had won rather handily in 1896. At that time the Democratic nominee had carried the Cornhusker State by more than thirteen thousand votes, but in the rematch, he lost by more than seven thousand. Bryan was not only defeated in his own state, but in his own city and precinct as well.

Table 11.1   The Election of 1900

Presidential candidate	Party	Home state	Popular vote Count	Percentage	Electoral vote
William McKinley (Incumbent)	Republican	Ohio	7,228,864	51.64%	292
William Jennings Bryan	Democratic	Nebraska	6,370,932	45.52%	155
John G. Woolley	Prohibition	Illinois	210,864	1.51%	0
Eugene V. Debs	Social Democratic	Indiana	87,945	0.63%	0
Wharton Barker	Populist	Pennsylvania	50,989	0.36%	0
Joseph F. Maloney	Socialist Labor	Massachusetts	40,943	0.29%	0
Other			6,889	0.05%	
Total			13,997,426	100%	447
Needed to win					224

Vice President Elect, Theodore Roosevelt, Governor (R-NY)

THE AFTERMATH

On September 6, 1901, six months after being inaugurated for a second term, President William McKinley was shot and mortally wounded by the anarchist Leon Czolgosz while shaking hands in a receiving line at the Temple of Music of the Pan-American Exposition in Buffalo, New York. He died eight days later. Ironically, neither man was supposed to be there.

The president appeared to be in the picture of good health. He kept up his busy schedule but was known as an avid cigar lover who neither smoked in public nor permitted himself to be photographed with a stogie. Longtime White House chief usher Ike Hoover stated, "McKinley had a passion for cigars and was perhaps the most intense smoker of all the presidents during my life. One never saw him without a cigar in his mouth except at meals or when asleep."

While William McMcKinley's profile had risen to the top of the national picture, the same could not be said of twenty-eight-year-old Leon Czolgosz. He was a loner who resided with his Polish immigrant parents in Cleveland. Instead of work, he set forth on a path evolving into an anarchist by becoming a disciple of Emma Goldman, a well-known agitator of the era. In May 1901, the impressionable Czolgosz got an opportunity to meet his hero when she delivered a speech at Cleveland's

Franklin Club. He later said that the address had a tremendous impact on him. That summer, the solitary outsider relocated to the community of West Seneca, New York, a suburb of Buffalo.

While Czolgosz was sinking deeper into the depths of an antigovernment mindset, the McKinleys traveled to the West Coast. The president delivered a speech in San Jose on May 13 and attended a parade in San Francisco the following day. The First Lady had accompanied her husband but became ill and often remained in her room. Stories circulated that she had contracted a blood infection.

While in San Francisco, President McKinley witnessed the launch of the battleship, USS *Ohio*. But Ida's condition continued to worsen to the point that the next leg of the tour that was scheduled for the Northwest was canceled. Additionally, the northeastern part of the journey included a stop at the Pan-American Exposition in Buffalo on June 13. It was decided to push that appearance to September as the First Couple returned to the White House.

In July 1901, Czolgosz traveled to Chicago where he met with Abraham Isaak, the publisher of the anarchist newspaper *Free Society*. He had wanted to visit with Goldman who also lived in the Windy City. However, she and her daughter were off to enjoy the Pan-American Exposition so Czolgosz escorted them to the train station. Even the radical Goldman was beginning to have concerns about her young acolyte.

The weeks during the summer of 1901 passed and on August 29, William McKinley performed his final administrative duty by signing an Executive Order promoting US Army brigadier general G. S. Gillespie to temporarily perform the duties of secretary of war. Meanwhile, Czolgosz had read in the newspaper that the president would soon be traveling to the Pan-American Exposition to make up for the trip that had been postponed in June. A few days earlier, on August 31, the vagabond anarchist arrived in Buffalo and checked into a hotel.

On Tuesday, September 3, Czolgosz went to Walbridge's Hardware Store on Main Street and purchased a .32-caliber Iver Johnson revolver. In his confession, he later stated, "It was in my heart, there was no escape for me. I could not have conquered it had my life been at stake. There were thousands of people in town on Tuesday. I heard it was President's Day. All those people seemed bowing to the great ruler. I made up my mind to kill that ruler."

The president and First Lady arrived by rail the next day. Although still frail, her health had improved to the point where her doctor allowed her to make the journey. The crowd cheered as the couple exited the train with a nearby cannon firing a welcome salute. But the big gun had been set up too close to the parked locomotive and the explosion blew out a number of its windows. Some of the spectators, believing that the incident had been the result of a bomb, began shouting "Anarchists!"

Among those in the crowd was an armed Leon Czolgosz who believed that the resulting confusion might provide the opportunity that he was seeking to get near the chief executive. As he made his way toward McKinley, his plan was foiled when he was unable to get past the presidential detail. Without a clear path, he was forced to continue to wait.

The McKinleys were taken to the home of John G. Milburn, the president of the Pan-American Exposition, which became their residence during their stay in Buffalo. On Thursday, September 5, the heavily guarded McKinley toured the fair as he conversed and shook hands with visitors. While attendance had been lackluster to that point of its run, it was hoped that an appearance by the popular US president would spur larger crowds. McKinley's presence was just what organizers had hoped for as the exposition broke its record by drawing more than one hundred thousand patrons that day.

On Friday morning, the president, his secretary George B. Cortelyou along with his wife and a few others in the traveling party were taken twenty miles by train to scenic Niagara Falls. They spent their time marveling at the natural wonder of the massive waterway and then toured a power plant. The group returned to the exposition that afternoon and at 4:00 p.m., the McKinleys arrived at the Temple of Music. It was a concert hall that had been built specifically for the fair and the place where the president was scheduled to shake hands in a receiving line.

As McKinley was greeting the guests, he was wearing his usual lucky flower. It was a red carnation, which was a custom that he started when he won his first election to Congress in 1879. The line of fairgoers steadily moved along until twelve-year-old Myrtle Ledger from Springbrook, New York, found herself standing before the nation's leader. He bent down and asked her name as they shook hands. After she replied, he told her, "In that case, I must give this flower to another little flower."

The president removed the carnation from his lapel and handed it to the young girl as just a few feet away, Czolgosz patiently waited in line with others. Myrtle and her mother then exited the building as the group moved forward.

At 4:07 p.m., Czolgosz was face to face with his self-created adversary and wasted no time executing his plan. When McKinley extended his hand, the anarchist slapped it away and drew his pistol, which was wrapped in a handkerchief. He got off two shots, the first hitting the president on the right side of the chest with the second entering his abdomen. Crowd members were immediately on top of the assassin, but it was Jim Parker, a former slave, who secured him for authorities.

As Myrtle and her mother walked through the grounds, they could hear a ruckus coming from the building, but they didn't turn back. The pair was on their way to the train station for their return trip to Springbrook. As they continued to walk, they heard the announcement that the president had been shot.

With chaos ensuing around him and his blood beginning to pool, McKinley's first consideration was once again for his wife. He told his bodyguards, "Be careful how you tell her, oh be careful." Czolgosz, who had been beaten and bruised by patrons, was taken into custody as the president was rushed to a unit where he could receive medical attention.

Despite rallying during one point of his convalescence, McKinley never left Buffalo alive and died eight days later. Czolgosz's fate was also sealed in New York as on October 29, 1901, just forty-five days following the murder, he was executed by electric chair at Auburn Prison.

After Czolgosz's execution, government officials wanted to destroy his corpse in order to detour any relic hunters. Those given the task first used quicklime, to hasten deterioration, but later decided to pour sulphuric acid into his grave to completely destroy the remains.

In 1907, the frail First Lady, Ida McKinley, died in Canton, Ohio, and was buried next to her husband and two daughters.

The postponement of President McKinley's scheduled appearance for June at the Pan-American Exposition became the catalyst that set the wheels in motion for Czolgosz's action. No one could have known that something as simple as a schedule change would have such a profound effect on American history. Perhaps had the original plan been carried out, the resulting tragedy might not have occurred.

However, McKinley's successor, Theodore Roosevelt, wasn't immune from dangerous situations. When touring New England, the new president was slightly injured when his carriage collided with an electric trolley on September 3, 1902, in Pittsfield, Massachusetts. During the accident, Secret Service agent William Craig lost his life making him the first from the agency to be killed in the line of duty. The president, a veteran of the Spanish-American War, emerged with a swollen face and injured leg, but continued the tour for the day, stopping in Bridgeport, Connecticut, to speak to a crowd of thirty thousand.

THE FOLLOWING ELECTIONS>

1904: Theodore Roosevelt won thirty-two of forty-five states for 336 electoral votes in a landslide win over New York Court of Appeals judge Alton B. Parker. The incumbent won the heavily populated northern states while the Democrats' nominee could only secure thirteen from the south. In the battle for their home turf of New York, and its precious thirty-nine electoral ballots, Roosevelt throttled the judge, 53 percent to 42 percent.

The election of 1904 marked the first in which the Socialist Party participated. Their candidate was former Indiana state senator Eugene Debs who picked up more than four hundred thousand votes.

Following his 1904 victory, Theodore Roosevelt promised publicly not to seek reelection in 1908.

1908: The election marked Democrat William Jennings Bryan's third attempt at the presidency. This time the opponent was Roosevelt's secretary of war William Howard Taft of Ohio.

When it came to public speaking in the early 1900s, few could match the eloquence or endurance of the Nebraska Democrat including Taft who was neither good nor enjoyed the practice. But he endured by delivering four hundred speeches over an eighteen thousand-mile whistle stop marathon. It marked the first time in the nation's history that both major party presidential nominees had crisscrossed the nation in search of votes. The new strategies of the twentieth century had dictated how campaigning had completely changed and would continue to do so into the future.

Even though his speaking skills were of a lesser quality than his opponent's, Taft dominated the election winning in a landslide with 321 of 483 electoral ballots. Overall, about 66 percent of voters who were registered turned out to make their choices as Taft became the nation's largest president tipping the scales at around 325 pounds.

12

The Election of 1912

William Howard Taft (Republican) vs. Woodrow Wilson (Democrat) and Theodore Roosevelt (Bull Moose)

"I think I might as well give up being a candidate. There are so many people in the country who don't like me."

—William Howard Taft, July 22, 1912

In terms of candidates, there had never been an election like that of 1912 and there hasn't been one since. It consisted of a three man field that included the incumbent president, a former president and Nobel Peace Prize winner, and a former university president who held a PhD.

William Howard Taft, who had preferred to be the chief justice of the Supreme Court over his wife's objection, announced his intention to run for a second term, but his first order of business was to win the nomination of his party. That wouldn't be easy as the opposition arrived in the form of his old boss and ex-chief executive Theodore Roosevelt.

By 1912, the one-time friends had become bitter partisans. Roosevelt was impulsive where Taft was cautious and would compromise with opponents. T. R. was bitter because he felt that Taft hadn't continued to advance his agenda such as his antitrust policy.

In 1910, Roosevelt became angered when Taft didn't welcome him home after returning from a big game hunting safari to Africa and a European tour. In turn, he rejected a later invitation for the two to meet at the White House. As the weeks passed, Roosevelt became more bitter and criticized Taft's performance in his speeches. He also took the opportunity to remind the public about his role in major events like the ongoing construction of the Panama Canal.

The ex-president boasted, "I took the Canal Zone and let Congress debate; and while the debate goes on, the canal does also."

73

Taft had faced two personal trials during his term. In May 1909, just two months following her husband's inauguration, Nellie Taft suffered a stroke that impaired her speech, along with her right arm and leg. Her dream of being the country's First Lady was carried out with the help of her four sisters and the president as she spent nearly a year recovering from her medical setback.

In the spring of 1912, both Taft and Roosevelt were dealt a blow with the death of their close friend, Major Archibald Butt. He had served as a military aide and adviser to both men and prior to 1912, the life of the forty-six year old had been trending upward as he had become a trusted confidant to those in the White House. But the pressures of his job were beginning to take a prodigious toll on him.

Toward the final months of his term, Taft observed the major's condition and confided in others, "I don't think Butt is looking very well." The president expressed his concerns to the hard working staff member and offered him a six week hiatus from the job. The major was conflicted because on one hand, he, too, realized that his health had deteriorated to the point of exhaustion. However, it was an election year and the first Republican primary was scheduled for March 19 in North Dakota, which was just a few weeks away. Although hesitant, Archie accepted the president's recommendation. However, from the moment that he made the decision, the military veteran began to have second thoughts about his choice.

While Butt traveled through Europe, spring had just begun and Washington, DC, was the recipient of a gift of Japanese cherry trees from Mayor Yukio Ozaki of Tokyo on March 27. The more than three thousand donated trees symbolized the growing friendship between the United States and Japan. Today, they are a major tourist attraction of the nation's capital.

However, the other news on the home front wasn't good for conservatives. Taft was soundly defeated in the North Dakota primary by Roosevelt and Senator Robert Lafollette of Wisconsin and over the next few weeks things got worse. The president lost three out of the next four contests as a rested and refreshed Archie Butt prepared for his return voyage from Europe.

On April 10, the major boarded his ship at the port of Southampton, England, bringing along seven trunks of clothes and gift purchases that he had made during his journey. He embarked on a brand new vessel from the White Star Line company that was making its maiden voyage and was hosting a number of prominent Americans and other travelers. That ship was the *Titanic*.

On the evening of April 14, after colliding with a massive iceberg, passengers who were fortunate enough to escape, took their seats on the lifeboats and departed the sinking liner. It was evident that whatever premonition had haunted Archie over the bygone weeks had come to fruition. He knew that there was no escape for him, and his final chapter was about to be written.

The major's courage in the face of impending death became a focal point for others who were involved in the tragedy.

One perspective came from survivor and first-class passenger Dr. Washington Dodge, a prominent banker from San Francisco, who gave credit to both Archie and fellow voyager, the famed multimillionaire businessman Colonel John Jacob Astor. "Throughout the whole panic and during the loading of the boats, Butt and Astor assisted the ship's officers. Like soldiers, they seemed. As I remember it, the two were together throughout the whole of the panic. I saw their figures outlined against the sky from the (life)boat."

Survivor Eleanor Cassebeer stated that shortly before the last rescue craft was away from the ship, Major Butt returned to his cabin to destroy "diplomatic papers" that were in his possession. It was a final act of duty to his job.

Just after midnight (there was a one hour time difference between the ship's position and Washington, DC), Taft telegrammed the offices of the White Star Line with the following message: "Have you any information concerning Major Butt? If you communicate at once I will greatly appreciate." William Howard Taft.

But on Friday, April 19, 1912, Taft met with the press who had gathered at the White House. He stated what he had known the tragic outcome from the beginning, "I never had any idea that Archie was saved at all. As soon as I heard that 1,200 people went down I knew he went too. He was a soldier and always on deck where he belonged."

His body was never recovered.

That afternoon, Taft was scheduled to throw out the ceremonial first pitch to open the Washington Nationals' baseball season. He had started the ritual two years earlier with his friend Archie Butt by his side. However, on this day, the nation's leader was so grief stricken that he couldn't bring himself to attend the game. He chose to send Vice President James S. Sherman in his place.

While the day went along, things continued to worsen as that evening, the president was informed that he had lost two more primaries, Oregon and Nebraska, in his quest for reelection. But for the moment that made little difference to Taft as he sank into a deep depression over his friend's death for whom he felt responsible for his demise after coaxing him into taking the trip.

On May 2, 1,500 mourners crowded into the opera house of Butt's hometown of Augusta, Georgia, to pay tribute to the local soldier who was loved by so many. Among the group were the two former friends turned political combatants, William Howard Taft and Theodore Roosevelt. For a few hours on that day, the election took its rightful place in the background as the life of the town's hero was moved to the forefront.

Once the mourning had concluded, the duo resumed their ambivalent behavior toward each other. T. R. referred to Taft as a "puzzlewit," while the president labeled his opponent a "honeyfugler." For 1912, those words bordered on the slanderous statements tossed around by John Adams and Thomas Jefferson more than a century earlier.

Roosevelt was riding a wave of momentum as the Republican National Convention opened in Chicago on June 18. He had decisively won nine of thirteen primaries (eight by landslide margins) while Taft could only muster two victories. Each man won the other's home state (Taft took New York while Roosevelt snagged Ohio) by landslide margins as La Follette captured the remaining two states of Wisconsin and North Dakota. With the numbers pointing in his favor, it appeared that T. R. was headed back to the White House for another term.

While scattered states had a history of conducting primaries and caucuses in the past, 1912 marked the first presidential election campaign where a larger number of contests were held. Thirteen of the forty-eight states conducted primaries that year.

However, when the gathering began their floor vote, the primary numbers didn't hold as neither man had the 540 delegates needed to win. Roosevelt had secured 411 with Taft holding 367 and minor candidates carrying 46, leaving 254 up for grabs. In typical convention back-room dealing, the Republican National Committee, which was controlled by the Taft team, awarded 235 delegates to the incumbent and a paltry 19 to Roosevelt, thus ensuring the current office holder's renomination.

A furious T. R. believed that he was entitled to seventy-two delegates from Arizona, California, Texas, and Washington that had been awarded to the president. The election was months away but the fact that Taft had beaten the former "Rough Rider," who had berated him for months, among the members of their own party, was tremendously satisfying to the big man from Ohio.

The following week, the Democrats came together in Baltimore, but their job was larger than refereeing a two man fight. With thirteen names placed in nomination the process resembled a battle royal rather than a political convention. The two top contenders were Woodrow Wilson and Champ Clark who had each won five of the twelve primaries.

Wilson was the sitting governor of New Jersey where he had served just half (two years) of his term. It was the only elected office on his resume after eight years as the president of Princeton University. He also knew something about competition as in 1877, as a sophomore student, he was named the school's first ever football coach.

The sixty-two-year-old Clark was a congressman from Missouri and the sitting Speaker of the House. He was the frontrunner coming into the convention with a majority of delegates pledged to his camp, but he failed to receive the necessary two-thirds of the vote on the first several ballots.

By the seventeenth round, Clark had increased his lead over Wilson to 554.5–356 but was some distance away from the necessary 726 needed for the nomination. The rounds continued as Wilson made a breakthrough on the thirty-ninth ballot going over the five hundred-vote plateau for the first time. From there, the party's power brokers began pushing for the governor who was confirmed with 990 delegate votes on the forty-sixth ballot, the most cast at a convention since 1860.

The choice for Wilson's running mate was far less dramatic and time-consuming as the Democrats quickly settled on Governor Thomas R. Marshall of Indiana after just two rounds of voting.

Weeks passed but time hadn't healed Roosevelt's wounds as he felt that the GOP nomination had been stolen from him. That anger prompted him to form his own party, the Progressives. Nicknamed the "Bull Moose Party," they were bankrolled by wealthy donors and even held their own impromptu convention in Chicago on August 5 where they nominated, by no surprise, T. R. as their candidate.

Taft for the most part did not stump as he believed that it wasn't necessary for an incumbent president to campaign. Meanwhile, Wilson delivered speeches around the east on policy while former candidate William Jennings Bryan was sent out west to carry the party message out west. Roosevelt returned to whistle stops with his vibrant speaking style, which was aimed primarily at the Taft administration.

But the biggest story of the campaign centered around the former battle-hardened veteran. During a stop in Milwaukee on October 14, 1912, Roosevelt was shot at close range by John Schrank, a psychotic New York saloonkeeper. The gunman had his .38 caliber pistol aimed at Roosevelt's head, but a bystander saw the weapon and deflected Schrank's arm just as the trigger was pulled.

Roosevelt did not realize he was hit until someone noticed a hole in his overcoat. When he reached inside, the former president found blood on his fingers.

The Spanish-American War combatant insisted on delivering his speech even though he had been shot. Still wearing the blood-stained shirt, audience members cheered the address but encouraged the former commander in chief to get medical attention. He lost a great deal of blood and spent a week in a Chicago hospital after completing his address.

Roosevelt was extremely lucky. He had the manuscript of the long fifty-page speech in his coat pocket, folded in two, which slowed the bullet as it passed through. He also had a steel spectacle case in his pocket that the bullet also traversed before entering the candidate's chest near the right nipple. Passing through those two items is what doctors believed saved his life.

However, the bullet was never removed and when T. R. died seven years later, he did so with the reminder of that close call still lodged inside him.

Although not as fortunate as Roosevelt was Vice President James S. Sherman. In 1904, he was diagnosed with Bright's disease (the same malady that claimed the life of former president Chester Arthur) and was in failing health throughout the 1912 campaign. Less than a week before the election, he died at his home in Utica, New York, just six days following his fifty-seventh birthday.

Sherman, who one year earlier had become the first vice president to fly in a plane, became the last to die in office. With no running mate on the ticket, Columbia University's president Nicholas Murray Butler was designated by the party to receive Sherman's electoral votes.

The final numbers from the election told an usual story about the candidates and the voters. Wilson won with fewer votes than Bryan had received in each of his three defeats in 1896, 1900, and 1908. He captured just 41.9 percent of the vote (6,296,284) to Roosevelt's 27.4 percent (4,122,721) and Taft's 23 percent (3,486,721). His runner up finish made T. R. the first ever third party candidate to finish ahead of a major party nominee in a general election. Socialist Party candidate Eugene Debs won 6 percent (900,672) giving him more popular votes than his past two efforts combined.

But the electoral college count told a different story as Wilson won in forty states, giving him 435 votes. Roosevelt carried only six states—California, Michigan, Minnesota, Pennsylvania, South Dakota, and Washington—compiling a mere eighty-eight votes. Taft won eight electoral college ballots from the two states that stayed loyal to him, Utah and Vermont. It was the worst performance by an incumbent president seeking reelection.

Perhaps the late major Archibald Butt had foreseen Wilson as the election's ultimate roadblock and stated it best when he told Taft in 1911, "he [Wilson] has got to be reckoned with."

Table 12.1   The Election of 1912

Presidential candidate	Party	Home state	Popular vote Count	Percentage	Electoral vote
Woodrow Wilson	Democrat	New Jersey	6,296,284	41.84%	435
Theodore Roosevelt	Progressive	New York	4,122,721	27.40%	88
William Howard Taft (Incumbent)	Republican	Ohio	3,486,242	23.17%	8
Eugene V. Debs	Socialist	Indiana	901,551	5.99%	0
Eugene W. Chafin	Prohibition	Illinois	208,156	1.38%	0
Arthur E. Reimer	Socialist Labor	Massachusetts	29,324	0.19%	0
Other			4,556	0.03%	—
Total			15,048,834	100%	531
Needed to win					266

Vice President Elect, Thomas R. Marshall, Governor (D-IN)

THE AFTERMATH

The election of 1912 was the first to include all forty-eight of the current contiguous United States. It was also the first for the most recent entrants, Arizona and New Mexico, and the last contest to feature three candidates who had served or would serve as president of the United States.

On March 4, 1913, Woodrow Wilson was sworn in as the twenty-eighth president of the United States. After the ceremony, a quarter of a million people watched the inaugural parade, which included students from the two major service academies—the Annapolis midshipmen (Navy) and the West Point cadets (Army). Among the group of future soldiers was one who would one day also take the presidential oath of office—twenty-two-year-old Dwight D. Eisenhower.

One day earlier, thousands lined Pennsylvania Avenue to view a different type of parade that called for a constitutional amendment guaranteeing women the right to vote. While females had been fighting for suffrage for more than sixty years, the gathering marked the first major national event supporting the movement.

William Jennings Bryan never became president, but he was appointed secretary of state by Wilson, serving for two years (1913–1915).

The election of 1912 devastated the once very close friendship between the two former presidents. However, the feud concluded when Taft and Roosevelt reconciled shortly before T. R.'s death in 1919.

In 1921, Taft finally got his dream job when he was nominated for chief justice of the Supreme Court. The appointment came from fellow Republican president Warren Harding upon the death of Edward White. Ironically, he had been chosen for the position by Taft in 1910 but many suspected that the president's selection held an ulterior motive.

There were those who believed that the choice of White wasn't totally based on his qualifications but rather his age. At the time he was picked, the Civil War veteran was sixty-five years old in an era when the average male lifespan was just over forty-eight years. There were rumors that Taft knew that his time in the position would be limited, either by retirement or death, which would pave the way for the president to one day assume the duties.

Toward the end, White was in terrible health suffering from cataracts that had already rendered him blind in one eye along with being almost deaf. Still, he refused to retire. He fell ill, had bladder surgery, and died a few days later in Washington on May 19, 1921. At the time of his death, the seventy-five-year-old jurist had served twenty-six years on the Court, his last ten were as chief justice.

There had been rumors circulating that if the opening came about, Harding would select the sixty-three-year-old Taft as White's successor, which he did.

In another example of history repeating itself, Taft had criticized former chief justice Melville Fuller for mistakes he had made when he administered the oath of office to him in 1909. Twenty years later, the former president found himself on the other side of the stage as he conducted the swearing in of the newly elected Herbert Hoover.

As thousands of spectators watched and listened, Taft erroneously recited the phrase "preserve, protect, and defend" as "preserve, maintain, and defend." The chief justice was told about his error in a letter from Helen Terwilliger, a thirteen-year-old eighth-grade student from Walden, New York. Taft admitted his mistake chalking it up to "the defect of an old man's memory."

Taft remains the only former president to administer the oath to an incoming chief executive. In fact, he did it twice. Along with the Hoover inauguration, he also swore in Calvin Coolidge in 1925.

Taft appeared to have finally found happiness as the head of the nation's highest judicial body as in that same year he wrote, "The truth is that in my present life I don't remember that I ever was president." William Howard Taft died in 1930 at the age of seventy-two.

13

The Election of 1916

Woodrow Wilson, Incumbent (Democrat) vs. Charles Evans Hughes (Republican)

"Never murder a man who is committing suicide."

—Woodrow Wilson's comments about his opponent during
the campaign of 1916

Between 1865 and 1916, seven of the ten men who served as president had wartime military experience. Only three did not: Grover Cleveland, William Howard Taft, and Woodrow Wilson.

Wilson was not a warrior. In fact, far from it. He was an academic and the first, and only, president to have earned a PhD. By the time he took office, the Virginia native had already written six books including *Congressional Government, A Study in American Politics* (1885), which served as his doctoral dissertation from Johns Hopkins.

Over the years, he taught at Bryn Mawr College, along with Wesleyan and Princeton Universities, the latter of which he served eight years as president. Amazingly, he had achieved all of this academic prowess despite the fact that he had dyslexia and struggled with reading his entire life. Although, instead of being overcome by his disability, the former professor used self-discipline not only to survive as a student but to excel.

Wilson had defeated an incumbent (Taft) and a former president (Roosevelt) to win the election of 1912, a feat that had never been accomplished previously. There were also several positives from his first term including:

- The Seventeenth Amendment (Amendment XVII) to the Constitution was ratified establishing the election of US senators by a direct vote of the people. The new law eliminated election to that office by state legislatures.
- The passage of the Federal Reserve Act giving the United States a central banking system.
- The Clayton Antitrust Act, which further sought to prevent anticompetitive practices.

But Wilson's reign had its share of low points beginning with a personal loss. On August 6, 1914, his wife Ellen died at the White House of Bright's disease. The couple had been married for twenty-nine years and had three grown daughters, two of whom were married at the presidential mansion.

While dealing with his wife's condition, one week prior to her death, World War I erupted in Europe surrounded by events pertaining to the assassination in Sarajevo of the archduke Franz Ferdinand, the heir to the throne of Austria-Hungary. The fact that the United States was yet to be directly involved didn't lessen their attention of the conflict.

In November, Wilson suffered through the same experience as many of his predecessors had during midterm elections. While the Democrats picked up three seats in the Senate, the Republicans turned sixty-two House seats to their favor. It was a less than stellar reflection on the incumbent who was already planning his own reelection.

In early May 1915, several New York newspapers published a warning by the German embassy in Washington that Americans traveling on British or Allied ships in war zones did so at their own risk. That notification became a reality on May 7 as the United States was drawn a step closer to war when Germany sank the British liner RMS *Lusitania* off the southern coast of Ireland. Of the 1,198 who died in the attack, 128 were Americans, which didn't sit well with many who would be voting in the next election.

There was much discussion in the passing weeks about the possibility of the United States joining the Allied Forces, but on October 6, 1915, the public received an unexpected notice when the president announced his engagement to Edith Bolling Galt, a wealthy Washington socialite. The news caught everyone by surprise as the press had not been privy about their three month romance. Attempting to avoid the pomp of a White House wedding, the new First Couple were married on December 15 at the bride's DC home in front of about fifty guests.

As the newlyweds were getting settled, Wilson faced another international crisis closer to home. On January 11, 1916, a group of bandits associated with the Mexican guerrilla leader Pancho Villa and his renegade band, stopped a train at Santa Ysabel in Chihuahua, Mexico, forcing nineteen mining engineers to get off before shooting all of them. One did manage to survive. The act was in retaliation of the United States recognizing Villa's rival Venustiano Carranza as the official head of the government of Mexico.

Three days afterward, while some citizens clamored for the president to send US military troops across the border, Wilson publicly defended his policy announcing that he would continue his "watchful waiting" of their southern neighbor and that the eighteen Americans recently executed there . . . and were specifically warned not to go to Mexico. Those statements brought criticism from a number of members of the citizenry as well as many Republicans.

It didn't take long before the president's plan was put to the test. On March 9, 1916, Villa personally led a raid on the small town of Columbus, New Mexico, located just three miles north of the border. American casualties included ten civilians and eight soldiers while the Villa forces incurred between one hundred to two hundred killed or wounded.

As the president was attempting to find a remedy for his Mexican headache, the Republicans had begun to arrive in Chicago for their convention. Former New York governor and sitting Supreme Court justice Charles Evans Hughes entered the proceedings as the favorite but had to deal with a familiar name from the past to solidify his position.

As the delegates convened, supporters for former president Theodore Roosevelt began making a push for their candidate. The fifty-seven year old had been busy over the preceding four years traveling the world and even beating back a bout of malaria that he had contracted in the Amazon, but through it all, he continued to comment and criticize the Wilson administration's handling of events at home and abroad.

However, for many Republicans, Roosevelt's time on the world stage had drawn to a close. His messy split from the party during the 1912 election had left a sour taste in the mouths of a number of GOP loyalists who felt that his actions had helped Wilson win the White House. It was the end of the political road for the old "Rough Rider" who died three years later. Hughes clinched the nomination on the third ballot with former vice president Charles Fairbanks tabbed as his running mate. On June 10, he finalized his candidacy with his resignation from the Court.

On June 14, Democrats arrived in St. Louis to rubber stamp the renomination of Wilson and Vice President Thomas Marshall. The overriding theme of the convention was, "He kept us out of war." It served as an accolade for the president as the United States had remained on the sidelines during the Great War of Europe. The slogan was the idea of the campaign's public relations director George Creel who was an expert at making Wilson and his record look positive in the public eye.

While he and other members of the president's reelection team attempted to keep the voter's focus on Europe, little was being said about the other problem. Since the raid on Columbus, an expeditionary force of more than 14,000 regular army troops under the command of Brigadier General John J. "Black Jack" Pershing had been sent to northern Mexico in pursuit of Villa. Meanwhile, another 140,000 regular army and National Guard troops patrolled the vast border between Mexico and the United States in order to prevent further raids as Democrats continued to chant, "He kept us out of war."

While incumbents often employ the same strategy that won their previous election, Wilson didn't have such a luxury. In 1912, he was victorious with 41.84 percent of the popular vote, the second lowest total ever! Taft and Roosevelt hurt each other splitting the Republicans and the Socialist Dems received more than nine hundred thousand votes. The chief executive couldn't depend on such a string of fortunate circumstances going his way again.

While trying to figure out what to do about the war in Europe, Pancho Villa and his Mexican outlaws, and trying to get reelected, another problem cropped up close to the president's former home. In July 1916, four people were killed by shark attacks off the coast of New Jersey forcing some resort towns to close. President Wilson called a cabinet meeting to deal with the matter agreeing to give federal aid to "drive away all the ferocious man-eating sharks which have been making prey of bathers."

The attacks were the inspiration of the best-selling book and legendary motion picture, *Jaws*.

Wilson did catch a major break in 1916, thanks to his opponent. In August, Hughes was busy campaigning in heavily Republican-laden California. Also on the stump was the state's popular governor Hiram Johnson who was seeking to become its next US senator. At one point, both men were staying at the same hotel in Long Beach, but Johnson became miffed when he didn't receive a courtesy call from the visiting candidate.

When the story went public, a number of California Republicans felt slighted and returned the snub three months later at the voting booth. On election night (November 7), the challenger, took an early lead in the eastern and midwestern states, and several newspapers, facing press deadlines, declared him the winner. However, Wilson refused to concede, and as returns came in from the south and west, the incumbent made a comeback and eventually took the lead.

The key state proved to be California, which Wilson won by only 3,773 votes out of nearly a million cast. Many believe that Hughes rebuff of Johnson sealed his fate. The electoral count was one of the closest in American history—with 266 votes needed to win, Wilson captured thirty states for 277 electors, while Hughes won eighteen states and 254 electoral ballots. The math could not have been simpler, if Hughes had carried California with its thirteen electors, he would have won the election.

It was also close in the overall popular vote as Wilson received 49 percent to Hughes' 46 percent. On election night, Hughes went to bed believing that he was the newly-elected president. When an *Associated Press* reporter tried to telephone him the next morning to get his reaction to Wilson's comeback, someone answered the phone and told the journalist that "the president is asleep." The scribe retorted, "When he wakes up, tell him he isn't the president."

Table 13.1 The Election of 1916

Presidential candidate	Party	Home state	Popular vote Count	Percentage	Electoral vote
Woodrow Wilson (Incumbent)	Democratic	New Jersey	9,126,868	49.24%	277
Charles Evans Hughes	Republican	New York	8,548,728	46.12%	254
Allan L. Benson	Socialist	New York	590,524	3.19%	0
Frank Hanly	Prohibition	Indiana	221,302	1.19%	0
No Candidate	Progressive	(n/a)	33,406	0.18%	0
Arthur E. Reimer	Socialist Labor	Massachusetts	15,295	0.08%	0
Other			462	0.00%	
Total			18,536,585	100%	531
Needed to win					266

Vice President Elect, Thomas R. Marshall, incumbent

Another piece of history took place with the election of 1916 as the first national opinion poll was conducted. *The Literary Digest,* a weekly magazine, compiled its survey, in part as a circulation-raising promotion, and correctly predicted the Wilson victory. Information was collected from postcards by participants and the publication went on to predict the wins by Warren Harding (1920), Calvin Coolidge (1924), Herbert Hoover (1928), and Franklin Roosevelt (1932).

THE AFTERMATH

Woodrow Wilson became the first Democratic president since Andrew Jackson to be elected to two consecutive terms of office. The other big winner that night was California's Hiram Johnson who captured the Senate seat and remained there until his death in 1945.

However, as the public was preparing to cast their ballots, there was maneuvering going on behind the scenes unbeknownst to those who were heading to the polls. As Election Day drew near, Wilson appeared to be on the brink of losing his bid for reelection. Two days before the vote, the chief executive had a sealed letter, which he had typed himself, hand-delivered to the secretary of state, who at that time was third in the line of succession to the presidency.

Wilson wrote that if he lost, he would appoint Hughes as secretary of state, at which point he and Vice President Marshall would resign, thus immediately making Hughes the new president and bypassing the four month transition period. Wilson said he was proposing the plan because those were not "ordinary times" and "no such critical circumstances in regard to our foreign policy have ever existed before."

The only other people who knew of the proposal were the First Lady and Secretary of State Robert Lansing, who first revealed it in his posthumously published memoirs in 1935.

With all that was going on in the United States in 1916, in addition to those problems, there were more than 7,000 deaths and 27,363 cases reported during America's worst polio epidemic.

Before Wilson took the oath for his second term, his self-indulging "He kept us out of war" theme was drawing to an end. In January 1917, a coded telegram from German foreign secretary Arthur Zimmermann was sent to the Mexican government seeking them as a Western ally in the war. In return, once the United States was defeated, Mexico would recover their former territory that consisted of Texas, Arizona, and New Mexico. The telegram was intercepted and decoded by British intelligence.

On January 22, speaking before the US Senate, Wilson proposed a negotiated settlement to the European conflict, a "peace without victory." In response, nine days later, on January 31, the German ambassador in Washington, DC, informed the US State Department that his nation would begin unrestricted submarine warfare on all ships in their path in the Atlantic Ocean at midnight.

On March 4, Woodrow Wilson was sworn in for his second term. One month later, the peace loving commander in chief asked a joint session of Congress to declare war against Germany, stating, "The world must be made safe for democracy." Four days later, the nation's legislators granted his wish. The president was able to keep the nation out of war but only during his first term in office.

While entering a military conflict is nothing to celebrate, one person who must have been looking forward to the opportunity was General John "Black Jack" Pershing. He and his forces had spent more than a year in Mexico trying to rout out Pancho Villa without success but would enjoy much greater accomplishments a few months later in Europe.

In 1930, Charles Evans Hughes returned to the Supreme Court, this time as chief justice as he replaced the retiring William Howard Taft. It meant that Wilson became the only candidate to ever defeat two chief justices in presidential elections.

THE FOLLOWING ELECTIONS

1920: Before Bill Clinton, there was Warren Harding who never turned away from a good time. Like Grover Cleveland, he fathered a child out of wedlock and used Secret Service agents to deliver the hush money to the mother.

After the Ohioan was elected in a landslide, he would hold weekly poker games in the White House where he once lost a set of the mansion's china during a hand. Additionally, the liquor flowed freely on the premises even though it was during Prohibition.

On August 2, 1923, the nation's leader was sitting up in bed in the eighth floor presidential suite of the Palace Hotel in San Francisco, listening to his wife read a flattering article about him from the *Saturday Evening Post.*

"That's good. Go on," he told her.

Suddenly, the president's body twisted and convulsed, and he passed out.

The First Lady called for the doctors. There were five in the travel party, but Dr. Charles Sawyer, Harding's personal physician took the lead as he attempted to revive the fifty-seven-year-old chief executive, but it was to no avail. He was declared dead at 7:35 p.m. The first official to reach the death scene was the secretary of commerce, Herbert Hoover.

1924: Upon Harding's death, Vice President Calvin Coolidge became the country's new leader. His stoic, short answer method of speaking had earned him the moniker "Silent Cal." Ironically, he played a role in a new form of campaigning that changed the way that candidates talked to voters. The Republicans were on a roll and in 1924 they began using the radio to get out their message. The GOP opened an office in New York City on October 21, 1924, to broadcast 24/7 on a dedicated station until Election Day, including messages from their candidate.

The Republicans also put a new twist on the traditional whistle-stop tour. It was called the "Coolidge-Dawes-Lincoln Tour," a car caravan that began in the president's hometown of Plymouth Notch, Vermont, and rolled on for more than 6,500 miles over fifty-seven days. The route followed the Lincoln Highway with more than one hundred thousand vehicles making stops in four hundred communities concluding Tacoma, Washington. Neither Coolidge nor vice presidential nominee Charles Dawes actually participated in the rally, but it did demonstrate that cross country motor travel was a realistic expectation.

Fifteen months in office had been a large enough sample size for the public to select Coolidge for a full term of his own. His management of the country with a red-hot economy satisfied an overwhelming number of voters.

When the ballots were counted, the end result resembled a map from the Civil War period as the president won all the former Union states while his opponent John W. Davis, a fifty-one-year-old former congressman from West Virginia, captured those that had made up the Confederacy. It remains the last election where anyone won the presidency without carrying any of the one-time slave states.

While the Republicans had been doing well in the early years of the twentieth century, several of their winning streaks came to an end in 1924. It was the last election in which they won both Massachusetts and Rhode Island in the same year until 1952. The GOP carried New York City, a feat they have not repeated since then, and was also the last election in which they carried Suffolk County, Massachusetts; Ramsey County, Minnesota; Costilla County, Colorado and Deer Lodge County, Montana, along with the city of St. Louis, Missouri.

It was also the final occasion that a Republican won the presidency without taking Florida, Oklahoma, and Tennessee, and the last time until 2016 that they did so without Virginia. Davis did not carry any counties in twenty of the forty-eight states, two fewer than James Cox during the previous election, and did not carry a single county in any state bordering Canada or the Pacific.

Another option for voters was the Progressive Party headed by Republican senator Robert La Follette of Wisconsin. He picked up a respectable 4.8 million popular votes along with his home state's thirteen electoral ballots. The Progressives were an off-shoot of Theodore Roosevelt's former Bull Moose Party.

1928: Even though Coolidge was not a candidate, the Democrat nominee New York governor Al Smith was forced to run against the incumbent's record. The economy had cooled somewhat but remained in good shape and with Herbert Hoover as a part of the administration, his campaign staff constantly reminded voters that those trends would continue under his watch.

On the night of November 6, Smith, who was known as the "Happy Warrior," transformed into a vanquished opponent. Hoover won forty of the forty-eight states, thirty-two of them by double digits. The electoral count of 444–87 completed the Election Day thrashing and kept the executive branch in Republican hands. In the most telling chapter of his demoralizing loss, Smith was not able to win his home state of New York.

Hoover's 21,427,123 popular votes were the most ever received by a presidential candidate to that point. It was also the first time that the electoral counts for North Carolina and Virginia had not been awarded to a Republican since 1872 although Texas was won by a GOP candidate for the first time in its history.

All "other" votes totaled just 1.08 percent of the national popular total with the Socialists dropping to just 267,478. With the popular Eugene Debs out of the picture, party members sought out other candidates to the point where, in seven states, there were no Socialist votes cast.

Smith was stunned by the margin of his defeat and the viciousness of the campaign against him. "I do not expect to run for office again," he told reporters. "I have had all I can stand of it."

14

The Election of 1932

Herbert Hoover, Incumbent (Republican) vs. Franklin D. Roosevelt (Democrat)

"This country has gotten where it is in spite of politics, not by the aid of it. That we have carried as much political bunk as we have and still survived shows we are a super nation."

—Will Rogers, November 1, 1932

Herbert Hoover was on top of the world when he took the oath of office on March 4, 1929. Over time, the former orphan had risen in personal wealth and was now the president of the United States.

The rest of the nation was also in pretty good shape. The stock market was roaring, jobs were plentiful, and people were buying big-ticket items like houses and cars at a record pace. While the outgoing president, Calvin Coolidge, prepared to move into retirement at Northampton, Massachusetts, he could feel pretty good about the condition that he was leaving the country as he departed the White House.

On September 3, 1929, the Dow Jones Industrial Average swelled to a record high of 381.17, more than double what it had been three years earlier. Economists and the public viewed the increase as a sign that everything was well as the numbers represented the largest bull market that the country had ever seen. That same month, Secretary of the Treasury Andrew W. Mellon confirmed to the nation, "There is no cause to worry. The high tide of prosperity will continue."

However, Hoover quickly learned that, from his perch atop the political mountain, there was nowhere to go but down. Those who were cautious about ongoing trends became concerned when it was announced that 60 percent of Americans had annual incomes below the poverty line (estimated at $2000). The first dark wave struck on October 24, known as "Black Thursday." when the New York Stock Exchange (NYSE) collapsed its stock prices as thirteen million shares were sold.

Efforts by wealthy businessmen like J. P. Morgan Jr. and John D. Rockefeller to prop up the faltering exchange were unsuccessful.

It was hoped that when the market closed for the weekend that sanity would return to the trading floor on Monday. But by Tuesday, October 29, the situation worsened as a record 16.4 million shares were sold at further declining prices.

Hoover attempted to keep the public calm during a November speech when he said, "Any lack of confidence in the economic future or the basic strength of business in the United States is foolish."

However, by December 1, shares offered on the NYSE were down $26 billion and the bad news didn't stop there.

During the 1920s, an average of 70 banks failed nationally per year. During the first ten months following the crash of 1930, 744 additional financial houses went under—ten times as many. In all, 9,000 of those institutions failed during the decade of the 1930s. Among them was the Bank of the United States in New York City, with its sixty branches and four hundred thousand ill-fated depositors. Those closings took place before the formation of the Federal Deposit Insurance Corporation (FDIC).

By the end of 1930, the national unemployment rate had reached 11.9 percent, but Hoover believed government intervention was not the solution. He argued that if banks and businesses demonstrated confidence by refusing to panic, the market would naturally follow suit and rebound. He wasn't alone in his thinking, but the strategy also had its critics.

In February 1931, Congress passed the Bonus Loan Bill over the president's veto. It allowed veterans, most from World War I, to obtain cash loans of up to 50 percent of their bonus certificates issued in 1924. When the government failed to honor the full value of the bonds, which were not scheduled to mature until 1944, nearly twenty thousand ex-servicemen descended upon Washington, DC, setting up a shanty town camp known as "Hooverville" near the Capitol. In July 1932, the president called upon General Douglas MacArthur to break up the protests.

Serving alongside MacArthur in the chaos were two future heroes of World War II—his then chief military aide Dwight D. Eisenhower and Major George S. Patton. Many veterans were injured when the evacuation turned violent.

Newsreels showing the unemployed waiting in soup lines and former soldiers being hauled away by MacArthur's troops shocked the public and stoked an interest in potential candidates from the opposition party. As the reporting of the array of bad news stories increased, Hoover's chance of reelection was becoming diminished and some Democrats saw it as their best chance of retaking the White House since Woodrow Wilson.

The Republicans staged fourteen primaries that year but Hoover only won four of them. His top competitor was Senator Joseph France of Maryland who captured seven contests. But when the convention played out from June 14–16 in Chicago, Hoover's campaign team took control of the party mechanism and despite the nation's woes, the president became the nominee on the first ballot.

A few months earlier, the city had witnessed an even more spectacular event with the tax evasion trial of mob kingpin Al Capone. Hoover had vowed to remove the underworld's most recognized figure and even though he was never convicted of any of his many alleged murders, he was found guilty on twenty-two counts of failure to pay his taxes and sentenced to eleven years in federal prison. There were those who viewed having the convention in Chicago was for Hoover, like taking a victory lap in Capone's backyard. However, the mobster's downfall couldn't provide the president with the needed element to be reelected.

There was one last-ditch effort to remove the incumbent on the ticket when a group of Republicans–who had lost all faith in Hoover's ability to return to office—attempted to replace him with former president Calvin Coolidge. When "Silent Cal" was told that his comeback would "be the end of this horrible depression," the former chief executive replied, "It would be the beginning of mine." Coolidge ardently refused to be drafted as a candidate and Hoover remained the nominee.

The Democrats fell into two categories as their convention got underway on June 27, 1932, also in Chicago. There was one group of potential candidates who could have run but decided to hold off until 1936 because there seemed to be no foreseeable solution to the financial crisis in the near future. In contrast, other prospects believed that 1932 was the time to make their move.

Although before any voting began, there was party business to work out, which turned into constant bickering between factions. Topics regarding rules and chairmanship took center stage while candidates sat and waited. Hours turned into days as the marathon of squabbling continued to fill the arena.

The first ballot finally began at 4:28 a.m. on July 1 as ten candidates were placed in nomination. Three dominated the voting: Governor Franklin D. Roosevelt (FDR) of New York (666.25); former governor Al Smith of New York (201.75); and Speaker of House John Nance "Cactus Jack" Garner of Texas (90.25). Nobody secured the 770 votes needed to gain the nod.

Many things had changed during the past four years, not just the economy. Smith was getting little attention from delegates as opposed to 1928 when his nominating speech was given by Roosevelt, which led him to being picked as the party's presidential hope. But politics has a way of ending friendships and it did so in the case of the former allies. As his hopes for the 1932 nomination faded, Smith became a vocal opponent of his one-time pal FDR.

Such was not the case of political humorist/actor/columnist Will Rogers who became a favorite-son candidate from the delegation of his home state of Oklahoma. At the time, he was arguably the most recognized person in the United States and its most respected. In his typical down home style, he summed up his feelings some years earlier by drawing laughter when he said, "I am not a member of any organized political party, I am a Democrat!"

Although the nomination wasn't pressed, the beloved Rogers did pick up twenty-two votes on the second ballot which had begun at 5:17 a.m. Meanwhile, there was little change among the three leaders, a trend that continued into the next round.

Roosevelt was in serious trouble on the third ballot as the Mississippi delegation, which had given him its twenty votes, was deeply divided and threatened to break away from the candidate. Eventually, Huey Long, the colorful governor of Louisiana, was able to keep his southern neighbors in the fold.

FDR's team was near the mandate but needed to find a route to close the deal for their candidate. The winning path seemed to be through California and Texas, which were providing strong support for Garner. They offered him the vice presidential spot in exchange for withdrawing and encouraging those delegates to vote for Roosevelt. Behind the scenes, FDR was getting help from two of the country's most powerful businessmen: newspaper magnate William Randolph Hearst and former RKO movie studio owner Joseph P. Kennedy Sr., the father of future President John F. Kennedy.

On the fourth ballot, things fell into place. California and Texas went for FDR although the Lone Star State made it close by a 54 to 51 count. That put Roosevelt at 945 and made him the nominee. To complete the agreement, as promised, Garner was chosen as his running mate.

The odds of Roosevelt winning a single stint in the Oval Office seemed remote as he delivered his convention acceptance speech on July 2, 1932. As a child, he had been a visitor to the Executive Mansion. His initial journey to the presidential estate was in 1887 when he was accompanied by his father James Sr. At that time, five-year-old Franklin met President Grover Cleveland who told him, "My little man, I am making a strange wish for you. It is that you may never be President of the United States." Cleveland didn't take his own advice as he ran for the office twice more—winning once. Young Franklin also ignored the warning.

FDR's own political career began in 1910 when he was elected as a state senator in New York. Two years later, he made his debut on the national stage when he was appointed assistant secretary of the Navy by President Woodrow Wilson. But his opportunity to rise to higher office almost ended on one summer night.

On June 2, 1919, seven US cities located within ninety minutes of one another were attacked with bombs carried out by the Galleanists, followers of the violent anarchist Luigi Galleani. Among their more noted followers were the high profile duo of Sacco and Vanzetti. The target areas included New York; Boston; Pittsburgh; Cleveland; Patterson, New Jersey; Washington, DC; and Philadelphia. The bombing in the nation's capital happened about 11:15 p.m. at the home of Attorney General Mitchell Palmer, a controversial figure who was known to often overreach his authority. The blast came from a package that had been left on his porch.

At the time, FDR lived across the street and had departed the Palmer residence just moments prior to the explosion. Had the device detonated earlier, there was a possibility that both men might have been killed, although one person did die—the bomber Carlo Valdinoci, a member of Galleani's inner circle. His remains were discovered by Palmer and Roosevelt after he had been blown apart by the charge. Investigators theorized that the bomb had triggered prematurely.

A roundup of suspects referred to as the "Palmer Raids" was carried out by the US Department of Justice and the Bureau of Immigration. It resulted in Galleani and eight of his fellow terrorists being deported three weeks after the bombings.

The following year, FDR resigned his post with the Navy and was selected as the vice presidential running mate of the Democratic nominee James Cox of Ohio. However, the pair were overmatched by their counterparts and were soundly defeated in the general election by Warren Harding and Calvin Coolidge.

In 1921, Roosevelt was diagnosed with infantile paralysis (i.e., polio). He was thirty-nine years old and had contracted a disease that was rare among adults but common with infants. His doctor believed that the malady had laid dormant in FDR's system since childhood and many concluded that his political career, and possibly his life, were over. There was little reason for optimism as the nation's death rate from polio in the 1920s was 47 percent.

However, after years of rehabilitation, much of which took place at the Warm Springs Foundation, a therapeutic center for polio sufferers in Georgia, Roosevelt had become a survivor and made his political comeback in 1928 being elected governor of his home state of New York. He was reelected in 1930 but with the country in the grips of the Great Depression and a Republican incumbent in office, he immediately began to plan his campaign for president.

The economy and prohibition weren't the only campaign issues, the Democratic candidate's health prompted much discussion. While FDR's handlers made their best effort to hide his paralysis from the public and the press, it was the worst kept secret of the campaign—voters didn't see the evidence, but they knew of it. Hoover was smart enough to stay away from the subject, but a number of his surrogates continued to plant seeds of doubt by questioning if Roosevelt's physical limitations would prevent him from effectively running the country.

Although he had yet to be elected, FDR was showing the nation that he was a master politician as he broke with precedent and flew to Chicago to accept the nomination. At the convention, Roosevelt spoke to the crowd in a strong and commanding tone dispelling the doubts that his crippled condition would prevent his effectiveness to lead.

In his convention acceptance speech, FDR introduced the "New Deal"as his plan to rebuild the nation's economy. It was a big risk to raise expectations so early in the process. At the time, it lacked details, but the public liked the fact that the candidate had a vision for the country and the speech did exactly what he wanted it to do—put the Hoover administration on the defensive.

FDR did the usual whistle stop tour giving stump speeches for thirteen thousand miles with little insight into the "New Deal." But that changed on September 23 when he delivered an address at San Francisco's Commonwealth Club, which gave the public a peak at the plan. Once again, it was short on details, but one thing was made clear: the federal government was going to play an active role in the recovery. With one-quarter of the United States out of work, FDR's timing for that speech could not have been better planned.

Hoover never recovered, and as time rolled on to November, things got progressively worse. The fact was that the incumbent didn't cause any of the economic dilemmas that put the Great Depression in motion, but, as always, when things go bad, the person in the White House must take the blame, and 1932 was no different. The man from Iowa would have to pay the price even if the mistakes had come from others.

Voters also extended their approval of FDR to his party, giving Democrats a substantial majority in both houses of Congress. These congressional majorities would prove vital in Roosevelt's first year in office.

In 1928, Hoover had pounded Smith in every election category for one of the biggest landslides in history. Four years later, he was on the receiving end as FDR's victory was even more decisive. He bested the Republican in the electoral college (472–59); the popular vote (57%–39%); and total states (42–6) in a dominant performance. The numbers told the story of the sad conclusion to the Hoover presidency.

Table 14.1 The Election of 1932

Presidential candidate	Party	Home state	Popular vote Count	Percentage	Electoral vote
Franklin D. Roosevelt	Democratic	New York	22,821,277	57.41%	472
Herbert Hoover (Incumbent)	Republican	California	15,761,254	39.65%	59
Norman Thomas	Socialist	New York	884,885	2.23%	0
William Z. Foster	Communist	Illinois	103,307	0.26%	0
William David Upshaw	Prohibition	Georgia	81,905	0.21%	0
William Hope Harvey	Liberty	Arkansas	53,425	0.13%	0
Verne L. Reynolds	Socialist Labor	New York	34,038	0.09%	0
Jacob Coxey	Farmer-Labor	Ohio	7,431	0.02%	0
Other			4,376	0.01%	
Total			39,751,898	100%	531
Needed to win					266

Vice President Elect, "Cactus" Jack Garner, Speaker of the US House (D-TX)

THE AFTERMATH

FDR became New York's governor in 1928, and in 1932, was the first—and to date only—handicapped individual elected to the presidency. However, he wasn't the last to lead a state as in 2015 Greg Abbott, who lost the use of his legs in an accident as a young man, was elected the governor of Texas.

On August 26, 1920, the Constitution's 19th Amendment was adopted when it was ratified by Tennessee and allowed for women's suffrage in all areas of the United States. It also meant that Franklin Roosevelt's mother, Sara, became the first female parent who was eligible to vote for her son for president. That's because the mothers of presidents Warren Harding (1920), Calvin Coolidge (1924), and Herbert Hoover (1928) had already died when their sons ran for office.

In November, FDR captured a landslide victory over the Depression-damaged incumbent Herbert Hoover. He had survived a bombing and polio to become president-elect. It appeared that all that was left to be done was to go through the transition period and prepare to take the oath. Three weeks before the inauguration, Roosevelt spent time relaxing aboard the yacht belonging to Vincent Astor (another member of the famous family) off the coast of Florida.

On February 15, 1933, he rode in an open car through Miami's Bayfront Park where he gave an impromptu speech to an enthusiastic crowd from the vehicle. It was common to spare him the challenging walk to a podium. After the address, Chicago mayor Anton Cermak walked over to shake hands with Roosevelt. Suddenly, five shots rang out that wounded four spectators along with Cermak. FDR was the intended target but was unhurt.

The gunman was an unemployed brick layer named Giuseppe Zangara who shouted, "Too many people are starving!" before beginning his rampage. No doubt good fortune was on FDR's side as being just twenty-five feet away, it should have been an easy shot for the assassin. But Zangara lost his balance standing atop a wobbly chair, and instead of hitting the president-elect, he fatally wounded Cermak. The mayor's last words to FDR were, "I am glad it was me instead of you."

Zangara was initially sentenced to eighty-four years in prison for attempted murder and injuring bystanders. But when Cermak died on March 3, the anarchist said, "I don't like no peoples," was tried and convicted for murder and given the death sentence. On March 20, 1933, sixteen days after Roosevelt's inauguration, Giuseppe Zangara died in the electric chair.

It is traditional on Inauguration Day for the outgoing and incoming presidents to ride together from the White House to the Capitol Building. The event always features lots of smiles and hand waving directed toward the cheering crowd but looks can be deceiving. In 1933, several months after a contentious campaign, the defeated incumbent Herbert Hoover and his successor Franklin D. Roosevelt were still so angry at one another that they did not speak during the drive.

Franklin Delano Roosevelt became president in 1933. In 1905, he married his cousin (fifth cousin, once removed) Eleanor but was not the first commander in chief to do so. Martin Van Buren had married his second cousin, Hannah Hoes, in 1807 but she died eighteen years before he was elected president.

After a busy day of inaugural activities, the new president decided to turn in early. At 10:00 p.m., the First Lady ushered several cars of VIPs, as FDR slept, to the Washington Auditorium, where the inaugural ball was held. Guests paid $150 (a steep price during the Depression) per ticket, which went to charity.

Roosevelt's *Fireside Chats* radio program was meant to inspire the public and, for the most part, was very popular. But that was just the beginning as every US president since FDR has delivered a regular communication via radio. *The Weekly Radio Address by the President* began in 1982 with Ronald Reagan and was carried on by his successors until October 2017.

With declining interest from radio stations and increasing methods of communications, President Donald Trump chose to discontinue the practice.

Following the victory, the FDR team took care of their own. When "Cactus Jack" Garner dropped out of the nomination process, he was promised the vice presidential slot. But it was clear that the plain talkin' Texan wasn't overly enthused about the deal stating, "It [the vice presidency] was not worth a quart of warm spit."

Businessman Joe Kennedy Sr. was rewarded for his efforts behind the scenes by being named the first chairman of the Securities and Exchange Commission.

Frances Perkins was the US secretary of labor from 1933 to 1945 (a record length of time for that office), making her the first woman appointed to the US cabinet. In 1913, she married economist Paul Caldwell Wilson but went to court, and won, in order to keep her maiden name.

On April 20, 1933, the famed aviator Amelia Earhart along with her husband, George Putnam, were invited to dinner at the White House. President Roosevelt was away during the occasion, so the First Lady was accompanied by her brother, Hall Roosevelt.

During the meal, Earhart suggested to Eleanor that they take a flight to Baltimore and back. The suggestion struck a fancy with Mrs. Roosevelt who had recently obtained her student pilot's license.

The group still donned in formal attire took off from the Hoover Field airport (now the site of Reagan International). The renowned pilot was at the controls sporting a white, silk-sewn evening dress with Mrs. Roosevelt sitting next to her in the copilot's seat. Among the passengers were the First Lady's Secret Service detail.

Following the short flight to Baltimore, the group returned to the nation's capital and the White House where they made their way back to the dining room for dessert.

America's favorite political commentator Will Rogers was killed in an airplane accident on August 15, 1935, along with record-setting pilot Wiley Post at Point Barrow, Alaska. President Roosevelt sent Charles Lindbergh to the site to oversee the retrieval of their bodies.

On January 1, 2014, Bill de Blasio was sworn in as mayor of New York City. For the ceremony, FDR's family Bible was used, which dated back to 1686. Former president Bill Clinton officiated the proceeding.

Shortly after the swearing in, the historic artifact, which was on loan from the Roosevelt Library, went missing sending fifty New York police detectives on the hunt. The Bible was found around 5:00 p.m., when it was discovered that it was never actually missing but was in someone's possession the whole time. It had been taken into City Hall for safe keeping after the inaugural ceremony outside had concluded.

THE FOLLOWING ELECTIONS

1936: *Literary Digest*, one of the most respected magazines of the time, made its presidential predictions based on polling. They had picked the correct winner in every election since 1916. However, for 1936, their poll predicted that the challenger, Kansas governor Alf Landon, would not just defeat the incumbent but would do so in a landslide, 57 percent to 43 percent!

That year another poll entered the fray. It was created by Dr. George Gallup, an Iowa statistician, who, in order to get newspapers to subscribe to his weekly research, promised that he would correctly predict the winner of the 1936 presidential election. Gallup told the editors and owners that if he were wrong, he would refund all their money. Based on fifty thousand respondents, Gallup predicted that Roosevelt would be reelected, 56 percent to 44 percent.

The final numbers had FDR with 60.8 percent to Landon's 36.54 percent in the popular vote. The error in the *Literary Digest* survey was the largest ever in a major public opinion poll. Practically all the erroneous sampling resulted from bias. It was one of the largest and most expensive polls ever conducted, with a sample size of around 2.4 million people!

It wasn't the last election where a polling company walked away with egg on its face as the worst was still yet to come.

Landon became the Republicans sacrificial lamb as he suffered the party's largest loss in presidential history. He was bested by FDR by 24.26 percent in the popular vote and was demolished in the electoral college, 523–8. The governor won just two states, Vermont and Maine, and lost his home state of Kansas. Sixty-one percent of the public participated in the election, a 4 percent increase over 1932.

1940: FDR won reelection in an electoral college landslide, 449 to 82 but his other numbers were also closer than in 1936. He won the popular vote by just 10 percent and captured eight fewer states during his latest effort. Even though challenger Wendell Willkie (R-NY) lost by nearly five million votes, he amassed more popular ballots than any other Republican nominee between 1928 and 1952.

A total of 62.5 percent of registered voters took part, a 1.5 percent increase over 1936. The president's latest victory was the final decree in the divorce between the squabbling tandem of FDR and his straightforward vice president "Cactus" Jack Garner of Texas. When the dust settled, the two-termer hitched up his wagon and headed home ending forty-six years in public life.

15

The Election of 1944

Franklin D. Roosevelt, Incumbent (Democrat) vs. Thomas Dewey (Republican)

"I am accustomed to hearing malicious falsehoods about myself. But I think I have a right to resent, to object, to libelous statements about my dog."

—President Roosevelt's comments during a speech to the Teamsters Union countering Republican attacks about his dog, Fala, on September 23, 1944. The remarks drew a great deal of laughter.

Franklin Roosevelt had been solving problems throughout his political career. As governor of New York (1929–1932) during the Depression, he started a relief system that became the model for the Federal Emergency Relief Administration (FERA) that was able to secure $20 million (a substantial amount for the time) in aid from the state legislature, which was used for public works projects.

During his second term, FDR founded the Seabury Commission whose investigations led to a number of corrupt public officials being removed from office. As president, he instituted the New Deal to address the massive unemployment and economic downturn.

When the Japanese bombed the US fleet at Pearl Harbor, Hawaii, on December 7, 1941, America was officially brought into the war. As expected, three days later, the other two members of the Axis powers, Germany and Italy, declared their aggressions on the United States, which would be forced to fight the enemy on two separate fronts of the world. It was something never attempted on such a scale in modern warfare.

Over his first eight years in office, FDR had faced down many problems—both foreign and domestic. But during his third term, an adversary that couldn't be stopped with the passage of a bill or the signing of an executive order mounted an all-out offensive against the commander in chief. It was a series of health issues that

President Franklin D. Roosevelt, Vice President-elect Harry S. Truman, and Vice President Henry Wallace in a car. President Roosevelt is returning to the capitol from Union Station during a downpour. A frail-looking FDR died six months later. Credit: Truman Library

targeted the country's only three-term president who became a shell of his former energetic self during the war years.

As FDR attempted to get the upper hand over his enemies like Adolf Hitler and Hidecki Tojo, Father Time had become his biggest antagonist. In 1937, Roosevelt was diagnosed as having systolic hypertension, the most common form of high blood pressure in the elderly, although he was only fifty-five at the time. That was followed in 1941 when it was discovered that he suffered from diastolic hypertension, which is associated with an increased risk of a cardiovascular event. Being that FDR was a heavy smoker who drank and enjoyed fried food, his chances of further health problems were an increasing probability.

Inadvertently, the Japanese had helped solve Roosevelt's unemployment problem. Prior to the attack on Pearl Harbor, the jobless rate was still near 9.9 percent. However, a year later with men going off to war and large numbers of women working outside their homes for the first time, the jobless rate quickly shrank to just 4.7 percent. It was the end of the Great Depression as many females were busy rebuilding the ships and aircraft lost in the island attack.

Meanwhile, the United States was making a comeback, albeit gradually, with victories at Midway (June 1942) and Guadalcanal (August 1942 to February 1943). It was good news for General Douglas MacArthur and his staff, although things weren't going so well for his boss in Washington, DC.

In addition to his continuing health issues, FDR's personal life was in turmoil. His years of philandering had finally reached a breaking point with Eleanor, who in 1926, moved into a private cottage, *Val-Kill*, on the Hyde Park estate. She also had a townhouse in New York City.

The president's adulterous history with other women was so well-known that Herbert Hoover considered using the information against him in the campaign of 1932. The couple remained married and in 1942, with his health failing, FDR asked his wife to return to the main house to be closer to him, but the staunchly independent First Lady refused.

In 1943, Roosevelt and Churchill watched as Hitler's troops continuously failed in their attempt to overthrow the Soviet Union. Like most armies, Nazi forces had not been trained to fight in the harsh conditions of the Russian winter and it was obvious that der Führer was no student of history or he would have known that other combatants, like Napoleon, had already attempted and failed to brave the frigid temperatures.

In 1854, during the Crimean War, Tsar Nicholas I bragged about his climatic ally over impending invasions when he stated, "I have two generals who will not fail me: Generals January and February." His ghost had returned to haunt Hitler and the Third Reich into a frozen trap that cost them any advantage that they had gained at the outset of the war along with the lives of thousands of soldiers. In the South Pacific, General MacArthur's troops continued to island hop their way toward the enemy's strongholds.

Not all of FDR's problems were on the other side of an ocean. In the summer of 1943, race riots broke out in Detroit, Michigan, New York City's Harlem, and Beaumont, Texas, leaving forty-three people dead and extensive property damage in each community. Because of the president's narrow social background, he lacked an understanding of the inner workings of the black community.

In one instance in 1941, A. Philip Randolph, the head of the Brotherhood of Sleeping Car Porters and a leading voice of the civil rights movement, planned a mass march on the nation's capital to protest the exclusion of blacks from World War II defense jobs and certain New Deal programs. Fearing that bad publicity from such a demonstration might damage his agenda, FDR met with Randolph a day before the event, and issued Executive Order 8802 creating the Fair Employment Practices Committee. It forbade discrimination against workers in the defense industry and government. In return, the union leader called off the planned march.

In 1944, FDR's only daughter, Anna, returned to the White House from her job as a journalist in Seattle to serve as her father's confidential assistant, substitute chief of staff, and quasi First Lady. She ran interference for the president, only allowing those into his presence whom she deemed absolutely necessary. Anna also served as White House hostess during her mother's absence and traveled with the president to the historic Yalta Conference.

As 1944 was an election year, major decisions had to be made. In the evenings during January, Roosevelt began complaining of headaches. Weeks later on March 27, Dr. Howard Bruenn, a cardiologist at the Bethesda, Maryland, naval hospital diagnosed the president with hypertensive heart disease. It marked the beginning of keeping the nation's leader sequestered as much as possible.

Also examining Roosevelt was one of Boston's top physicians, Dr. Frank Lahey who went one step further and advised him not to seek a fourth term as he was in seriously declining health that included the possibility of cancer as well as advanced heart disease. He was convinced that FDR would not survive another four years in office. Over the following weeks, his weight dropped from 188 to 165 pounds.

On March 30, crackles were discovered at the base of both lungs signaling a problem with his airflow. Bruenn also diagnosed the president with congestive heart failure and placed him on digitalis for the rest of his life.

The doctor ordered FDR to leave Washington, DC, and rest. While recuperating at the South Carolina plantation of his friend and multimillionaire campaign donor Bernard Baruch, the president developed severe abdominal pains on April 28 that were diagnosed as acute cholecystitis (inflammation of the gallbladder). All the while, fighting in Europe and Japan continued as the war raged onward.

On D-Day, June 6, FDR went through a series of meetings at the White House that included General George Marshall and Speaker of the House Sam Rayburn (D-TX). That evening, the president did a ten minute radio broadcast at 9:57 p.m. to update the public on the invasion, which included a prayer for the troops. After a historic and demanding day, the sickly chief executive retired about 11:00 p.m.

The Republican National Convention began on June 21 in Chicago. Not since the days of FDR's cousin Theodore Roosevelt had the GOP nominated a war hero, but there was a possibility that could change. General Douglas MacArthur, the supreme allied commander for the War in the Pacific, was in the thick of the Republican race even though he had been out of the country since 1935. He won two of the thirteen primaries and garnered almost 29 percent of the popular vote, more than any other candidate.

However, the respected general faced a dilemma. He wanted the nomination but also intended to complete his job against the enemy in the Pacific who was now on the defensive. Some of his followers believed that "Mac" could emulate the strategy of Mexican-American War hero Zachary Taylor and have his staff run his campaign while he finished his military obligation. It was a longshot, but as news about FDR's failing health became a larger issue, it meant that for many Republicans, MacArthur for president became a real possibility.

But on April 30, 1944, the general ended all hopes of being the latest candidate to go directly from the battlefield to the White House when he issued a statement that closed with the passage, "I request that no action be taken that would link my name in any way with the nomination. I do not covet it nor would I accept it."

There was also something that MacArthur feared might become known if he became a candidate. In 1929, the then forty-nine-year-old general fell in love with sixteen-year-old Isabel Rosario Cooper, a Scottish and Filipino Chinese beauty, who was attempting to become an actress. When Mac was appointed army chief of staff and returned to Washington, DC, he relocated his new girlfriend in a nearby apartment.

Five years later, with the relationship ended, MacArthur was being blackmailed by reporter Drew Pearson of the *Washington Post* who threatened to expose the relationship. He made a $15,000 payoff to the journalist to kill the story, but it wasn't because he feared the reaction of the president or the public rather he was concerned that his demanding and overbearing mother, Mary, might find out about his carousing with a teenager.

As the Republicans convened, FDR had already been at Hyde Park for six days attempting to keep up with his responsibilities while, in some way, adhering to his doctor's orders. When MacArthur decided not to pursue the nomination, the happiest person in Chicago was Thomas Dewey. He had been the special prosecutor for a grand jury investigation into vice and racketeering in New York City that eventually convicted the famous mob boss Charles "Lucky" Luciano in 1936. From there, he rode the guilty verdict into becoming the state's governor in 1943 and, after falling short four years earlier, had his eyes squarely again on the White House in 1944.

With MacArthur out of the running, Dewey claimed an easy first ballot nomination with fellow governor James Bricker of Ohio selected as his running mate.

The Democrats' convention ran from July 19–21 and, like their opposition, was also assembling in Chicago. However, FDR had departed the nation's capital a week prior and was far away in sunny San Diego with family members when the gavel struck the podium to begin the meeting. Against his doctor's advice, he was renominated for another term and accepted the distinction via a radio address to the nation. He had again made history, this time by becoming the first president to be nominated for a fourth term. Although his health continued to be a problem, as during his time in the Southern California coastal community he suffered a seizure.

The real question back in Chicago was who would be Roosevelt's running mate? Due to his failing health, the decision for the fourth term would be more important than it had in the past. The popular Henry Wallace was the sitting vice president and wanted to be retained as did FDR who said, "I like him and I respect him and he is my personal friend. For these reasons, I personally would vote for his renomination if I were a delegate to the convention."

But a couple of weeks preceding the convention, the party bosses, headed by the outgoing Democratic National Committee chairman Frank C. Walker, met with Roosevelt because they felt that Wallace was too politically liberal and lenient toward labor unions. He had also made enemies of some of the more powerful voices on Wall Street.

They favored nine-year US senator Harry Truman of Missouri, who was chairman of the Senate's Special Committee to investigate the National Defense Program, for the ticket's second spot. FDR, who barely knew Truman, balked at the choice, and countered with former senator and ex-Supreme Court justice James F. Byrnes, but the party's hierarchy knew that the labor unions would never accept the South Carolinian due to his conservatism.

Days earlier, while traveling to San Diego, Roosevelt had sent the following message to Robert Hannegan, the new Democratic National Committee chairman, which said:

Dear Bob:
  You have written me about Harry Truman and Bill Douglas [Supreme Court chief justice William O. Douglas]. I should, of course, be very glad to run with either of them and believe that either one of them would bring real strength to the ticket.
  Always Sincerely,
  Franklin D. Roosevelt

FDR relented but only if Sidney Hillman, chairman of the Congress of Industrial Organization's Political Action Committee and the party's chief fundraiser, approved the nomination, which he did. It was a sign of just how far the president's power had fallen since the last election in 1940 when he personally chose Wallace as his running mate. As opposed to his previous run when he was making every major decision, Roosevelt was now being told by others how the process was going to work and, at that stage, simply didn't have the energy to fight back.

Truman was reluctant to accept the agreement, which became known as the new Missouri Compromise, although there was still the matter of winning over the delegates. At the start of the convention, a Gallup Poll asked potential voters who they wanted on the ticket as vice president. Sixty-five percent of potential voters chose Wallace while only 2 percent said they wanted Truman.

On the convention's third day, FDR called Hannegan in Chicago to find out if Truman was on board with the nomination. When he was told that he wasn't, the angry president responded, "Tell him if he wants to bust up the Democratic Party in the middle of a war, this is his responsibility." Shortly afterward, Truman, who overheard the call, accepted the offer.

On the first ballot (July 21), Wallace lead Truman 429.5 to 319.5 with the remaining votes scattered among several others. The magic number for nomination was 589 and it appeared that the incumbent was in good position. At that point Hannegan released the message that he had received from FDR about Truman to the conventioneers, which caused a dramatic shift on the second ballot as the senator surged into the lead 477.5 to 473. That position change began the usual arm twisting and deal cutting that was prevalent at every convention. When it was over, and the second ballot was retaken, Truman had amassed 1,031 delegates and his party's blessing as its vice presidential nominee. His acceptance speech, one of the shortest in American political history, lasted less than a minute.

For Henry Wallace, it was the ultimate case of so close yet so far away. Following the first ballot, he was just 159.5 votes from being renominated. With FDR's death the following April, that delegate count showed how close he came to becoming the thirty-third president of the United States. Although, instead of the White House,

Wallace's next, and last, post was an eighteen-month stretch as secretary of commerce (1945–1946).

While the Democrats were attempting to decide on their vice president, an unsuccessful attempt was made on Hitler's life in East Prussia. It was evident that time was also running out for the German dictator as some of his inner circle were making their own plans to defect to a safe haven. As the summer pressed on the president visited Hawaii and Alaska, which was billed as a military tour but it was primarily done to help FDR rest, as there were long stretches where little work was getting done.

The entourage returned to Washington, DC, on August 17 and FDR held his first meeting with Truman, as his running mate, the next day over lunch. Afterward, the new nominee told the press, "The president looked fine and ate a bigger lunch than I did. He's still the leader he's always been and don't let anybody kid you about it. He's keen as a briar." However, privately he told those who were close to him a different story, "His hands were shaking and he talks with considerable difficulty. . . . It doesn't seem to be any mental lapse of any kind, but physically he's just going to pieces."

The two men met only eight times, most of which took place in the company of legislative leaders. The campaign received some good news on August 25 as Allied forces liberated Paris although, when it came to most matters, Truman soon learned that the protocol around FDR was not business as usual.

"I was handicapped by the lack of knowledge of both foreign and domestic affairs due principally to Mr. Roosevelt's inability to pass on responsibility," said the Missourian. "Roosevelt never discussed anything important at his Cabinet meetings. Cabinet members, if they had anything to discuss, tried to see him privately after the meetings."

Truman had served as a captain during World War I, so he understood about doing one's duty, which currently meant helping get FDR reelected. Therefore, when it was time to hit the road, which he did on August 31, he started at a familiar location, his birthplace of Lamar, Missouri.

As August gave way to September, Dewey was on the offensive, and enjoying a small lead (51% to 49%) in the Labor Day polls. As opposed to his former challengers Landon and Willkie, FDR genuinely disliked the New York governor although aides were concerned if Roosevelt still had the fire in his belly to endure a final campaign. At one point, he told Margaret Suckley, his archivist at Hyde Park, that he would not be surprised if Dewey won in November because Democrats seemed too confident of success.

The contest was bruising but there was also trouble behind the scenes. The First Lady had played a prominent role in the previous three campaigns but had disagreements with Robert Hannegan, the current campaign manager, in terms of strategy. She thought he was more focused on winning rather than on the reasons for reelection. The two reached a point where they barely spoke to one another as Mrs. Roosevelt's focus centered on her own priorities such as domestic issues rather than the campaign's prevailing theme of foreign conflict.

The president's failing health had become a major topic and there were some who demanded a full accounting. Dewey considered making the issue public, but his handlers stopped him fearing a voter backlash. They also realized that the press wouldn't cooperate because of FDR's power as a wartime president.

The polls changed frequently as on September 6 when a *Fortune* survey showed Roosevelt enjoying a small lead at 52.6 percent. A Gallup Poll, released the following day, had Dewey with 51 percent support. Despite the problems in their marriage, as the race grew closer, Eleanor Roosevelt urged FDR to go public and campaign vigorously away from the radio microphone and not just hunker down in his office at the White House.

While touring the western United States, the Dewey campaign got a jolt on September 19, but it had nothing to do with FDR. At 11:50 a.m. (PST), the candidate's train that was en route to Portland, ploughed into the rear of a Great Northern passenger express near the small town of Castle Rock, Washington. A few passengers in some of the railway cars suffered minor injuries. The Deweys were shaken but uninjured.

If the Democrats were lackadaisical, the events on September 22 quickly slapped them back into reality. Dewey addressed a highly partisan crowd of ninety-three thousand at the cavernous Los Angeles Memorial Coliseum. He delivered the address under a fifty-two-foot American flag and was accompanied by an array of Hollywood celebrities that included Ginger Rogers and Walt Disney.

Dewey's massive West Coast gathering inspired the president to give, as his aides assessed it, one of his best speeches ever the following evening. The address was delivered to the Teamsters Union in Washington, DC, and, for the first time in a long while, the old FDR with his well-known wit and energy, reemerged. When the night concluded, the overlying question was if it were a trend that would carryover for the campaign's final weeks or just a one night show?

Beginning in early October and continuing through Election Day, Truman spoke in more than fifteen states and over twenty large cities proving that his plain-talking style could be a valuable campaign asset. But Roosevelt knew that Eleanor was correct and, no matter his declining health, if he were going to win a fourth term, he would have to go out on the road.

That strategy changed from the past campaigns. Rather than appearing at numerous communities with a whistle-stop tour, he made fewer appearances but in larger venues like athletic stadiums. His campaign stops included: October 21, New York City; October 27, Camden, New Jersey; October 27, Wilmington, Delaware; October 27, Philadelphia; October 28, Fort Wayne, Indiana; October 28, Chicago; October 29, Clarksburg, West Virginia; November 2, radio campaign speech from the White House; November 4, Hartford, Connecticut; November 4, Springfield, Massachusetts; November 4, Bridgeport, Connecticut; November 4, Boston; November 6–7, informal remarks during Dutchess County campaign tour and election night at Hyde Park.

Even after the failed assassination attempt in 1933, the president continued riding in open cars at most of his tour stops.

On November 6, 1944, the last campaign speech of Franklin D. Roosevelt was broadcast from his estate in Hyde Park, New York. Two days later, he gained his fourth term by a smaller margin than any of his previous elections, especially in the popular vote where Dewey lost by only three and one half million votes. A shift of five hundred thousand votes in a few states (including Michigan, New York, Illinois, Massachusetts, New Hampshire, Missouri, and Pennsylvania), all of which had Republican governors, would have given Dewey an electoral college win and the presidency. FDR won seven states by 4 percent or less of the popular vote and it was the first time since Grover Cleveland's reelection in 1892 in which Ohio went to the losing candidate

The weather on Election Day 1944 was clear and mild throughout the country, but the turnout of 55.9 million was down 6.6 percent from 1940.

Roosevelt received 53 percent of the popular vote (and 432 electoral votes) to Dewey's 47 percent (and 99 electoral votes). That count was almost identical to the *New York Daily News'* final poll (New York voters only) of the campaign that had FDR holding a 50.8 percent to 49.2 percent lead on November 3. The final Gallup Poll had the incumbent leading 51 percent to 48 percent.

The biggest improvement for Republicans came in the county votes. During Roosevelt's first presidential election in 1932, he carried 2,721 counties—more than any other candidate for president up to that time. The incumbent, Herbert Hoover, carried only 372. In 1944, Roosevelt's last election, Republicans won 1,344. While Democrats still held a majority of the nation's counties (1,750), most of them came from the south. Outside that region and the mountain (where Republicans tied Democrats) section, Democrats carried only 390 counties.

Overall, the president carried a majority of the women's vote, which was the largest participation block in the country, as well as the black and city votes. Dewey was the choice of more men and rural population residents. Interestingly, the challenger also carried FDR's hometown of Hyde Park, New York, and Truman's community of Independence, Missouri although 80 percent of all voters maintained that Dewey had waged the most negative campaign.

It took FDR longer than usual to close the deal as 31 percent of the electorate said that they made their final choice in the last four to six weeks of the campaign. There were no debates between the candidates, and it was the last election in which a Democratic presidential candidate carried every state in the south.

Even with the election concluded, Governor Dewey couldn't escape from the giant Roosevelt shadow. Shortly after 3:00 a.m. on November 8, he appeared in Manhattan to concede defeat. He said all the expected words in a brief address during the appearance that was made from the ballroom of a historic luxury hotel located on 45 East 45th Street. The establishment was the famous Roosevelt Hotel, named in honor of FDR's cousin Theodore.

Table 15.1   The Election of 1944

Presidential candidate	Party	Home state	Popular vote Count	Percentage	Electoral vote
Franklin D. Roosevelt (Incumbent)	Democratic	New York	25,612,916	53.39%	432
Thomas E. Dewey	Republican	New York	22,017,929	45.89%	99
(none)	Texas Regulars	(n/a)	143,238	0.30%	0
Norman Thomas	Socialist	New York	79,017	0.16%	0
Claude A. Watson	Prohibition	California	74,758	0.16%	0
Edward A. Teichert	Socialist Labor	Pennsylvania	45,188	0.09%	0
Other			11,816	0.02%	â€"
Total			47,977,063	100%	531
Needed to win					266

Vice President Elect, Harry Truman, US Senator (D-MO)

THE AFTERMATH

Four years after his defeat in 1940, Wendell Willkie remained a popular figure, but on October 8, 1944, he died after suffering a heart attack. Both FDR and Dewey wanted his endorsement, but he died before backing either of them.

By 1945, sixty-three-year-old FDR was tired and very ill. The stress of the job, in addition to his polio and other health issues, had aged him greatly beyond his years. His heavy smoking also added to his ailments.

Roosevelt's final inauguration was historic. It was held on Saturday, January 20, 1945, and was the first time that an individual publicly took the oath of president for the fourth time. Due to the chief executive's weakened state, the ceremony was held on the south portico of the White House, rather than the Capitol, where his inaugural address was one of the shortest in American history lasting just six minutes.

FDR recited the same Bible verse at all four of his inaugurations: "Though I speak with the tongues of men and of angels, and have not charity, I am become as sounding brass, or a tinkling cymbal" (Corinthians).

The parade and inaugural ball were canceled in deference to the troops who were still at war. The gravely ill Roosevelt died eighty-two days into the term with Truman ascending to the presidency.

On April 12, FDR was sitting for a portrait at the presidential retreat at Warm Springs, Georgia, when he complained of a headache. He then lost consciousness, collapsed, and was pronounced dead two hours later. In the end, it wasn't an assassin with a gun; or a bomb-toting anarchist; or even a misguided torpedo fired from one of his own ships as had happened in 1943 that finally ended FDR's time on earth but rather a biological stalker that couldn't be thwarted—a cerebral embolism. Among those who were with him at the time was his long-time mistress Lucy Mercer Rutherfurd.

Conspicuous by his absence at the Roosevelt funeral was his good friend and ally, Winston Churchill, who was urged to remain at home as the war in Europe was drawing to an end. In later years, he regretted that he had allowed himself to be persuaded not to go. Following V-E Day, on July 26, 1945, the prime minister resigned after the decisive defeat of the Conservatives when the Labour Party picked up 229 seats in that summer's British election.

The old adage that the deaths of the famous go in threes held true in April 1945.

Following FDR, Italian dictator Benito Mussolini was murdered by a mob in the village of Giulino di Mezzegra on April 28 and, two days later, Germany's strongman Adolf Hitler took his own life in his Berlin bunker. None of the three lived to witness the surrender on May 7. The other central figure, Japan's minister of war Hideki Tojo was hanged as a war criminal on December 23, 1948.

In addition to all the previous close calls, there was another item where FDR might have again changed history. On September 2, 1945, the Japanese surrendered drawing a conclusion to World War II. Aware of his declining health, Roosevelt had planned to see the war through to its end and then retire to his estate at Hyde Park. Had that scenario played out, in addition to winning four terms, he would also have become the first president to leave office of his own accord before concluding a term.

Even though Roosevelt was the only president of the United States to be elected to four consecutive terms, many believed that he had acquired too much power over his decade plus in office. Some observers likened him closer to a king than a president. That was the reason that, following his death, Congress wasted little time passing the Twenty-second Amendment to the Constitution in 1947, which limits the chief executive to two terms. It was ratified in 1951, and unless there is a change in the law, FDR's record of four terms will stand forever.

Some have speculated who might have been the Democrats' nominee if FDR hadn't run in 1944. The party didn't have the next political star waiting in the wings. The best bets may have been Truman, Senator Harry Byrd of Virginia, or Vice President Henry Wallace. Each would have provided Dewey with a better chance at victory than facing the entrenched Roosevelt.

During his twelve White House years, Roosevelt set the all-time presidential record of 243,827 miles traveled by rail.

16

The Election of 1948

Harry S. Truman, Incumbent (Democrat) vs. Thomas Dewey (Republican)

"You want a friend in Washington? Get a dog."

—Harry Truman

On April 12,1945, Franklin Delano Roosevelt complained of a headache, a short while later he was dead.

That afternoon, Eleanor Roosevelt, who had remained in Washington, DC, rather than accompanying her husband to Georgia, sent a request to Harry Truman at the Capitol Building asking him to meet her immediately at her study in the White House. At 5:30 p.m., she greeted the administration's newest vice president, who had not yet been told the news. The outgoing First Lady then calmly told him, "Harry, the president is dead."

Truman recalled his first reaction when he was informed of FDR's passing, "I felt like the moon, the stars and all the planets had fallen on me." Regrouping his thoughts, he asked the newly-widowed Eleanor if there was anything that he could do for her, to which she replied with a note of caution in her voice, "Is there anything we can do for you? For you are the one in trouble now."

From 7:08 p.m. to 7:09 p.m., the Cabinet Room, which had been the place where many of history's important decisions had been made, became the site of the changing of the guard at the Executive Mansion as Harry S. Truman was sworn in as the nation's thirty-third president. "Boys, if you ever pray, pray for me now," he told reporters. One departing journalist told him, "Good luck, Mr. President," and Truman replied, "I wish you didn't have to call me that."

Like FDR, Truman also had a close call years earlier that almost kept him out of the White House. On Sunday, March 27, 1938, while serving as a third year US senator, the man from Missouri was returning to the nation's capital from Hagerstown, Maryland, with his wife and daughter. The future commander in chief was driving his 1936 Plymouth when he ran a stop sign at an intersection.

As the senator's vehicle blew through the cross streets, another car broadsided Truman's sedan causing it to roll over several times. Fortunately, no one in either car was hurt as he later exclaimed that his view of the stop sign had been blocked by a parked car. Although Truman's automobile was a total loss, no citations were issued by the police. His daughter Margaret recalled, "It was a miracle that we escaped alive. Dad had a cut over his forehead and Mother had a wrenched back." She also said that her father always drove too fast.

Unfortunately for the new president, his predecessor had few confidants and Truman had never been allowed into the Roosevelt inner circle. Among those issues that were under discussion was perhaps the most crucial, the development of the atomic bomb.

When Truman became the chairman of the Senate's Special Committee to Investigate the National Defense Program in 1941, he took his responsibility quite seriously. So much so that in 1944, a record showing a large amount of untraceable cash drew his attention. There were billions of dollars going into something called the "Manhattan Engineering District" but he couldn't get any answers to his inquiries pertaining to it.

He confronted Secretary of War Henry L. Stimson who told him that the money was funding for a top secret project and that was all that he would be told. It took another year and the death of the president for Truman to find out that what he had stumbled upon was the financing for the Manhattan Project and the development of the first atomic bombs. Even as the head of the committee and as vice president, Truman had been kept completely out of the loop by Roosevelt's inner sanctum.

But it didn't take long for the new president to get up to speed about America's emerging superweapon. He ordered that the project be continued and shortly thereafter, on August 6, 1945, the first bomb was dropped on the Japanese city of Hiroshima. It was the single most powerful man-made force that the world had ever seen, instantly killing an estimated seventy-thousand people.

Three days later, after Japan rejected an opportunity to surrender, a second explosion destroyed the city of Nagasaki that killed at least another forty thousand. The two nuclear blasts had instantly ended four years of fighting for the United States, but they also had a secondary effect propelling Harry Truman from a little known senator from Missouri into one of the primary individuals on the world stage. The weapon may have started with FDR, but it was his successor, who had been in the dark just weeks before, who used it to drop the final curtain on World War II.

With the Japanese surrender, Truman's postwar focus was primarily on the spread of Communism in Europe, the deteriorating relationship with the Soviet Union, and the recovery of Japan and Europe from the war. With 1948 on the horizon, he also needed to make a decision about his candidacy for the upcoming election.

On the other side of the aisle, the Republicans were busy trying to find the person who could end the twelve-year Democrat reign of the executive branch. Their first ploy was the same as 1944, when they attempted to draft Douglas MacArthur, prior to turning their attention to the mastermind of the D-Day invasion, General Dwight D. Eisenhower. However, before the bandwagon for the European commander could begin rolling, Eisenhower, also known as Ike, put the brakes on the proposal declining all overtures and sending the GOP brain trust back to the drawing board.

The primaries got underway in April 1948 with one of the more intriguing figures making an impact. Former Minnesota governor Harold Stassen had been elected to office in 1938 at the politically youthful age of thirty-one. During his 1942 reelection campaign, Stassen announced that, if he won again, he would resign to serve on active duty with the US Naval Reserve. True to his word, following his victory, he left his office and reported for active duty.

In the eleven contested primaries that year, Stassen won four of them, more than any other candidate. But California's governor Earl Warren topped the contenders with 27 percent of the popular vote. Each candidate had their factions but there was no clear-cut favorite as spring morphed into summer.

Some believe that the first presidential debates took place between John F. Kennedy and Richard Nixon in 1960. That's partially true as Kennedy-Nixon featured the nominees of the two major parties. But on May 17, 1948, there was a primary debate between Republican candidates Thomas Dewey and Harold Stassen in Portland, Oregon. The national radio broadcast of the initial presidential debate attracted nearly forty million listeners.

That event helped Dewey, in his third run for president, win the Oregon primary, which was held the following day. It was one of his two primary wins, the other was New Jersey. Some years afterward, on May 21, 1956, the Democrats hosted their first primary debate between hopefuls Adlai Stevenson and Estes Kefauver from Miami, Florida.

The 1948 Republican Convention was held June 21–25 in Philadelphia. Even though Stassen had the momentum of his primary victories on his side, Dewey had the experience and name recognition going for him. When the balloting began, the New Yorker took the lead over US senator Robert Taft of Ohio and Stassen. On the third ballot, the other hopefuls withdrew, and Dewey received all 1,094 delegate votes.

On the fifth and final day of the convention, the nominee selected Earl Warren as his running mate. It would be the governor's second time as his party's nominee.

The Democrats were also gathering in Philadelphia from July 12–14 and for good reason. The idea behind the City of Brotherly Love hosting both conventions was so that each event could be televised without having to move and set up equipment in two separate locations. Two of the three new television networks, NBC and CBS, had the ability to telecast along the East Coast with complete live coverage of both conventions.

Truman had served almost all of FDR's final term allowing him time to make an impression on voters for his own four-year stint. His handling of the duties satisfied the delegates who named him as the nominee with a first ballot confirmation. The party's running mate was Alben Barkley, the Senate minority leader from Kentucky.

However, the count wasn't without its own drama. During the tally, Alabama delegate Leven Ellis announced his strong disapproval of the party's civil rights measure and proclaimed, "We bid you good-bye," as thirteen members of his state's delegation marched out of the hall followed by members from Mississippi who shouted, "Good-bye Harry!"

The balloting for both offices took place on July 13 and for good reason. The high temperature inside the convention hall had gotten worse since the Republicans left town, as a blistering heat wave was causing havoc in the nonair-conditioned facility sending 108 people to the aid station for treatment of heat prostration.

Truman and Dewey had squared off four years earlier but, at that time, the Missouri native was in the role of Franklin Roosevelt's understudy. Even though the Democrats' number two man landed some sharp jabs on the campaign trail, this time around, he and his record would be on the receiving end as the former New York prosecutor would once again attempt to make his case to the American people.

Truman had another concern. The south had always been a Democrat stronghold. Even in the elections that they lost, the party could always rely on the former Confederacy to come through at the polls. But that changed in 1948 as a Democrat faction known as the Dixiecrats, who opposed Truman's efforts to integrate the military, had broken away from the party's mainliners. Also, the president was not on the ballot in Alabama because the state's Supreme Court ruled that any statute requiring party presidential electors to vote for that body's national nominee was void.

The Dixiecrats were led by South Carolina's segregationist governor Strom Thurmond who became their presidential nominee. It meant that in the upcoming campaign, Truman had to keep one eye on Dewey and the other on Thurmond as the once reliable southern states were now in play. Another former Roosevelt vice president, Henry Wallace, who had also wanted to be the Democrats' choice, was in the field running on the Progressive Party ticket.

The Democrat election team divided Truman's campaign into two phases. The first came in June with a whistle stop tour that began in Ohio and wound its way to the West Coast. There were some good moments, but the nearly nine thousand-mile journey was a necessity as in May, Truman had a 36 percent approval rating according to the Gallup Poll, as many American voters viewed him as being soft on Communism.

If Truman didn't believe that Dewey, Thurmond, or Wallace represented a challenge, all he had to do was to read the numbers. The postconvention Gallup Poll didn't pack much good news for the incumbent as Dewey officially started the campaign with a 49 percent to 36 percent lead. August was better for Truman, but he still trailed 47 percent to 39 percent although in September, Dewey's lead had been reduced from 46 percent to 40 percent.

On September 9, two full months before voting took place, another major pollster Elmo Roper, announced that his organization was discontinuing surveying for the remainder of the election cycle. He had Dewey leading 53 percent to 38 percent and assumed that the race was over and any further polling was just a waste of time and money.

Truman's seventeen-car campaign train nicknamed *"Magellan"* pulled out of the nation's capital on September 17 for the latest cross-country expedition. Over the next thirty-three days, it covered an astounding 21,928 miles as the candidate gave 352 speeches. In an era when television coverage was still a rarity, the election team was putting the president on display at as many stops that they could squeeze into their schedule.

When the October polls were released, Gallup had Dewey ahead 50 percent to 44 percent as he conducted his final survey almost two weeks before the election. Another national poll from Archibald Crossley had Dewey at 49.9 percent to 44.8 percent but he had stopped polling by October 25.

Election Day fell on November 3, and by all appearances Harry Truman would soon be returning to Independence, Missouri, as a private citizen. He trailed in every poll and almost all that remained for the pundits and newspapers was to write the epitaph for the Truman presidency. Perhaps FDR had been correct four years earlier when he suggested that either Henry Wallace or James Byrnes should be his vice president.

Team Truman was hunkered down at Kansas City's upscale Muehlebach Hotel's presidential suite. The day before the election, the president's close friend Tom Evans came up to the penthouse to talk. "What do you actually and honestly believe?" Evans asked Truman. "Do you think you can win?" "Yes, I'm going to win," Truman responded. Evans was not so sure. "I've always said you ought to be the international president of the Optimist Club," he remarked.

If Truman was sure, that was not the case with everyone else around him as the outcome of the election was so uncertain that the Secret Service detail had already been split between himself and Dewey. For his part, the president was staying away from the confusion at his headquarters and was relaxing at the nearby Elms Hotel in Excelsior Springs, Missouri.

Later, Truman recalled the most interesting evening that a presidential election had seen,

> On election day I voted at an hour that was convenient to the White House photographers, so they wouldn't have to get up too early. I had my sandwich and glass of buttermilk, and went to bed at six-thirty. And along about 12 o'clock, I happened to wake up, for some reason or other, and the radio was turned on, to the National Broadcasting Company [NBC]. And Mr. [H. V.] Kaltenborn and Mr. [Richard] Harkness were reporting the situation as it then developed.
>
> Mr. Kaltenborn was saying, "While the President is a million votes ahead of the popular vote, when the country vote comes in, Mr. Truman will be defeated by an overwhelming majority." At that point, Truman went back to sleep.

About 4 o'clock in the morning, the Chief of the Secret Service came in and said, "Mr. President, I think you had better get up and listen to the broadcast. We have been listening all night." And I said, "All right." I turned the darn thing on, and there was Mr. Kaltenborn again. Mr. Kaltenborn was saying, "While the President has a lead of 2 million votes, it is certainly necessary that this election shall go into the House of Representatives. He hasn't an opportunity of being elected by a majority of the electoral votes of the Nation!"

I called the Secret Service men in, and I said, "We'd better go back to Kansas City, it looks as if I'm elected!"

Along about 10 o'clock (the following day), I had a telegram which said that the election was over, and that I should be congratulated on the fact that I had won the election"

I am highly appreciative of the electors who voted—the 303 electors who voted for me as President—and I am not in any way interested in the analyses which have been made of the vote . . . when those analyses were made by Mr. Gallup, and Mr. Kaltenborn, and Mr. Harkness.

However, George Gallup Jr., cochairman of the Gallup organization, made no excuses for his company's mistake, "We stopped polling a few weeks too soon. We had been lulled into thinking that nothing much changes in the last few weeks of the campaign."

In New York, the day after the election at 11:14 a.m. (EST), Dewey sent a telegram to Truman: "My heartiest congratulations to you on your election and every good wish for a successful administration. I urge all Americans to unite behind you in support of every effort to keep our nation strong and free and establish peace in the world."

At 1:00 p.m., Dewey met with the members of the press and they were looking for answers. One reporter asked, "What happened, Governor?"

"I was just as surprised as you are," he responded, and concluded by saying that he wouldn't run again.

The outcome seemed so certain that the *Chicago Tribune*, facing its evening deadline, printed its famous edition with the blaring headline, "*Dewey Defeats Truman*." In 2018, a copy of this well-known journalistic blunder, which is considered to be a collector's item, sold at auction for $1,800.

After another stinging defeat, Dewey not only had to go home to lick his wounds but had to listen to jokes about it. This was one that made the rounds:

On election night, Governor Dewey asked his wife Frances, "How will it be to sleep with the President of the United States?" She replied, "A high honor, and quite frankly, darling, I'm looking forward to it."

The next morning at breakfast, after Dewey's defeat, Frances inquired, "Tell me Tom, am I going to Washington or is Harry coming here?"

Table 16.1 The Election of 1948

Presidential candidate	Party	Home state	Popular vote Count	Percentage	Electoral vote
Harry S. Truman (Incumbent)	Democratic	Missouri	24,179,347	49.55%	303
Thomas E. Dewey	Republican	New York	21,991,292	45.07%	189
Strom Thurmond	States' Rights Democratic	South Carolina	1,175,930	2.41%	39
Henry A. Wallace	Progressive/ American Labor	Iowa	1,157,328	2.37%	0
Norman Thomas	Socialist	New York	139,569	0.29%	0
Claude A. Watson	Prohibition	California	103,708	0.21%	0
Edward A. Teichert	Socialist Labor	Pennsylvania	29,244	0.06%	0
Farrell Dobbs	Socialist Workers	Minnesota	13,613	0.03%	0
Other			3,504	0.01%	—
Total			48,793,535	100%	531
Needed to win					266

Vice President Elect, Alben W. Barkley, former US Senate Minority Leader (D-KY)

The campaign of 1948 has been reevaluated numerous times over the decades but, in the end, November 2 boiled down to the outcomes in three states—California, Illinois, and Ohio. In the Golden State, Truman defeated Dewey by just 17,865 votes out of more than four million cast. That winning margin of 0.44 percent was good for twenty-five electors. The Republican candidate was hurt by the presence of former vice president Henry Wallace on the ballot who received 190,381 votes.

Earlier in the evening, Truman won Illinois by only 33,612 (0.84% margin) for twenty-eight electoral votes. The incumbent also edged his way to victory in the Buckeye State by a scant 7,107 (0.24%) scoring another twenty-five electoral votes. It also kept the streak intact where no Republican candidate had won the presidency without capturing Ohio.

In total, had Dewey won those three states with their seventy-eight electors, instead of losing the electoral college 303–189, he would have won the presidency 267–225, just one vote over the mandated total. Truman took the crucial trio by an overall total of 219,369 popular votes which came to 0.5067 percent.

THE AFTERMATH

Some were surprised that General MacArthur never made a serious bid for the presidency, but it was understandable because he was busy ruling Japan. The general had been put in charge of rebuilding the former enemy of the Allied Powers following the surrender.

Part of that responsibility was establishing his new headquarters in Tokyo. He chose a building owned by the Dai-Ichi Insurance Comapny, one of only a few intact structures left in the city at the end of the war, which stood across the street from the Imperial Palace.

MacArthur requisitioned the building, permitted the company three days to pack up, move out, while he and his staff relocated into a sixth floor office. The real attraction for the new American shogun was the view, because from his perch, Mac could look across a moat and high walls onto the palace grounds from above.

The general refused to call on the emperor. Eventually, Hirohito made the pilgrimage across the street to MacArthur's office, making it clear to all who was in charge, which raised the question: why run for president when you can rule like an emperor?

There was perhaps no other president who enjoyed driving more than the man from Missouri. Even after his vehicular close call in Hagerstown during his Senate years, Truman always enjoyed getting into the driver's seat.

On July 6, 1947, on a return trip to Washington, DC, from Charlottesville, Virginia, President Truman took over the wheel of the presidential limo and drove back to the White House! He was also known to have driven on other occasions while serving in office.

It is a practice that is no longer allowed by the Secret Service.

Strom Thurmond, the nominee of the States Rights Party in 1948, did not win but received thirty-nine electoral votes, an effort that tied for third at that point of history, and 2.4 percent of the national popular vote in the election. He never became president, but in 1954 the World War II veteran became the first person to be elected to the US Senate as a write-in candidate against ballot-listed opponents.

Thurmond switched to the Republican Party in 1964 and remained in the Senate for forty-eight years until 2003. He died a few months after his retirement at the age of one hundred.

Perhaps the biggest winner on election night was Stuebenville, Ohio, native Jimmy Snyder. Nicknamed "The Greek," the thirty year old placed a $10,000 bet on the underdog Harry Truman to defeat the challenger Thomas Dewey. At 17:1 odds, Snyder won $170,000, which is $1.7 million when adjusted for inflation.

The Greek relocated to Las Vegas where he became the country's best known sports handicapper and a national television personality.

THE FOLLOWING ELECTIONS

1952: It was expected that at least one of the big names from World War II would be a serious candidate in 1952, and when the field was sorted out, it was the Republicans who nabbed General Dwight D. Eisenhower.

He won an easy victory over Illinois governor Adlai Stevenson Jr. But the real excitement took place on Inauguration Day.

In most political campaigns, the bad feelings and harsh words normally end when the election results are confirmed. But that wasn't the case in 1952 and the problem wasn't between the candidates. The hostilities were between the outgoing and incoming chief executives.

Eisenhower was sworn in as president on January 20, 1953. The tradition of the president-elect going to the White House on inauguration morning to meet the outgoing president before proceeding to the Capitol began in 1877 with Rutherford B. Hayes and incumbent Ulysses S. Grant.

That ritual continued until January 20, 1953, when Ike and his wife Mamie refused to go inside the mansion to join the Trumans for coffee. Even though he won the election, Ike was still upset over remarks that his soon-to-be predecessor had made about he and Senator Joe McCarthy during the campaign.

After being spurned, Truman emerged on the White House steps after a few moments wearing a bogus smile, but several veteran reporters on the scene understood what had just taken place. The contentiousness continued in the car on the way to the Capitol.

Once both men were seated, Eisenhower asked Truman who had released his son John from active duty in Korea so he could attend the inauguration. John, a West Point graduate like his father, was embarrassed that he had been called home. Truman stated that he had given the order, which infuriated the top Allied strategist of the D-Day invasion.

After the ceremony, the Trumans went directly home to Independence, Missouri.

Over the years, the long-distance sparring continued as each man did his best to avoid the other. On November 25, 1963, the two old rivals found themselves together once again sharing a limousine—this time they were among the mourners at President Kennedy's funeral. When it was over, the two ex–world leaders returned to Blair House for food and fellowship. They sat and talked about the past for over an hour, and at the conclusion of the afternoon, the pair of old soldiers buried the hatchet. It was their final face-to-face meeting.

1956: Four years later, Eisenhower and Stevenson were rematched by their parties, but things got worse for the Democrat the second time around.

On Tuesday, November 6, more than sixty-two million citizens went to the polls to make their voices heard. Ike picked up about 1.5 million more popular votes than he had in 1952. Stevenson lost almost a million over that same period.

The incumbent's electoral count went from 442 in his first victory to 457 in 1956. Stevenson dropped from 89 in 1952 to 73.

Eisenhower won forty-one states including all of those that he captured in 1952. Four years later, he added Kentucky and West Virginia to his win column. Ike and Vice President Richard Nixon also captured Stevenson's home state of Illinois. To date, Dwight David Eisenhower is the last general to be elected president.

17

The Election of 1960

John F. Kennedy (Democrat) vs. Richard Nixon (Republican)

"Just think what my margin might have been if I had never left home at all."

—President-Elect John Kennedy, commenting on the fact that he had campaigned hard in Alaska and lost, but won Hawaii handily without visiting it

For eight years, from 1952 to 1960, Dwight D. Eisenhower dominated the presidential landscape. For the most part, the country had prospered during his two terms and had begun to make inroads into civil rights issues. However, his time in the White House was expiring and both parties were shopping for his successor.

From one perspective, it was easier to see who wasn't available. There were no major military heroes like Eisenhower who fit the criteria. General MacArthur was still around but he was eighty years old. Former general Omar Bradley was also retired and General George Marshall, the former chief of staff, had died a year earlier.

The possibilities from the list of nation's governors and members from both houses of Congress were thin. It meant that the party bosses would be forced to go in another direction with younger candidates who appealed more to television audiences as the days of capturing large blocks of voters via radio had pretty much gone by the wayside.

For the Democrats, there was a name floating around that most of the party faithful were familiar with. Adlai Stevenson, who had been soundly defeated by Eisenhower in 1952 and 1956, still had a group of supporters but not enough to mount a legitimate third campaign. Although he did draw the interest of America's antagonist during a meeting with Soviet ambassador Mikhail A. Menshikov in January 1960, as the former Illinois governor was told if he again became a candidate, that the USSR would back him financially.

John F. Kennedy and Richard Nixon during their postelection transition meeting in Key Biscayne, Florida. Credit: National Archives

Stevenson's response was immediate stating that such an arrangement was "highly improper, indiscreet, and dangerous." He went on to express "grave misgivings about the propriety or wisdom of any interference, direct or indirect, in the American election."

In the search for a presidential candidate, John F. Kennedy (JFK) dominated the primary season winning ten of sixteen contests along with 31 percent of the popular vote. The Democrat Convention began on July 11 at the new Los Angeles Memorial Sports Arena where JFK was nominated on the first ballot. For vice president, the Kennedy team took a page from Franklin Roosevelt's playbook when, like FDR, they accepted a Texan for the second spot on the ticket.

Lyndon Johnson, the Senate Majority Leader, was chosen to bring the southern vote to the team. FDR made a similar move in 1932 when Speaker of the House John Nance Garner, who also hailed from the Lone Star State, was brought on board. Easterners like Kennedy and Roosevelt understood the necessity of covering other parts of the country on the party's ticket even if they personally disliked them as running mates.

After the delegate voting was done, JFK's campaign staff decided to move the festivities for the final event, the candidates' speeches, across the street to the massive Los Angeles Coliseum. The near one hundred thousand seat venue had originally played host to the 1932 Olympic Games. Attendance estimates that evening varied from fifty thousand to eighty thousand. Among those who had been skeptical about the big move into the stadium was the candidate's brother and campaign manager, Robert Kennedy, but he went along with the idea.

As JFK prepared to tell thousands why they should vote for him, those who were close to the Massachusetts senator had to be amazed at the fact that he was in his newly anointed position.

Four decades earlier as a two year old, the second son of Joe Sr. and Rose Kennedy contracted scarlet fever and almost died. He also overcame whooping cough and chicken pox during the same period. Young John battled various illnesses through out his childhood and teen years but by 1941 with conflict on the horizon, he was healthy enough to enlist in the US Navy.

The story of his heroic exploits as a PT boat commander during World War II have been chronicled in books and later became a successful motion picture.

In August 1943, at Blackett Strait in the Solomon Islands, a Japanese destroyer rammed JFK's ship, *PT-109*. The young lieutenant, with some other crew members, swam to a nearby island but found it held by the enemy. At that point, he and a fellow officer continued swimming to another small island, where they persuaded the inhabitants to send a message to US forces, who rescued them. For those actions, the twenty-six-year-old PT boat commander received the Navy and Marine Corps Medal along with the Purple Heart.

JFK's wartime saga served as the perfect springboard for a career into politics, and in 1946 the decorated hero was elected to the US House of Representatives. It was well documented that Kennedy suffered from back ailments which were thought to be related to his military service, but he was actually afflicted with Addison's disease. The condition caused a withering of the adrenal glands, which was a terminal disease until maintenance treatments were discovered in the late 1940s. In 1947, the physician who examined JFK and diagnosed his condition as Addison's, told one of Kennedy's friends, "He hasn't got a year to live."

That prognosis appeared to be accurate because in September 1947, the Catholic born JFK became so gravely ill that he was given the last rites aboard the ocean liner *Queen Mary* while returning from London where he had been diagnosed with the malady.

However, the young congressman proved the medical experts wrong and by the late 1950s, the new treatments for the disease made it possible for him to lead a normal life for the first time. So much so that in 1952, he won the US Senate race in his home state.

But in October 1954, Kennedy appeared to be at death's door once again as he underwent major back surgery resulting in a postoperative urinary tract infection that put him in a coma. In a repeat of history from seven years prior, a priest was called in to perform the sacrament of last rites.

Once again, Kennedy defied the odds and made a full recovery even though he was hospitalized several times during the decade of the 1950s for a continuous assortment of back ailments. But by 1960, he was healthy enough to make a run at the nation's highest office

The Republicans were also conducting a candidate search, but it appeared that a number of GOP hopefuls were not interested in following the popular Eisenhower as the nation's leader. But that didn't apply to Ike's vice president Richard M. Nixon who, on January 9, 1960, made it official by announcing his candidacy. It was a bold move from a guy who the president had attempted to oust from the number two position just four years earlier.

Nixon entered eleven primaries, won them all, captured 87 percent of the popular vote and on March 16, Eisenhower formally endorsed him. He was nominated on the first ballot at the convention with former senator Henry Cabot Lodge Jr. of Massachusetts as his running mate. That set the stage for a campaign that would feature two guys who knew each other pretty well.

In some ways, Kennedy and Nixon were mirror images of each other as they had both served in the Navy during World War II. Following the conflict, they entered the House of Representatives as freshmen congressmen in 1947. Although they didn't serve in the Senate together, they had both been members in the early 1950s. The men, who were just four years apart in age, became friends and JFK's father, Joe Kennedy Sr., a staunch Democrat, donated $1000 to the Republican Nixon's 1950 Senate campaign.

While there were similarities, there were also pronounced differences like social standing as Kennedy was raised in a wealthy family while Nixon grew up poor. Because he hailed from a prominent Boston clan, JFK attended and graduated from the prestigious Harvard University as Nixon earned his degree from tiny Whittier College in California. Each man was devout although Kennedy was a Catholic and Nixon a Quaker. Finally, on a social scale, the outgoing JFK enjoyed living large especially when it came to the company of a number of young women while his opponent was an introvert who preferred his privacy.

The early polls had been close. The first Gallup survey in December 1959 had Nixon holding a 48 percent to 43 percent lead, but over the following months that position shifted back and forth. However, voters were talking about another important campaign issue other than just the candidates.

As summer progressed, stories were spreading through the news that the networks were working with the nominees and their campaign staffs attempting to put together a series of history making debates. The television stations viewed such programing as a money making bonanza and were eager to provide whatever incentives were necessary to close the deal.

On July 28, during a press conference at Chicago's Sheraton-Blackstone Hotel following his nomination, Nixon surprised the audience and the media by accepting the invitation of network executives to participate in the debates. Kennedy, who had already confirmed his intention to take part, was working with a smaller budget than the GOP nominee and saw the faceoff as an opportunity for national television exposure that he wouldn't have to pay for from his campaign funding.

It was agreed that the contenders would take part in four debates. The first was held on September 26 from the studio of WBBM-TV, the CBS affiliate, in Chicago. The buildup to the contest was reminiscent of a heavyweight title fight rather than two fellas having a political discussion. It was the first televised presidential debate in American history and the first between the two major candidates of a presidential election since the seven Lincoln-Douglas pairings a century earlier, which were also held in Illinois.

In the weeks leading up to the first debate, Nixon's run of luck was mostly bad. On August 17, just forty days before the initial matchup, he scraped his left knee on a car door while campaigning in North Carolina. The injury developed into a Staphylococcus aureus infection and the Republican candidate was admitted to Walter Reed Army Medical Center for twelve days of treatment that included surgery.

Just as he was getting back on track, the GOP's nominee then had a bout with the flu that developed on September 14. He refused to rest, and the following day gave a speech in St. Louis while running a 103 degree fever. On the day that he arrived at WBBM for the initial debate, the vice president reinjured the knee while getting out of his car. He had lost twenty pounds and looked tired and ill.

In contrast, when Kennedy appeared at the studio, he appeared rested, tanned, and refreshed. Realizing the importance of the debate, he had taken a few days off from the road to rehearse his responses with aides.

For aspiring politicians, JFK's debate strategy was so groundbreaking that it continues to be studied decades later. All aspects were analyzed including the fact that he wore make-up for the camera while Nixon refused, which showed him perspiring under the warm stage lights; how he sat (legs crossed); and to look directly at Nixon whenever the vice president was speaking. For a televised debate, JFK's performance was a masterpiece.

But perhaps no area came under more scrutiny than the candidate's choice of clothing. Each man was dressed in a business suit, but Nixon chose a light colored outfit that blended into the background of the studio's stage. Since the transmission of the majority of America's television sets were in black and white, colorless picture tubes were often drab and dull.

To combat the technology of the day, Kennedy selected a dark suit with matching tie that made him stand out against the gray background. It was a small item, but it helped make him the focal point for the viewers of the three people, including moderator Howard K. Smith, who were on stage.

Broadcast Magazine estimated that an audience of 74 million (the country's entire population at the time was 180.7 million) watched the faceoff on television while another 61 million tuned in on the radio. In the postdebate survey, the majority of television viewers stated that they believed Kennedy had won the contest while most radio listeners sided with Nixon. After the conclusion of the history-making program, Nixon's mother, who had watched the contest on TV, called her son afterward to ask if he was ill?

Gallup's Poll, that was taken two weeks prior to the debate, had Nixon leading 47 percent to 46 percent. The first postdebate survey saw a 4-point swing toward Kennedy as he went up 49 percent to 46 percent. It was evident that as more voters had televisions in their homes than in the past, an increasing number of the public was going to be voting with their eyes. It was the beginning of a trend that became a permanent part of politics.

There were three more debates (October 7, 13, and 21) but the polls held in Kennedy's favor even though Nixon had learned his lesson and wore makeup and a dark suit for his other appearances. He also followed those practices in his future campaigns. JFK told J. Leonard Reinsch, a former television executive, "Television may be the most important part of the campaign. It may decide the election."

Throughout October, the candidates zigzagged across the country following a hectic pace. Meanwhile, back in New York, Cuban dictator Fidel Castro had arrived on September 18 for a ten-day stay that included delivering a 4.5 hour speech to the United Nations on the same day as the first debate. He also met with Soviet premier Nikita Khrushchev and activist Malcolm X during his visit. The last thing that the candidates needed as the election drew closer were the symbols of Communism taking up their airtime on the evening news.

On November 4, four days prior to Election Day, two men carrying guns were arrested during a Kennedy appearance in Chicago. No one was injured although such was not so the following day when forty-four-year-old Victor Rojas, a Democrat, wanted to see JFK on television. But his wife, Norma Jean, age thirty-four and a Republican, preferred to watch the popular *Lawrence Welk Show* (a musical variety program on the ABC network). An argument ensued at their home in El Cajon, California, that resulted in Mrs. Rojas fatally stabbing him with a paring knife. It is the only murder officially attributed to the election of 1960.

The results of Gallup's final poll came just a few days before voters went to the polls. It gave JFK a slight 51 percent to 49 percent advantage. The last Roper Poll had it 49 percent to 47 percent for Nixon. After all the money spent and miles traveled, the candidates were essentially back to the point where they had started as a toss-up.

At midnight on November 8, 1960, nine voters gathered in the "Ballot Room" at the Balsams Hotel in Dixville Notch, New Hampshire. Since then, the tiny community has held midnight votes for every presidential election and basked in the national publicity that comes with it. The village claims to have the longest continuous record of midnight voting and is often first to report its returns. Those participating unanimously voted for Nixon.

On election night, the three networks (CBS, NBC, and ABC) used their new computers to make projections to their viewers. CBS had the IBM 7090 while ABC used a Univac, and early on both announced that Nixon would be the next president. NBC was equipped with the RCA 501 and had it right from the start as the "Peacock Network" projected JFK's popular vote at 51.1 percent.

Table 17.1   The Election of 1960

Presidential candidate	Party	Home state	Popular vote Count	Percentage	Electoral vote
John Fitzgerald Kennedy	Democratic	Massachusetts	34,226,731	49.72%	303
Richard Milhous Nixon	Republican	California	34,108,157	49.55%	219
*Harry Flood Byrd	Democratic	Virginia	116,248	—	15
(unpledged electors)	Democratic	(n/a)	494,161	0.42%	—
Eric Hass	Socialist Labor	New York	47,522	0.07%	0
Rutherford L. Decker	Prohibition	Missouri	46,203	0.07%	0
Orval Faubus	States' Rights	Arkansas	44,984	0.07%	0
Farrell Dobbs	Socialist Workers	New York	40,175	0.06%	0
Charles Sullivan	Constitution	Mississippi	(TX) 18,162	0.03%	0
J. Bracken Lee	Conservative	Utah	(NJ) 8,708	0.01%	0
Other			11,128	0.02%	
Total			68,832,482	100%	537
Needed to win					269

Vice President Elect, Lyndon B. Johnson, US Senate Majority Leader (D-TX)

*Senator Harry F. Byrd (D VA) received fifteen electoral votes from unpledged electors: six in Alabama, eight in Mississippi, and one in Oklahoma.

Kennedy won with 303 electoral votes to Nixon's 219. But those numbers don't explain how actually close that the election had been. A shift in just two states, 4,480 votes in Illinois and 25,000 on Johnson's home turf of Texas, would have given Nixon the presidency, 270–252.

Kennedy won five states, each by a margin of less than 1 percent that accounted for sixty-three electoral votes (Hawaii, 0.06%; Illinois, 0.19%; Missouri, 0.52%; New Mexico, 0.74%; and New Jersey, 0.80%). Had Nixon won those, he would have been elected 282–240. The Republican also had his own close call winning his home state of California by just 0.55 percent, which hasn't been won by the GOP since 1988.

In defeat, Nixon received more votes (34,108,157) than Eisenhower won in his first race for the White House in 1952 (33,778,963).

This was the only presidential election where both major candidates were under the age of fifty.

THE AFTERMATH

On January 20, 1961, US Senator John F. Kennedy of Massachusetts was sworn in as the thirty-fifth president of the United States. At the age of forty-three, he was the youngest chief executive to have been elected in the nation's history.

Throngs witnessed JFK take the oath from Chief Justice Earl Warren either live or via television. It was the first time that the inauguration was broadcast on TV in color. But since pulling off one of the closest election victories in history, much has been learned.

Most of the credit for Kennedy's victory can be attributed to his powerful father, Joe Kennedy Sr. It had been his plan dating back decades, that his oldest son would become the country's first president of Irish Catholic descent. That responsibility fell upon the shoulders of his first born, Joseph Jr. When he was a young man, everything was going according to plan as the athletic and Harvard educated offspring was chosen as a delegate to the 1940 Democratic National Convention.

But those dreams were scuttled on August 12, 1944, when the father's namesake, a US naval aviator, was killed in combat during World War II. Because he had completed twenty-five missions, the twenty-nine-year-old Kennedy was eligible to return home but had volunteered for *Operation Aphrodite*, a bombing run from Great Britain to France. However, the explosives on board his BQ-8 aircraft detonated prematurely in flight over Blythburgh, England, claiming his life and that of another crew member.

The death of Joe Jr. didn't detour his father's quest as he simply shifted his attention to his next oldest son, John Fitzgerald. The names may have changed but the script never did. After returning from the war, Joe Sr. made sure that JFK got elected to the House and the Senate while assuring that he was getting an ample supply of positive publicity from the media. In 1957, the former ambassador paid $75,000 (more than $683,000 value in today's market) to the editors at *Time* magazine to place JFK's picture on their cover.

Joe Sr. understood the importance of image, having successfully run the RKO movie studio in the 1920s. He stayed busy keeping JFK's public persona as that of someone that was appealing to voters. Although on January 24, 1947, the thirty-year-old naval hero went behind his dad's back and was secretly married to Palm Beach socialite Durie Malcolm by a justice of the peace. The groom had just taken his seat for his first term in the US House of Representatives twenty-one days earlier.

The fact that his son would clandestinely wed a two-time divorcee infuriated Joe Sr., a devout Catholic. He quickly and quietly moved to have the nuptials annulled by the powerful Cardinal Richard Cushing, the archbishop of Boston.

Later reports stated to insure Durie's silence, she was paid a significant sum of cash by Joe Sr. who arranged for her to quickly get married again. Not quite six months later, she wed Thomas H. Shevlin, the son of a wealthy Minneapolis lumberman. JFK and Durie were granted the annulment from the Catholic Church without getting a civil divorce. In 2008, she died at the age of ninety-one and continued to deny that they had ever married.

She wasn' the last woman that Joe Sr. had to address on his son's behalf. Shortly before JFK was sworn in as president, his wife Jackie had finally had enough with his constant philandering and began making plans for a divorce. After a meeting with her father-in-law in New York City, she reconsidered and opted to accept his offer of $1 million in cash to remain with him.

Kennedy's opponents got a small taste of what was to come during the Democratic primaries. They targeted West Virginia as a key state for its large number of members of the powerful coal miner's union. Estimates ran as high as $2 million ($11 million in today's dollars) that was disbursed in a vote buying scheme. Among those in the middle of the action were JFK's younger brothers and future senators, Robert and Ted. The victory in the Mountaineer State for Kennedy ended the presidential hopes of his nearest competitor Senator Hubert Humphrey of Minnesota.

Joe Sr. realized that Illinois was also an important state that could go either way in the general election, which boiled down to winning one specific location, Cook County. It was a place with one of the shadiest reputations in the nation for election fraud dating back to the early 1900s with their unscrupulous US senator William Lorimer and later with criminals like Al Capone.

Kennedy Sr. wasn't about wasting an opportunity and asked his old friend, Chicago judge William J. Touhy, to arrange a meeting with local mob boss and former Capone associate Sam Giancana. The family patriarch sought the gangster's influence with local labor unions to mobilize the rank and file's turnout for his son at the ballot box. Not to be overlooked was Chicago mayor Richard Daley and his Democrat machine who were also prominent players in the voter roundup.

Whatever exactly took place between Joe Sr., Giancana, and Daley, is unknown as each took the details of their part of the plan to the grave with them. Even though, Joe Sr. got the result he was seeking, the election in Illinois did produce some rather unusual numbers. JFK won the state by 8,858 votes but he carried Cook County by

318,736. The voter "turnout" in Daley-machine controlled Chicago was an unusually high 89 percent.

A follow-up investigation by the state's special prosecutor Morris Wexler resulted in the indictment of 677 election officials. However, the results were minimal as in 1962, one election worker confessed to witness tampering in Chicago's 28th Ward, where three precinct workers pleaded guilty and served jail sentences.

Investigative journalist Earl Mazo visited the Windy City following the election and found a Chicago address where fifty-six Kennedy voters "lived" even though it was a demolished house. He also found a cemetery where all the tombstone names were registered voters. In Ward 27, Precinct 27, the 376 voters cast 397 votes; in the 15th precinct of Ward 2, Kennedy beat Nixon 74 to 3 but only twenty-two people were registered to vote.

However, Illinois had nothing on Texas when it came to political shenanigans in 1960. In one precinct of Angelina County, only 86 people voted yet the final tally was 147 for Kennedy and 24 for Nixon while in Fannin County, the 4,895 registered voters were busy casting 6,138 votes (75% for Kennedy).

Under Texas law, discarded spoiled ballots were to be placed in "ballot box 4" for later reexamination, but many counties simply discarded them, and did *not* store them, making any further evaluation of those ballots impossible. When it was over, the 100 percent Democrat-controlled Texas Election Board refused to conduct a recount.

Following JFK's election, he appointed his brother and campaign manager Robert as US attorney general although no one seemed to mind that he had never argued a case in a courtroom. One of the first duties that he performed was to shut down all federal investigations into voter fraud and any questions that lingered about what did, or did not, take place.

As the losing team, there was no shortage of second guessing the Nixon campaign. He was criticized for not utilizing Eisenhower more, but he may not have had much say-so in that area. First Lady Mamie had told Nixon's wife, Pat, early in 1960 that she wanted to limit her husband's exertion during the campaign as he continued to exhibit heart problems.

When Eisenhower finally appeared on the trail with Nixon in mid-October, the polls began to tighten and suddenly, the Republican was slowly closing the gap on Kennedy. There were some who felt that the fact the two had never been close was the real factor as during a August 24, 1960, press conference where Ike was asked for an example of a major idea of Nixon's that been had adopted, and he replied "If you give me a week, I might think of one. I don't remember." The backhanded endorsement was meant as a joke but certainly didn't help the vice president's dilemma.

Among those who encouraged Nixon to seek a recount was Herbert Hoover as well as Ike. But in his 1978 memoirs, the vanquished candidate argued that a recount would have taken more than a year and a half, "during which time the legitimacy of Kennedy's election would be in question," which he claimed would be "devastating to America's foreign relations."

A challenge, he told others, would cause a "constitutional crisis," "hurt America in the eyes of the world," and "tear the country apart." Besides, he added, pursuing the claims would mean "charges of 'sore loser' would follow me through history and remove any possibility of a further political career."

When they emerged to meet the waiting reporters at a post-election meeting in Florida on November 14, a Kennedy quip made it clear there would not be a challenge. "I asked him how he took Ohio, but he did not tell me," Kennedy joked. "He's saving it for 1964."

There was one statewide recount that took place, but it drew little attention. On November 17, in their first presidential election as a state, Hawaii gave its three electoral votes to Nixon by 117 popular votes. On December 16, as the recount continued, Kennedy pulled ahead by 21 votes. Finally, on December 27, Judge Ronald Jamieson declared JFK the winner in Hawaii by 115 votes.

From that point forward, Kennedy kept a note in his pocket with the numerals 118,574, the number of popular votes by which he won.

THE FOLLOWING ELECTION

1964: With JFK's death, Lyndon Johnson finally realized his political dream of being elected president of the United States. He soundly defeated his former Senate colleague, Barry Goldwater (R-AZ), in the electoral college, 486–52.

Although, with the Vietnam War dividing America, Johnson's dream soon turned into a nightmare. While Goldwater never became commander in chief, his leading disciple was beginning to carry his conservative message to the populace and soon after Ronald Reagan became the new voice on the Right.

18

The Election of 1968

Richard Nixon (Republican) vs. Hubert Humphrey (Democrat)

"If people look at me and say, 'That's a new Nixon,' then all I can say is well, maybe you didn't know the old Nixon."

—Richard Nixon while campaigning in New Hampshire, 1968

When Lyndon Baines Johnson (LBJ) entered the Oval Office on January 21, 1965, it was the beginning of a period that he had dreamed of for years. It was the first full day of his term as his own president. He was no longer a substitute for the bygone John F. Kennedy after winning the election of 1964 in an impressive landslide.

With his victory, LBJ had become the ruler of the kingdom. Once, when he landed at an Air Force base and a young officer attempted to direct the commander in chief to a helicopter while stating, "Sir, your helicopter is over here," Johnson replied, "Son, they're all my helicopters."

That one sentence told the nation everything they needed to know about the thirty-sixth president of the United States. But what Johnson hadn't realized was how much the nation had changed over the years while he was busy climbing the political mountain.

LBJ knew about difficult times. He was a World War II veteran who had gone through the Great Depression. During that conflict, Americans understood who the enemy was and why the United States was fighting them. Such was not the case with the country's latest battlefield struggle. The Vietnam War had started in the 1950s with American military officials acting as advisors.

In the beginning, most Americans knew very little about Vietnam; where it was located; what the French had to do with the conflict; or why it was the United States' responsibility to fix whatever was broken in southeast Asia. At the time, Americans continued to be more concerned about the possibility of a nuclear strike from the Soviet Union.

By 1963, the United States had 16,300 troops fighting in the region. During Johnson's first full year in office (1964), troop strength grew to 23,300 and the next year that number increased dramatically to 184,300! The war bond rallies of a supportive public that had been part of the landscape of the 1940s had turned into rioting and mass draft card burnings on college campuses during the 1960s.

In part, the government became its own worst enemy. In an age dominated by television and viewer interpretation, no one in either the administration or Congress had found an effective method of explaining the reason why the United States was engaged in a dispute where it had not been attacked. In the 1950s, President Eisenhower attempted to describe the strategy as the "Domino Theory," stating that if one southeast Asian country was allowed to fall to the Communists, the others would follow just like cascading dominoes.

Ike's pep talk fell flat, and he handed the problem off to Kennedy when he left office in 1961, at which point Vietnam got shoved into the background. Other items such as the civil rights movement, nuclear issues with the Soviets, and the space program became a higher priority. Those seemed to be the issues that voters were showing the most concern. With JFK's death, Johnson inherited Vietnam and all the problems that went with it.

LBJ had been a champion of civil rights, signing major legislation in 1964 and 1968. But he also had to endure inner city rioting in places like New York's Harlem (1964); Watts in Los Angeles (1965); Chicago (1966); and 159 others in 1967. Johnson's program to combat urban poverty, known as "The Great Society," had been launched in 1964–1965 but wasn't moving fast enough to satisfy those who needed its help.

With the war and rioting dominating the evening news across the nation during most broadcasts, 1968 turned into a continuous, event-filled cavalcade where history was being made on a consistent basis. Some had to do with the upcoming election while much attention went to sudden occurrences that arrived on television screens without warning. Among those stories from 1968 that grabbed the most headlines included:

- *January 30:* The first phase of the Tet Offensive was launched in South Vietnam. The Viet Cong, along with Communist sympathizers, attacked military bases, government offices, and foreign embassies. In addition to military combatants, the enemy also executed thousands of civilians. There were more than forty-five thousand casualties in the first of three phases, which concluded in September. It was a major setback for the South Vietnamese government.
- *February 1:* The return of Richard Nixon. The former vice president who retired from politics six years earlier after delivering a stinging belittling of the media during a press conference, announced his return by confirming his rumored candidacy for the Republican Party's nomination for president.

Richard Nixon on the campaign trail in 1968.
Credit: Richard Nixon Foundation, Library, Museum

Nixon had obviously been spending his hiatus measuring voter trends as in the 1966 midterm elections, a key indicator for his decision—Republicans added forty-seven House seats, three in the Senate, and eight governorships. Like the phoenix of Greek mythology, Richard Nixon had also been resurrected.

- *March 12:* New Hampshire started the primary season with Nixon dominating the Republican field capturing move than 77 percemt of the vote. But it was the Democrats who staged the attention-grabber.

As expected, LBJ was the winner in the Granite State but surprisingly with only 50 percent of the vote. Even more astonishing was that the runner-up, Senator Eugene McCarthy of Minnesota, netted an impressive 42 percent of his party's support. At the conclusion of the tally, the media quickly manned their typewriters to write about, what they believed would be, the final chapter in the saga of Lyndon Baines Johnson.

- *March 16:* Johnson's poor showing didn't go unnoticed as Senator Robert (Bobby) Kennedy (RFK) of New York announced his candidacy for the Democrat nomination. The notification came as no surprise to many and was expected by most observers. His brother's murder had pushed RFK into the background at the White House when Johnson moved into the Oval Office. There was no way that the two rivals could ever work together after JFK was assassinated and LBJ succeeded him, so Kennedy left the administration.

In 1964, Bobby Kennedy was elected to the US Senate seat from New York as Johnson captured the presidency after serving the remainder of his predecessor's term. Over the next four years, the Vietnam War played a critical role in each man's future. LBJ battled Congress as he attempted to find a solution that would bring peace with honor but wouldn't appear that the United States had deserted the citizens of South Vietnam.

RFK had served in the US Naval Reserves during World War II and had supported the administration's stance over the conflict in Southeast Asia during his tenure as attorney general. However, over time, he became a strong opponent against the escalation of the war thus making him a favorite among those who opposed it.

On the same day as Kennedy entered the race, President Johnson announced that he would send an additional thirty-five thousand to fifty thousand troops to fight in Vietnam.

- *March 31:* Through the years, there have been political differences between the president and some of the television networks. On February 27, following an on-air editorial by the influential CBS newsman Walter Cronkite criticizing the US effort in the Vietnam War, Lyndon Johnson said, "If I've lost Cronkite, I've lost Middle America."

  In the minds of political observers, Kennedy's entry into the race would set up a showdown between he and his nemesis Johnson that would be played out on the national television stage. It also meant that the nation's commander in chief would now have to fend off two antiwar candidates from his own party in Kennedy and McCarthy.

  But Lyndon Johnson had made his name as a master politician during his days in the US Senate. His reputation for persuading colleagues to switch sides during a critical vote had made him a powerful voice and he had one last card to play as his party's primary process was underway. At the conclusion of a nationally televised speech on March 31 about the Vietnam War, LBJ stunned the nation by announcing, "I shall not seek, nor will I accept, the nomination of my party for another term as your president." The declaration was not part of the original written address so it came as a complete surprise to everyone. It also meant that there would be no showdown with Robert Kennedy.

- *April 4:* Civil rights leader, Dr. Martin Luther King Jr. was shot and killed in Memphis, Tennessee. He had been in the city to support African American sanitary public works employees, who had been on strike for nearly a month seeking higher wages and better treatment. His death touched off rioting in thirty-seven US cities including Washington, DC, Chicago, and Baltimore.

- *April 27:* With LBJ out of the election picture, Vice President Hubert Humphrey announced his candidacy for the Democratic nomination for president.

- *May 28:* Robert Kennedy had won the primaries in Indiana and Nebraska but on May 28, McCarthy defeated RFK, 44 percent to 38 percent, in Oregon.

That made California's vote casting on June 4 loom even larger as a West Coast victory for the Kennedy campaign might force McCarthy out of the race.

- *June 3:* The acclaimed artist Andy Warhol was shot three times in the lobby of his popular studio, The Factory, in New York City. The attempt was carried out by Valerie Jean Solanas, a radical feminist writer.

    Warhol, who barely survived, never fully recovered and for the rest of his life wore a corset to prevent his injuries from worsening. Solanas turned herself in to the police and was charged with attempted murder. Pleading guilty, she received a three-year sentence as Warhol refused to testify against her. The artist died in 1987 and Solanas passed away a year later.

- *June 5:* Robert Kennedy captured the Golden State's contest 46 percent to 42 percent and as the midnight hour approached out west, he and his wife Ethel prepared to make their way to the podium to deliver his victory address. A large crowd had gathered in the ballroom of the Ambassador Hotel in Los Angeles, which served as the campaign headquarters, to hear RFK's victory speech. It was a "winner take all" primary, which meant that all of the state's 174 Democrat delegates were now pledged to support RFK at the convention. The magic number required for the nomination was 1,312 and, with his big win, Kennedy had 393.

    At 12:10 a.m. (PDT), the victorious New York senator made his way to the microphone facing toward a robust crowd in the hotel's Embassy Room ballroom. There was nothing historic about his speech—no catchy lines or phrases that would be inscribed on a monument. He simply wrapped up the brief address by saying to the enthusiastic audience, "So my thanks to all of you, and now it's on to Chicago, and let's win there. Thank you very much." His reference to the Windy City was the upcoming and important Illinois primary that was just one week away.

    It was at this point that events began to take an abnormal turn. Traditionally, when he would conclude a speech, Kennedy would depart through the crowd shaking hands with supporters along the way. Former FBI agent Bill Barry, who served as Kennedy's chief of security, had prepared for the usual departure route but saw the candidate being led away to the kitchen area by the hotel's assistant maître d' Karl Ueker. Barry was normally very close to RFK whenever he was on the move but in the confusion of the moment, the two had become separated and Ueker now served as the senator's unofficial guide.

    They soon entered the pantry where Kennedy was greeted by members of the kitchen staff. Suddenly, a series of shots rang out in the confined area creating pandemonium as the entourage scattered away from the blast area. There were approximately eighty people in the room, six of them had been wounded, but the most serious of the group was the candidate. He was laying on the floor, bleeding profusely, as officials began working on him. In the blink of an eye, it was November 1963 all over again.

Just a few feet away, a suspect was being subdued. He was a twenty-four-year-old Palestinian immigrant named Sirhan Sirhan who had lived in the United States for twelve years. However, the slightly built assassin with an empty pistol was no match for his captors as he was immediately apprehended by former professional football star Roosevelt Grier and Rafer Johnson, the 1960 Olympic decathlon gold medalist. Both of whom were Kennedy supporters. Ueker secured Sirhan's .22 caliber weapon.

Kennedy suffered three wounds including one to the brain, which led to his death twenty-six hours later. Like his brother's assassination, there have been numerous theories about conspiracies and involvement of another gunman. But to this day, no one other than Sirhan has taken credit for the crime. As of 2020, he remains at California's Donovan Correctional Facility where he is serving a life sentence.

- *June 8:* James Earl Ray, the accused assassin of Dr. Martin Luther King Jr. was arrested at London's Heathrow Airport while he was attempting to leave Great Britain using a false Canadian passport. He had escaped from the Missouri State Penitentiary in 1967 prior to murdering the famed civil rights leader and Baptist minister in Memphis that past April. British officials quickly extradited the fugitive back to Tennessee.

- *August 5–8:* The Republican National Convention was held in Miami. The reinvigorated Richard Nixon was nominated on the first ballot even though California governor Ronald Reagan, a late entry into the mix, had earned more total popular votes during the primaries. The big surprise was Nixon's, and the party's, choice of Maryland governor Spiro Agnew for vice president.

  Because he was such an unknown, when House Minority Leader Gerald Ford of Michigan was told of the decision, he laughed believing that someone was joking. Ford had been one of the candidates who was considered for the position. Nonetheless, Agnew won a first ballot nod over Governor George Romney of Michigan.

- *August 26–29:* The year 1968 marked the tenth time that the Dems convened in the Windy City for the Democratic National Convention, and it was a gathering that wouldn't be forgotten.

  As the proceedings got underway, the most evident aspect of the assemblage was not who was there but who wasn't. Neither Lyndon Johnson nor Robert Kennedy, arguably the party's two top contenders just a few weeks before, were both nonfactors when the gavel struck the podium. That put vice president Hubert Humphrey into the favorite's role for the nomination.

  On the first night of the convention, protesters clashed with police and National Guard troops in the streets. Inside the convention hall, tensions ran rampant as delegates argued among one another long into the night.

  The following evening the unrest intensified as antiwar forces held a rally in Grant Park that drew more than ten thousand people, which quickly got out of hand. The television networks continued to cut away from the convention speakers, preferring to focus on the riot taking place on Michigan Avenue. Police dragged protesters into paddy wagons while moving them back with their billy clubs. Violence reigned through the streets as demonstrators chanted, "The whole world is watching!"

Back inside the hall, delegates continued to shout down one another. Among the worst was Chicago mayor Richard Daley, who could be seen hurling obscenities toward some of the speakers.

An estimated eighty million Americans viewed the confusion live on national television.

On August 29, the night of a scheduled tribute to Robert Kennedy, fans and supporters sang, "*The Battle Hymn of the Republic*" but continued after its conclusion, which irritated the Humphrey delegates who began booing in protest. An angry Mayor Daley shut it down and ordered the band to begin playing "*Chicago.*" Fighting then broke out between RFK and Humphrey delegates on the arena floor.

Humphrey accepted the nomination as violent protests raged outside with police using tear gas on the demonstrators who attempted to march toward the convention site—the International Amphitheater. Of the 2,607 delegates who voted, Humphrey garnered 1,759 of them.

The Democratic National Convention in Chicago was a complete disaster. Police responded and clashes occurred leading to 668 arrests. There were 192 officers injured, of whom 49 required hospitalization. Fortunately, through the televised mayhem, no one was killed although a total of 1,381 were injured.

- *September 4:* One week after the riotous convention, Richard Nixon triumphantly rode through the streets of Chicago in a tickertape parade before an estimated crowd of four hundred thousand. The first postconvention Gallup Poll had Nixon with a comfortable 43 percent to 31 percent over Humphrey.
- *September 16:* In a move that was a complete contradiction to his public image, Republican nominee Nixon made a brief guest appearance on NBC's hit comedy program *Rowan & Martin's Laugh-In.* The candidate only had four words of dialogue ("Sock it to me") but it showed him in a nonpolitical setting, which apparently was favorable to some voters.

  Vice President Hubert Humphery declined an invitation to be on the program. "Nixon said . . . that appearing on *Laugh-In* is what got him elected—and I believe that," said the show's creator George Schlatter. The Republican's poll numbers increased to 43 percent to 28 percent following his guest appearance.
- *September 17:* The right-wing American Independent Party nominated former Alabama governor George Wallace for president.
- *October 16:* During a medal ceremony at the Summer Olympic Games in Mexico City, African American athletes Tommie Smith and John Carlos each raised a black-gloved fist and bowed their heads during the playing of the US

national anthem. They were protesting the treatment of black citizens in the United States. Smith and Carlos had won the gold and bronze medals, respectively, in the 200-meter run.

However, International Olympic Committee president Avery Brundage ordered the duo suspended from the US team and banned them from the Olympic Village. Shortly afterward, they were sent back to the United States.

- *October 17:* Nixon's one-time double digit lead was down to 44 percent to 36 percent.
- *November 2:* In the final Gallup Poll before the election of 1968, Nixon's lead had shrunken to just a single point, 43 percent to 42 percent.
- *November 5:* Election Day in America. The weather was good across most of the nation as voters headed to the polls with the exception of the Gulf Coast of Texas. An F3 tornado hit the town of Victoria damaging twenty-five homes. Another twister, officially rated F0, touched down northeast of downtown Houston and tore the roof from a dormitory at Southern Bible College. An F1 destroyed six units in a trailer park and rolled several others. Fifteen people were injured but there were no deaths.
- *November 6:* It had been a long night as the count spilled over to the following day. At 5:00 a.m., Nixon called Agnew and New York governor Nelson Rockefeller to tell them that he had won. At 8:30 a.m., after confirming that he had secured Illinois, ABC-TV was the first of the networks to announce that Richard Nixon, who was at the bottom of the political abyss in 1962, would be the next president of the United States.

Table 18.1 The Election of 1968

Presidential candidate	Party	Home state	Popular vote Count	Percentage	Electoral vote
Richard Milhous Nixon	Republican	New York	31,783,783	43.42%	301
Hubert Horatio Humphrey	Democratic	Minnesota	31,271,839	42.72%	191
George Corley Wallace	American Independent	Alabama	9,901,118	13.53%	46
Other			243,258	0.33%	—
Total			73,199,998	100%	538
Needed to win					270

Vice President Elect, Spiro T. Agnew, former Governor of Maryland (R-MD)

With solid poll numbers, along with the sting of 1960 in his memory, Richard Nixon went debateless, sat on the lead, and won. It is impossible to know just how much his refusal to debate influenced voters. But the 1968 presidential race became extremely close during its final weeks, and on Election Day, the Republican was victorious by a razor-thin margin of 43.4 percent to Humphrey's 42.7 percent.

Among those other than Agnew that Nixon was considering for vice president was the legendary Green Bay Packers football coach Vince Lombardi who had stepped down from that post after his teams had won the first two Super Bowls ever played. The Republican nominee had gone as far as to order background checks on the gridiron great. But the idea was scrubbed when it was discovered that Lombardi was a Democrat and had been a major supporter of President Kennedy.

Today, the trophy that goes to the winning team in the Super Bowl is named in honor of the legendary Packer's coach.

Out of all the states that Nixon had carried in 1960, Maine and Washington were the only two that did not vote for him in 1968. As in several elections, a small group of states played key roles again. Nixon won California, Ohio, and Illinois, all by three percentage points or less. Had Humphrey carried all three of those states, he would have won the election.

Had the sitting vice president taken only two of them or just California, the decision would have been given to the House of Representatives which, at the time, was controlled by the Democrats.

On the evening that he was assassinated, June 5, 1968, Robert Kennedy had just won the California primary. It was a major step toward securing his party's nomination. Had RFK utilized the departure route that had been planned by his security detail, rather than exiting via the kitchen at the Ambassador Hotel, it would have taken him away from the area where gunman Sirhan Sirhan laid in wait.

That scenario would have probably meant another Kennedy-Nixon showdown where two critical states in that race would have been Nixon's home turf of California (forty electoral votes) and Texas (twenty-five, which were won by eventual Democrat nominee Hubert Humphrey). Also, George Wallace, running as a third party candidate captured five states worth forty-five electors. However, could the liberal Kennedy have won any of those conservative southern states?

THE AFTERMATH

Lyndon Johnson had a rocky relationship with a number of members of the press especially those in the national media. But there was one TV station where the president didn't have to worry about negative remarks. It was KTBC in Austin, Texas. The reason was that he and his wife, First Lady Lady Bird Johnson, owned it.

If Robert Kennedy had become the Democratic candidate for president in 1968, he would have faced the same man in the general election that his brother defeated in 1960—Richard Nixon.

In 1968, Sirhan Sirhan used a .22 caliber pistol to shoot and kill Senator Robert Kennedy. Because of its lack of striking power, the small handgun is usually not the weapon of choice to be used in an assassination.

Even though the shots were fired at close range, one of the surgeons who worked on the fallen presidential candidate reflected that had the fatal bullet struck him just a centimeter further back, RFK would not just have survived but most likely fully recovered.

It wasn't the only instance where a member of the famous family nearly escaped death by assassination.

Five years earlier in Dallas, Dr. Tom Shires, who was a member of the medical team that worked on Robert's brother President John F. Kennedy said that if JFK had not been hit by a second shot, he would have survived his initial wound.

What might have happened had Kennedy not exited through the kitchen area? Overlooked in the events of the day was the fact that RFK had also won the primary in South Dakota. At the time of his death, the delegate count was Humphrey (561), Kennedy (393), and McCarthy (258) of the 1,312 required for nomination. But many felt that with his strong following in the eastern states along with the experience of Team Kennedy running the campaign that the former attorney general's odds of securing his party's top spot were very promising.

In 1964, Johnson had considered McCarthy, a Catholic (like Kennedy), as his potential running mate before finally choosing Hubert Humphrey, the other senator from Minnesota.

Among those who received votes at the Democratic National Convention was the University of Alabama's famous football coach Paul "Bear" Bryant who picked up the support of 1.5 loyal Crimson Tide delegates.

Calvin Coolidge and Lyndon Johnson each succeeded presidents who died while in office. Then, they both ran for a term of their own and won (Coolidge in 1924 and Johnson in 1964). Four years later, each man announced that he would not be a candidate for reelection.

At the time, Los Angeles' Ambassador Hotel, where RFK was shot, was one of the most respected establishments in the city. It had hosted six Academy Award presentation shows and had been the campaign headquarters during Ronald Reagan's run for governor in 1966. Years earlier, Marilyn Monroe had applied for a job with the Blue Book Modeling Company, which kept an office at the building. It has been widely speculated that the actress had personal relationships with both of the Kennedy brothers before her death in 1962.

A group of wealthy Texas GOP backers had asked actor John Wayne to run for national office in 1968. He declined, joking that he did not believe the public would seriously consider an actor in the White House. However, he did support his friend Ronald Reagan's runs for governor of California in 1966 and 1970.

Wayne was one of the Republican convention's speakers on its opening day in 1968.

RFK's wife, Ethel, was three months pregnant when he was killed. On December12, 1968, their eleventh and final child, a daughter named Rory was born. Sirhan Sirhan was convicted of premeditated murder on April 17, 1969 and sentenced to death. His sentence was commuted to life imprisonment three years later due to the California Supreme Court ruling in *People v. Anderson*, outlawing the state's death penalty.

The Chicago Seven was a group of antiwar demonstrators who were among the leaders of the disturbance that took place during the Democrat National Convention in Chicago. David Dellinger, Rennie Davis, John Froines, Tom Hayden, Abbie Hoffman, Jerry Rubin, and Lee Weiner were charged by the federal government with conspiracy, inciting to riot, and other charges.

The trial lasted five months and ended in February 1970 with a split verdict. All charges of conspiracy were dismissed. Froines and Weiner were found innocent on all counts. The rest were found guilty of crossing state lines with the intention of starting a riot. Within three years, all convictions were overturned.

The entire episode turned some of the Seven like Hoffman and Rubin into celebrities, but Hayden became the most prominent. He served sixteen years in the California State Assembly and from 1973 to 1990 was married to movie actress and outspoken radical Jane Fonda.

At the time that Lyndon Johnson announced that he wouldn't be a candidate for reelection, the Gallup Poll measured his approval rating at a disappointing 36 percent of the American people. However, by the time that he left office ten months later, January 1969, his standing raised to 49 percent, proving that the American people are forgiving.

Johnson packed up his belongings and headed home to his Texas ranch. He wrote two books; resumed smoking after quitting fifteen years earlier; grew his hair long like those who had demonstrated against him; and gained twenty-five pounds. The former president endured heart attacks in 1970 and 1972 before suffering a final fatal cardiac event in 1973 at the age of sixty-four.

19

The Election of 1972

Richard Nixon, Incumbent (Republican) vs. George McGovern (Democrat)

"Always remember others may hate you, but those who hate you don't win unless you hate them, and then you destroy yourself."

—Richard Nixon's Final Remarks to the White House
cabinet and staff August 9, 1974

On Monday, January 20, 1969, an estimated crowd of sixty-five thousand spectators along with millions viewing on television watched Richard Nixon take the oath of office as the nation's thirty-seventh president from the steps of the east portico at the US Capitol Building. While the ceremony was full of its usual pomp and circumstance, there were also a full cast of detractors.

Most of their organizers were from a group called MOBE—the National Mobilization Committee to End the War in Vietnam. The new president, along with his Republican faithful, received a small dose of what their Democrat counterparts had experienced during their convention. The protesters didn't let the wintery mix interfere with their demonstration as about one thousand antiwar activists hurled rocks, bottles, and smoke bombs while shouting obscenities at Nixon's motorcade as Secret Service agents were kept busy avoiding the projectiles. American flags were burned while police clashed in the streets with neo-Nazis.

As opposed to the situation in Chicago, the Capitol Police were well prepared as a security force consisting of more than three thousand District law enforcement, five thousand regular troops, and one thousand National Guardsmen were deployed along the parade route and throughout the city. Some eighty-one persons were arrested during the disorderly event while twelve individuals were injured, including one police officer.

The inauguration turned out to be a trial run as on the following November 15, approximately half a million people turned out in Washington, DC, for the largest antiwar protest in United States history. During the campaign, President Nixon had promised to begin a troop withdrawal, but ten months after taking office he had yet to take action and those against the war were growing more impatient.

Over his first four years in office, Nixon watched two wars taking place: The first was against the Viet Cong in Southeast Asia. The other was the parade of antiwar demonstrations that became common, mainly on college campuses. The worst of those took place on May 4, 1970, at Kent State University in Ohio, where a clash between protesters and National Guard troops resulted in the deaths of four students who were gunned down during the melee.

Nevertheless, despite Vietnam and the campus protests, after two years as president, Nixon's approval rating hovered near the 60 percent mark. Part of that had to do with his formation of the Environmental Protection Agency in July 1970, which was welcomed by many, especially those on the left, as a positive first step toward preserving natural resources, wildlife, and habitat.

Over the next two years, the peace talks in Paris dragged on with little progress. Back home, as 1972 drew nearer, the political parties began to take their positions for their upcoming primaries. On January 7, 1972, Nixon announced his intention to run for reelection. The Democrats ended up with a contingent of fifteen candidates ranging from the famous like Hubert Humphrey and George Wallace to little known challengers such as Patsy Mink, a congresswoman from Hawaii.

In the primaries, Humphrey, the 1968 Democratic nominee, got off to a slow start as the field worked its way into a two-way battle between Senator George McGovern of South Dakota and Senator Ed Muskie of Maine. But there came a point where the memory of a tragic event from the last campaign impacted the latest crop of candidates.

On May 15, 1972, former Alabama governor George Wallace was shot and seriously wounded during a campaign appearance in Laurel, Maryland. As opposed to Robert Kennedy four years earlier, Wallace survived the attack, but the assassination attempt left him paralyzed and in a wheelchair for the rest of his life.

The attempted assassin was Arthur Bremer, a twenty-one year old who lived in a Milwaukee apartment near Marquette University who was already under the care of a psychiatrist. He was arrested, tried, found guilty, and sentenced to sixty-three years in prison for shooting Wallace and three other people. Bremer was released from prison on November 9, 2007, at the age of fifty-seven, having served just thirty-five years of his original sentence.

What was lost in the headlines from that day in 1972 was that Wallace was a serious candidate for the Democratic Party's nomination. He had won three of the twelve primaries that were held before the shooting and finished second in two others. He had also won five states and garnered forty-five electoral votes as a third party candidate in the 1968 general election.

On the day after the assassination attempt, Wallace won the Maryland and Michigan primaries. But that was the end of the trail as he was unable to physically endure any further campaigning as the momentum that he had built up gradually dissolved.

Wallace had been a staunch segregationist but had renounced his ways of the past. There was also a stark political contrast between the Far Right southerner and the liberal senator, and eventual nominee, George McGovern.

By the time the Democratic Convention began on July 10 at Miami Beach, a great deal of the delegates' work had already been done. As part of the selection process, the number of primaries had increased to twenty-two as eleven others held caucuses. By June 15, McGovern had 1,000 committed delegates of the 1,509 required for nomination. He was followed by Wallace—367, Humphrey—354, and Muskie—171 with all others totaling 110.

The Democrats had a well-known celebrity following with them in Florida, led by feminist spokesperson Gloria Steinem, along with actors Shirley MacLaine and Henry Fonda who made appearances. Also among the speakers was the recently wounded Wallace who addressed the gathering from his wheelchair and, technically, remained a candidate right up to the gathering's conclusion.

The 1972 convention didn't feature the upheaval that had reigned supreme four years prior in Chicago, but like large groups with differing opinions, there was ample debate inside the convention hall on such topics as women's rights, gay rights, abortion, and the ongoing war in Vietnam.

McGovern had been a World War II pilot before returning home and entering politics. Originally a Republican, he admired Franklin Roosevelt and became a Democrat. He won a House seat from his native South Dakota in 1957 and then moved to the Senate in 1963. Over the years, he became an outspoken advocate for the antiwar movement and, at the convention, earned a first ballot nomination.

There was also the matter of selecting a vice presidential nominee. On the evening of July 13, a floor fight ensued over the choice of his running mate. McGovern was scheduled to address the delegates and the nation at 9:00 p.m. (eastern time) but the war of words between delegates and others dragged into the wee hours of the night and the following morning.

In a compromise, it was eventually decided that Senator Tom Eagleton of Missouri would be the choice even though no one in the party had taken the time to properly vet the candidate. However, that didn't seem to matter as Eagleton was voted in by the delegation as time continued to roll on.

An anxious McGovern finally took the stage at 2:30 a.m. in front of a gathering of exhausted delegates, some of whom were falling asleep, and a small television viewing audience. Many agreed that it was the nominee's best speech of his career, but it followed what had been a disastrous selection process for vice president. McGovern later joked that his speech had gotten a very good rating in Guam where it was shown in prime time.

The lack of vetting came back to haunt the campaign as Eagleton's nomination was withdrawn two weeks later when it was revealed that a few years earlier, he had checked himself into the hospital three times for physical and nervous exhaustion, receiving electroconvulsive therapy twice. He is also known to have suffered from depression along with rumors of a drinking problem.

The Democrats moved quickly into damage control mode as Eagleton was replaced on the ticket with R. Sargent Shriver Jr., the former US ambassador to France, who was also the brother-in-law of John and Robert Kennedy.

While McGovern attempted to get control of his campaign, Nixon and the Republicans arrived in Miami the following month for his final coronation. But that wasn't what originally had been planned.

On June 17, police arrested James McCord, Frank Sturgis, and three accomplices inside the Democratic National Committee headquarters located in Washington, DC's Watergate Hotel. They confiscated cameras, wiretapping materials, and $2,300 in cash. The initial story drew little attention with most of those who saw it referring to it as a third-rate burglary, but it marked the beginning of the end for the Nixon administration.

Meanwhile, the convention was supposed to have originally been held in San Diego with one of its sponsors, the giant communication company International Telephone and Telegraph (ITT), playing a prominent role. It was agreed by party officials that, in return for a $400,000 convention donation, Nixon would make some pending antitrust litigation against the company disappear. When news of the scheme began to leak out with only three months before the start of the convention, the event was quietly moved to Miami Beach.

Nixon had years of experience with agitators, which continued into his presidency. On August 22, 1972, the convention's second day, he arrived at Miami International Airport as protesters attempted to force open the front gate of the convention center while others began laying in the street. They also harassed delegates at the scene.

Demonstrators caused further havoc by blocking the Fontainebleau Hotel, the convention's headquarters; burning the American flag; blocking traffic; trashing downtown Miami Beach; breaking windows; and tearing down signs. Law enforcement was eventually forced to use tear gas against the unruly crowd to restore order. By the end of the day, police had made 212 arrests. It was evident that Miami had learned a tough lesson from Chicago and was ready four years later when the Republican convention came to their city.

Nixon and Agnew were renominated on the first ballot. Prior to the convention, the chief executive had enhanced his resume becoming the first president to visit China and the USSR earlier in the year. When the post-Labor Day portion of the campaign began, the incumbent charged out of the gate in Gallup's first after-convention poll that measured Nixon with a 61 percent to 33 percent lead even though more details about the Watergate break-in continued to seep into the news.

Meanwhile, Agnew traveled across the country in his familiar role as the White House's attack dog growling at protesters and the media with whom he would use one of his favorite phrases referring to them as the *"nattering nabobs of negativism."* It was all for public consumption as the reports from a war, along with the corresponding events at home, were combined to be played out on the nightly television news. For the demonstrators, the only person more detested by the Left more than Nixon was the tough talking Agnew.

The final Gallup Poll projected 61 percent of the vote would go for Nixon, 35 percent for McGovern, 3 percent remained undecided, and 1 percent for minor party candidates. The last Harris Survey called the race 59 percent–35 percent for Nixon, with 6 percent undecided. On the eve of the election, attempting to show strength and rally his supporters, McGovern downplayed his standing in the polls and predicted that he would upset the incumbent.

When it was over, Nixon, who barely lost and then barely won in his two previous bids for the Oval Office, carried a record forty-nine states for 521 electoral votes. Only Massachusetts and the District of Columbia went for McGovern, combining for a meager total of only seventeen electoral votes, as he also lost his home state of South Dakota.

The margin of Nixon's electoral victory was the third largest in the nation's history, eclipsed only by the elections of 1820, when James Monroe won 231 electoral votes to 1 over John Quincy Adams, and 1936, as Franklin D. Roosevelt shellacked Alf Landon 523 to 8. Only two presidential candidates had ever taken 60 percent or more of the popular vote: Warren G. Harding in 1920 (60.3 percent) and Roosevelt's 1936 landslide (60.8 percent).

Another feature of the Nixon victory was that it was the first Republican sweep since Reconstruction of the once solid Democratic South. It was also the first time since 1944 that the South had gone solidly for any single candidate. By runaway margins, Nixon took all eleven states of the old Confederacy, plus all the border states. His victory in Arkansas marked the first presidential race since 1872 in which the Razorback state had gone Republican.

The 1972 presidential election was the first since the ratification of the 26th Amendment, that was ratified a year earlier, which reduced the voting age from twenty-one to eighteen years of age.

Table 19.1   The Election of 1972

Presidential candidate	Party	Home state	Popular vote Count	Percentage	Electoral vote
Richard Milhous Nixon (Incumbent)	Republican	California	47,168,710	60.67%	520
George Stanley McGovern	Democratic	South Dakota	29,173,222	37.52%	17
John G. Schmitz	American Independent	California	1,100,868	1.42%	0
Linda Jenness	Socialist Workers	Georgia	83,380	0.11%	0
Benjamin Spock	People's	California	78,759	0.10%	0
Louis Fisher	Socialist Labor	Illinois	53,814	0.07%	0
Gus Hall	Communist	New York	25,597	0.03%	0
Evelyn Reed	Socialist Workers	New York	13,878	0.02%	0
E. Harold Munn	Prohibition	Michigan	13,497	0.02%	0
John G. Hospers	Libertarian	California	3,674	0.00%	1
John Mahalchik	America First	New Jersey	1,743	0.00%	0
Other			26,880	0.04%	—
Total			77,744,027	100%	538
Needed to win					270

Vice President Elect, Spiro T. Agnew, incumbent

On January 20, 1973, many of the individuals who had gathered on the steps of the Capitol Building four years earlier reassembled for the second inauguration of Richard Milhous Nixon. Like 1969, there was plenty of celebrating among Republicans, protesting by antiwar demonstrators, and the weather was cold and cloudy. That evening there were several inaugural balls around the city which, for the most part, made the occasion look like a replay of his first presidential swearing-in.

One of the balls took place at the Smithsonian Institute's American History Museum where, among the exhibits, was one dedicated to American farm life, which included the use of live chickens. During the festivities, one of the birds escaped its confines and made its way across the dance floor where it attacked a guest who was sitting in a $1,000 VIP box. The escaped fowl was captured by the Smithsonian's secretary S. Dillon Ripley and returned to its exhibit.

Following the inauguration, Nixon and Agnew had much in common with the Smithsonian chicken as the nation's two top elected officials were also being perused on several fronts.

While the vice president had no links to Watergate, he had other serious problems of his own. In 1973, the Justice Department began investigating Agnew for improprieties dating back as far as the early days of his political career as Baltimore County executive. It had begun looking into charges that included extortion, bribery, and income tax violations related to illegal kickbacks from companies seeking state contracts. Some of the alleged activity had taken place while he was governor of Maryland.

The list of charges also included payments that Agnew received while vice president for assisting companies in obtaining federal construction contracts. In all, he was charged with having accepted bribes totaling more than $100,000. Even with overwhelming evidence against him, Agnew vowed to remain in office. With their own issues relating from Watergate growing, members of the Nixon legal team pushed for the VP's resignation hoping to avoid a potential Constitutional crisis from the presidential line of succession, but he refused to budge.

With the walls closing in around him, Agnew attempted one final legal maneuver to save himself. He requested that Speaker of the House Carl Albert (D-OK) bring charges of impeachment against him believing that a House investigation would clear his name. As strange as it sounded, Agnew's appeal had precedent as in 1826 Vice President John C. Calhoun had asked for and secured a House Select Committee to look into bribery charges stemming from his tenure as secretary of war. A month and a half inquiry returned a verdict in Calhoun's favor. But Agnew wasn't as fortunate, as on September 26, 1973, the Speaker denied the request on the grounds that Agnew's case "relates to matters before the courts."

With that decision, the involved parties consisting of Agnew's criminal defense team, the prosecutors, along with the presiding federal judge, worked out a plea bargain during a meeting in a motel room in Alexandria, Virginia. In return for a plea of no contest, he would be cited to a single federal count of failing to report $29,500 of unreported income on his 1967 tax return while governor of Maryland. In addition,

Agnew was fined $10,000 and sentenced to three years of unsupervised probation. The major provision of the sweetheart deal was that he would have to resign as vice president of the United States.

As the details were being put into writing, Agnew made a last visit to confer with Nixon. The president assured him that he was doing the right thing and when the meeting was over, the former running mates never spoke again. On October 10, 1973, while Agnew appeared in federal court in Baltimore, his letter of resignation was being delivered to Secretary of State Henry Kissinger. Inside the courtroom, he pled "Nolo contendere" (Latin for "no contest") to the charges to which Judge Walter Hoffman stated that the plea was the same as guilty.

Agnew was not the first vice president to quit office. Once again that distinction went to Calhoun whose political differences with President Andrew Jackson coupled with an opportunity to fill a vacant Senate seat in South Carolina became major factors for his 1832 resignation.

Three days following the court appearance, Congressman Gerald Ford who laughed in 1968 when he was told that Nixon had chosen Agnew as his VP was selected as his replacement.

Agnew wasn't the only one with a tax issue as Nixon was forced to pay $465,000 in back taxes in April 1974. But that was just the tip of his problems.

Over the nineteen months following the 1973 inauguration, an array of congressional hearings, lawsuits, and court rulings painted a picture of a presidency that was in serious trouble. Time was running out as the options were increasingly limited for Nixon and his team with the courts and public opinion stacked fully against him.

On August 7, 1974, US senator Barry Goldwater, (R-AZ), US House Minority Leader John Rhodes, (R-AZ), and US Senate Minority Leader Hugh Scott, (R-PA) minced no words during a White House meeting with the president. The lawmakers told the embattled chief executive that if he didn't resign, he faced all-but-certain impeachment, conviction, and removal from office in connection with the Watergate scandal. At that moment was the stark reality that it was finally over for Nixon.

The following evening he announced his resignation on national television and radio. At noon (EDT) on August 9, 1974, Richard M. Nixon became the first and only US president to resign from office. It was the final chapter of the greatest political comeback and downfall in the nation's history.

Nixon departed the nation's capital the following afternoon making Gerald Ford the new president. In just nine months, he had gone from House Minority Leader to vice president to commander in chief without being elected to the final two offices.

THE AFTERMATH

Following his departure after leaving office, Richard Nixon returned to his beachfront home in San Clemente, California. In 1979, he wanted to return to New York City where he had lived during the 1960s. However, there were residences that didn't want the president who had resigned in disgrace.

He was rejected by two co-op boards, one on East 72nd Street and another at 817 Fifth Avenue, before settling on a property that required no board approval. It was a townhouse on East 65th Street that Nixon bought for $750,000. As opposed to Watergate, the former commander in chief got the last laugh during a second transaction that took place less than two years later when he sold the home for $2.6 million.

From there, he and his wife moved to an estate in Saddle River, New Jersey.

Nixon was the first former president to cash-in financially after leaving office. He agreed to write his memoirs for $2.5 million, which went on to become a best seller. In 1977, he gave a four episode interview to British television personality David Frost for $600,000. The Nixons also sold their properties in Florida, which helped pay off many of the bills accumulated from his legal issues.

Since then, his successors have taken similar paths in parlaying their time in the White House into wealth and security. Richard Nixon died in 1994.

After leaving office, former vice president Spiro Agnew ran into financial problems primarily as a result of his legal troubles. Among those who came to his aid was his friend, entertainer Frank Sinatra who loaned him $200,000.

Since Agnew was never connected to Watergate and had he not been convicted on the other charges brought against him by the Justice Department, upon Nixon's resignation he would have become the thirty-eighth president of the United States. Agnew died in 1996.

Arthur Bremer's assassination attempt did not end George Wallace's political career. He was subsequently elected governor of Alabama twice again, in 1974 and 1982. Wallace died in 1998.

Miami Beach hosted both the Democratic and Republican conventions in 1972. Even though the city attempted to serve in the role many times since then, that year was the last time that it hosted the event for either party. In 1996, San Diego finally got its opportunity and welcomed the GOP convention.

In 1972, Congresswoman Shirley Chisholm of New York became the first African American female to become a candidate for president for one of the major parties.

Twenty-five-year-old Bill Clinton moved to Dallas in 1972 to work on George McGovern's presidential campaign. Another young mover-and-shaker who worked with Clinton for the Democratic Party nominee was future movie director Steven Spielberg.

THE FOLLOWING ELECTION

1976: The campaign, featuring the incumbent Gerald Ford (R-MI) and former Georgia governor Jimmy Carter (D-GA), had the first presidential debates since Kennedy and Nixon in 1960. Lyndon Johnson never saw a reason to participate in such an exercise since he held such a commanding lead in 1964 and Nixon had learned from his earlier experience how easy it was to make a mistake on television that could be unrecoverable, so he stood pat in 1968 and 1972. After the first debate, which went off without any major moments, Carter's lead had shrunk from 51 percent to 40 percent. The Plains, Georgia, native's strong point with voters was the fact that he was a true Washington, DC, "outsider" having never held office in the nation's capital. However, by early October, he clung to a narrow 47 percent to 45 percent edge in the Gallup Poll.

But the dreaded mistake that Nixon had feared became Ford's nightmare during the second meeting. Responding to a question from journalist Max Frankel of *The New York Times* about the Soviet control of Eastern Europe, Ford responded surprisingly, "there is no Soviet domination of Eastern Europe and there never will be under a Ford administration."

The fact was that the Soviets had resided in Eastern Europe since the end of World War II and had even erected the symbolic Communist barrier, the Berlin Wall, to keep citizens from seeking freedom.

Carter was so stunned by the unexpected answer, that he grinned before responding having not believed what he had just heard. It was one of the biggest debate gaffes in history and was the lead story on the next day's news. There were those who believed that the misstatement was the knockout punch delivered to the Ford campaign by their own candidate.

Even though the count was close in the popular vote, 50.08 percent to 48.02 percent, it was little known Jimmy Carter who won the biggest election of the Bicentennial.

20

The Election of 1980

Jimmy Carter, Incumbent (Democrat) vs. Ronald Reagan (Republican)

"A recession is when a neighbor loses his job. A depression is when you lose yours. And recovery is when Jimmy Carter loses his."

—Candidate Ronald Reagan, Labor Day address at Liberty State Park,
Jersey City, New Jersey September 1, 1980

Once the election of 1976 had concluded, its three main candidates went their separate ways. After serving twenty-eight years in public office, Gerald Ford was done with politics. He had always been an avid sportsman who enjoyed skiing and golf and divided his retirement years between two homes that could provide the best of both of those worlds, one in Vail, Colorado, and the other in Rancho Mirage, California. While delivering speeches for a hefty fee and playing in an occasional charity golf tournament with other celebrities, the thirty-eighth president stayed busy in his featured role of the former commander in chief.

Meanwhile, one-time Georgia governor Jimmy Carter, from the tiny town of Plains (population 231), settled into his position as the person behind the desk of the most demanding job in the world. He got off to an optimistic start in September 1978 when he helped negotiate the Camp David Accords, bringing peace between Middle East foes Israel and Egypt. It was one of his accomplishments that was cited when Carter was awarded the Nobel Peace Prize in 2002.

However, the economy at home wasn't cooperating with his agenda. By 1980, inflation had risen to 13.5 percent; unemployment stood at 7.2 percent; and the country's prime interest rate rose to a staggering 21.5 percent. Shortages of Middle East oil continued to cause a lack of gas at filling stations across the country. But there was another event that may have sealed the president's political fate several months before his reelection effort.

On November 4, 1979, militant Iranian students seized the American Embassy in Tehran taking fifty-three US citizens as hostages. From that point until election night 1980, the public watched in disappointment as networks broadcasted daily reports on the lack of progress that was taking place to gain freedom for the captives. It had all the makings of an international terror novel, but unfortunately for the Carter administration, the entire drama had fallen on its watch.

After his unsuccessful bid at the Republican nomination in 1976, the trifecta's final member, Ronald Reagan, returned home to California where he lived like the former movie star that he was, in the exclusive area of Pacific Palisades, while splitting time up the coast at his sprawling 688 acre ranch near scenic Santa Barbara.

The former governor received his share of criticism from conservatives who believed that his campaigns for president in 1968 and 1976 were lackluster. It was at that juncture that Reagan reverted back to the quality that had made him a household name—communication. He had burst upon the political stage in 1964 with his speech in support of Barry Goldwater, but his two White House runs never lived up to the drama of that initial address. It was after his bitter loss to Ford at the 1976 GOP convention that he began to lay the foundation for his 1980 campaign.

Reagan had always had the ability to communicate. Prior to becoming a well-known Hollywood actor, he got his start in the entertainment business as a radio sports broadcaster. After John F. Kennedy's notable performance in the debates of 1960, most candidates who followed viewed television as the key to opening the gates to the White House. However, Reagan knew that radio listeners were a different breed who relied on what they heard instead of what they thought they saw. He needed to point no further than ABC news broadcaster Paul Harvey whose fifteen-minute daily broadcasts reached more than twenty million listeners via more than 1,200 radio stations.

Reagan had begun a daily five-minute radio commentary in 1975 but halted the series to campaign the following year. After his defeat, he returned to the microphone with the zest that had made him a hero of the Right in 1964. The actor-turned-governor gave 1,027 addresses to an audience of twenty to thirty million listeners each week. In a throwback to the days before computers and iPhones dominated the scene, the Eureka, Illinois, college graduate wrote at least 679 of those commentaries in longhand on yellow legal pads.

While Carter dealt with the economy and the hostages, Reagan used the radio networks as his personal bullhorn in a call to the conservative wing of the Republican Party along with the undecided to unify in mass against all enemies, at home and abroad. A fervent anti-Communist, the Soviet Union was often a convenient target of the Goldwater deciple who pulled no punches whenever freedom was on the table as the topic of the day. But not all of Carter's opposition was gathering on the Right.

On November 7, 1979, US senator Ted Kennedy of Massachusetts announced his entry into the Democratic race. While the move caught some off-guard, the timing could not have been better to challenge the sitting president as he continued to struggle with problems both on the home front and on foreign soil.

In contrast to the country's early days, it had become increasingly rare for an incumbent chief executive to face a primary challenge from a prominent member of its own party and Kennedy wasn't just another hack politician looking to enhance his name recognition. In fact, he was the latest entrant from the heralded Bay State dynasty that had already produced a president, a US attorney general, and an American ambassador.

For those who had been waiting eleven years for another Kennedy to make a run for the Oval Office, Senator Ted was the answer to their prayers, and the early numbers supported their ambitions. In the summer of 1979, the Gallup Poll had Kennedy holding sizeable leads over all three of his potential opponents. For the Democratic nomination, he had a thiry-point advantage against President Carter and also held large margins over Reagan (59%–36%) and Ford (60%–38%).

According to some in the media, it appeared that the youngest Kennedy son had already wrapped up the general election before the first primary ballots were tabulated, but that was before the questions began.

In August 1979, the senator gave, what would be, his first televised interview of his campaign. He fielded a series of questions from journalist Roger Mudd of CBS News, none of which were considered particularly hard-hitting but when asked, "Why do you want to be president?" he appeared to be totally lost for a reply.

It seemed like such a simple and direct query, but it caught Kennedy completely off guard. He stammered and stumbled through the moment without ever giving a coherent response. It was evident that he didn't possess the natural verbal talent of his older siblings, JFK and Robert, who always appeared to be cool and calm, with an explanation for any question even if it was just an assortment of words parceled together that sounded acceptable.

Although, as bad as the moment was, things got worse. From the time that speculation began that Kennedy would run, everyone expected more questions about a decade-old incident that continued to haunt the candidate.

In the early hours of July 19, 1969, the state's senior US senator was involved in a one-car automobile accident resulting in the death of his twenty-eight-year-old passenger, Mary Jo Kopechne, a former campaign aid of Robert Kennedy. Kopechne had been attending a party, along with other staffers, on Chappaquiddick Island, off the coast of Martha's Vineyard, Massachusetts. She accepted a ride from Ted Kennedy in order to catch the last ferry back to Edgartown, where she was staying.

Along the darkened road, the senator, whose reputation for partying to excess around the nation's capital was no secret, drove his 1967 Oldsmobile Delmont 88 off a bridge and into Pocha Pond where the vehicle overturned. Kennedy was able to escape but didn't report the mishap until the following morning past 9:00 a.m. resulting in a delay, which made any opportunity to rescue Kopechne impossible. During a national television address a few days afterward, the troubled official called his conduct "indefensible."

Kopechne's tragic death didn't derail the senator's career objectives. In a controversial ruling that followed, Kennedy pled guilty to a charge of leaving the scene of an accident and received a two-month suspended jail sentence. While those in his home state continued to return him to the Senate every six years, the court's verdict didn't sit well outside of Massachusetts and was a factor in his decision not to seek the presidency in 1972 and 1976. From there, the bottom fell out of the Kennedy campaign.

Whatever the apprehensions were over Kopechne's demise, those questions were visible in the results of the Democrat primaries. The beleaguered Carter, who was hampered by the hostage crisis and a disastrous economy, defeated Kennedy in nine of their first ten encounters

Meanwhile, by April 23, Reagan had won ten of fifteen Republican primaries and caucuses with his nearest competitor being George H. W. Bush, the former congressman from Texas and ex-director of the C.I.A., who captured the other five. With each passing week, the gap between the two candidates grew wider with Reagan starting to gear his effort away from Bush to focus directly on Carter.

As attempts failed to free the captives, the problems in the Middle East were taking their toll on the president's campaign. Overall, Kennedy won ten states during the primaries but was unable to secure the party's nomination. Even without claiming the ticket's top spot, many felt that the damage had been done through the challenger's attacks on Carter's record. In the end, as Lyndon Johnson had encountered, some bad luck in foreign policy along with an election challenge from a member of the Kennedy family, proved to be a distasteful mix in the political blender for Jimmy Carter.

It was at that point that the incumbent decided to take a risk that, if successful, could free the hostages and provide an electoral advantage for himself. On April 24–25, 1980, Carter ordered *Operation Eagle Claw,* an attempt to rescue the fifty-two American prisoners that continued to be held inside the enemy's stronghold at the US Embassy in Tehran. Unfortunately, the effort was a debacle from the beginning with disagreements between the president and his commanders on how it should be carried out. In the end, no hostages were freed. Eight troops were killed, four others were wounded, one helicopter and one transport aircraft destroyed, and five other helicopters were abandoned or captured.

In a country that accepted nothing less than total victory, whether it be in sports or war, the rescue attempt was viewed as an embarrassment by much of the American public.

To make a bad situation even worse, billionaire businessman Ross Perot had put together a successful self-funded clandestine mission in 1979 when two of his employees were being held in an Iranian prison. Perot safely got his people out, along with a number of others who were captive, with the aid of former Vietnam War hero Colonel Arthur "Bull" Simons. The courageous exploits of the duo were turned into a bestselling book and then a movie.

The only thing that the Carter rescue plan had provided was a mountain of negative press. Republican nominee Reagan didn't have to harp on the failed mission, as that message was being taken care of by the media's political analysts. Instead, the GOP challenger continued to travel around the country lamenting the continuation of the administration's poor economic news.

A few weeks later, the Californian cinched the nomination on May 26 when Bush withdrew from the race. However, he had yet to name a running mate as the party's convention was getting underway on July 14 in Detroit. The hottest rumor making the rounds through Joe Louis Arena was that the Reagan team's first choice was their former rival Gerald Ford, even though the ex-president was viewed as a moderate while the new nominee was a rock-ribbed conservative.

After some behind-the-scenes meetings, it was evident that the match couldn't be made as Ford went on national television during the convention to announce that he had no interest in returning to his old job. A few hours later on July 16, the Republicans presented Bush as the second half of the ticket. Although he had originally referred to Reagan's budget plan as "voodoo economics" during the campaign, with his new anointment, he was soon on board as its most vocal cheerleader.

On August 14, President Carter won renomination from the Democratic National Convention at New York's Madison Square Garden. After the state of Texas finally put the chief executive over the nominating majority, chants of "'four more years'" broke out from the background of delegates throughout the hall.

With 1,666 votes needed to conclude the nomination, the first-ballot roll call gave Carter 2,129 votes to his nemesis Kennedy's 1,146.5. After a rough and tumble campaign, the pair appeared for the traditional photo-op handshake at the podium area but there was no hiding the bitterness that had developed between the two over the preceding months.

The next issue that needed to be addressed were the debates. Since Ford's gaffe four years earlier, the public wanted to see their nominees stand on a stage and recite facts from memory as they awaited an embarrassing blunder that might decide the election. However, there was a stumbling block in the form of third party candidate John Anderson (I-IL), a US congressman from Illinois. Simply put, Reagan thought that Anderson, who was polling well, should be included in the dialogue while Carter objected and threatened to bypass the forum if the third party politico was included.

When the candidates took the stage on September 21 in Baltimore, there were two of them there, but one was not the president. He had held to his word and refused to appear as long as Anderson was included in the mix. Reagan took advantage of the opportunity with a strong performance that boosted his poll numbers the following day. For the next few weeks, each of the campaigns moved along toward Election Day.

By October 23, Carter held a small lead over Reagan (39%–38% with 9% support for Anderson). The numbers had been consistent since Labor Day but his refusal to participate in the first debate had backfired and so he approved a one-time showdown between he and the Republican who immediately seized the offer.

The frontrunners met on October 28 at the Public Auditorium in Cleveland. In 1976, Carter had been the beneficiary of Ford's error about the Soviet dominance of Eastern Europe, but in an ironic twist, the role was about to be reversed. In the Cleveland forum, when the topic turned toward negotiating a weapons treaty with the Soviet Union, Carter responded, "I had a discussion with our daughter, Amy, the other day before I came here to ask her what the most important issue was. She said she thought it was nuclear weaponry, and the control of nuclear arms."

At the time, Amy Carter was a thirteen-year-old middle school student with no experience in either domestic or foreign policy. It was then that Reagan, a master of television communication, took full advantage of the mistake and finished the evening with a strong close. Many considered it the best summation from any presidential debate:

> Next Tuesday is Election Day. Next Tuesday all of you will go to the polls, will stand there in the polling place and make a decision. I think when you make that decision, it might be well if you would ask yourself, are you better off than you were four years ago? Is it easier for you to go and buy things in the stores than it was four years ago? Is there more or less unemployment in the country than there was four years ago? Is America as respected throughout the world as it was? Do you feel that our security is as safe, that we're as strong as we were four years ago? And if you answer all of those questions yes, why then, I think your choice is very obvious as to whom you will vote for. If you don't agree, if you don't think that this course that we've been on for the last four years is what you would like to see us follow for the next four, then I could suggest another choice that you have.

With his nonsensical anecdote, Carter had placed himself in serious trouble and his staff knew it. In essence, what the debate had giveth in 1976, the debate had now taken away four years hence.

Three weeks before the election, the polling firm of Yankelovich, Skelly and White, produced a survey of 1,632 registered voters showing the race as almost dead even, as did a private survey by Carter pollster Pat Caddell. Two weeks later, a survey by *CBS News* and the *New York Times* showed almost the same breakdown.

Some pollsters at that time, however, were getting results that showed a slight uptick for Reagan. *ABC News-Harris Surveys*, for example, consistently gave the challenger a lead of a few points until the climactic final week of October.

"On the Saturday before the election, the race had rebounded into a tie or slight Carter lead. And then it all fell apart," recalled Caddell. "My polling for the [Carter] campaign told the story. By Sunday night November 2] President Carter was 5 points down and by Monday night the margin had exploded to 10 points down. The uniqueness of 1980 is this: In the history of American polling this was the only presidential election that entered the last weekend close and finished in a landslide. The only one!"

The hostage issue was again in the news thus reviving the public's frustration with the incumbent. The public opinion industry christened Caddell's thesis as the "big bang" theory of the campaign, which had eight million voters moving to Reagan in the final forty-eight hours.

Table 20.1   The Election of 1980

Presidential candidate	Party	Home state	Popular vote Count	Percentage	Electoral vote
Ronald Wilson Reagan	Republican	California	43,903,230	50.75%	489
James Earl Carter Jr. (incumbent)	Democratic	Georgia	35,480,115	41.01%	49
John Bayard Anderson	Independent	Illinois	5,719,850	6.61%	0
Ed Clark	Libertarian	California	921,128	1.06%	0
Barry Commoner	Citizens	Missouri	233,052	0.27%	0
Gus Hall	Communist	New York	44,933	0.05%	0
John Rarick	American Independent	Louisiana	40,906	0.05%	0
Clifton DeBerry	Socialist Workers	California	38,738	0.04%	0
Ellen McCormack	Right to Life	New York	32,320	0.04%	0
Maureen Smith	Peace and Freedom	California	18,116	0.02%	0
Harley McLain	Natural People's	North Dakota	18,116	0.02%	0
Other			296	0.0003%	—
Total			86,509,678	100%	538
Needed to win					270

Vice President Elect, George H. W. Bush, former director of the CIA (R-TX)

When the election was over, Reagan had carried forty-four of the fifty states and won 489 electoral votes versus only 49 for Carter. The incumbent ran well in Alabama, Arkansas, Delaware, Kentucky, Massachusetts, Mississippi, New York, North Carolina, South Carolina, and Tennessee losing each state by less than 3 percent. However, Reagan dominated the larger populated states like California, Texas, Florida, and Illinois. In the end, it could only be speculated if a successful outcome of *Operation Eagle Claw* would have earned Jimmy Carter a second term.

THE AFTERMATH

Gerald Ford wasn't the only current or former president to maintain a residence in California. Other members of that exclusive fraternity have included Herbert Hoover, Richard Nixon, Ronald Reagan, Barack Obama, and Donald Trump.

The hostages in Iran were released on January 20, 1981, just a few moments after Ronald Reagan was sworn into office. Terrorist leaders refused to allow them to go free until Jimmy Carter was officially out of power. It was the final stain on the record of the outgoing president over the 444 day crisis.

Neither Carter nor Ford ever ran for office again after 1980. In fact, they went on to become close friends and together served on diplomatic missions for the government in later years.

Jimmy Carter's hometown of Plains, Georgia, has a population of 231. By comparison, there are 377 employees who work in the White House. Carter spent his retirement years writing, giving speeches, and doing charity work.

After failing to secure the Democratic nomination in 1980, Ted Kennedy was elected to five more terms in the United States Senate. He never again ran for president and was involved in other incidents that involved young women and alcohol. The longtime Senator died in 2009 at the age of seventy-seven having never apologized to the parents of Mary Jo Kopechne.

THE FOLLOWING ELECTIONS

1984: After taking a successful, no nonsense approach with the Soviet Union and putting the pieces in motion for an economic recovery, Ronald Reagan faced off against Walter Mondale (D-MN), Carter's former vice president.

In one of the biggest landslides in history, the incumbent retained the office with an overwhelming 525–13 electoral victory. Mondale's only two wins came from his home state of Minnesota and that of Washington, DC.

1988: The frontrunner for the Democrats became Senator Gary Hart of Colorado. Surprisingly, in a February 1987 *Los Angeles Times* poll, he was leading Bush 42 percent to 34 percent. However, there was trouble on the horizon.

On April 27, 1987, the *Miami Herald* received an anonymous tip that the fifty-year-old Hart had attended an overnight trip on a rented yacht appropriately named *Monkey Business*. According to the tipster, the former senator had sailed from Miami to Bimini, with an unrecognized woman.

By May 1, reporters staked out Hart's DC townhouse where he was seen departing with the woman who, once again, was not his wife and then leaving with her again the next evening. Two days later, the story appeared in *The Herald* with photos from the stakeout. The female in question was a twenty-nine-year-old model, Donna Rice.

During a press conference in New Hampshire, Hart was asked whether he had ever committed adultery. "I don't have to answer that," he quipped. Meanwhile Rice was doing her own damage control telling another gathering of reporters that she and Hart were "just pals."

Two weeks later, the tabloid *National Enquirer* published a photo of Rice sitting on Hart's lap. It was later revealed that he and his wife of twenty-eight years, Lee, had previous marital difficulties and had reconciled twice. Hart continued to portray himself as a dutiful husband who continued to deny there was anything improper about his friendship with Rice.

On May 8, 1987, a week after the story broke, Hart suspended his campaign although in December he returned to the race, but the damage was already done. He competed in the New Hampshire primary where he received just 4,888 votes, about 4 percent of the total.

Meanwhile, away from the scandal, Vice President Bush (R-TX) rode Reagan's coattails to an easy 426–111 electoral conquest over Governor Michael Dukakis of Massachusetts. During the primary season, Super Tuesday became more critical as it had expended to twenty-one states.

21

The Election of 1992

George H. W. Bush, Incumbent (Republican) vs. Bill Clinton (Democrat) and Ross Perot (Independent)

> *"Bill Clinton appeared at a televised town hall meeting on April 19 during the 1992 campaign when he was asked by an audience member about his preference in underwear, 'Is it boxers or briefs?' Clinton laughed, and conceded, 'Usually briefs.'"*

In most cases, everyone who is running for office has a campaign manager. It doesn't guarantee victory but it can make a difference for the candidate the more qualified the individual is who is helping to plan strategy.

There is also another tried and true method for those who wish to be elected, or reelected, president of the United Sates, and that is to win a war. It can be something big like World War I or II, or a smaller confrontation where the enemy is taken down in a quick and efficient manner. But most of all, Americans love their winners.

After just two months in office for George H. W. Bush, on March 24, 1989, the oil tanker *Exxon Valdez* ran aground in southeastern Alaska. It dumped 240,000 barrels of oil into the pristine waters around Prince William Sound causing extensive environmental damage. Clean-up crews were rapidly deployed to the damaged ship to reduce the amount of crude that leaked into the ocean. The clean-up cost for Exxon was more than $2 billion.

But most of what took place during Bush's first two years in office had to do with foreign incidents. In June 1989, the Chinese government used military weapons to put down a prodemocracy demonstration at Tiananmen Square in Beijing. Many Americans were horrified as they watched their evening news, as an estimated two thousand protestors were killed by the Communists. In response, Bush announced a number of condemnatory actions, including the suspension of sales of American weapons to China.

On November 9, 1989, the Berlin Wall, which had been in place since 1961, was torn down bringing a symbolic end to Communist rule in Eastern Europe. East

Germany fully opened its borders touching off a jubilant celebration illustrating the great changes taking place as freedom began to spread to the former barricaded zone.

About a month later, the new American leader and Soviet president Mikhail Gorbachev held their first summit meeting of Bush's tenure aboard the cruise ship *Maksim Gorkiy* at harbor in Valetta, Malta, to discuss nuclear disarmament and the strengthening of Soviet-American trade relations. To the relief of the rest of the world, both leaders announced that the Cold War was effectively over.

Three weeks afterward on December 20, 1989, American armed forces invaded Panama to capture Manuel Noriega, the country's military dictator. Noriega, who had been indicted in the United States on drug trafficking charges, surrendered on January 3, 1990, after years of allowing smugglers to use his country as a safe haven. He was convicted on drug charges on April 9,1992 and sent to a US prison.

With the Panamanian strongman's surrender, Bush's approval rating reached an astonishing 80 percent while the Democrats were busy searching for the candidate who could retake the Oval Office. A 1990 *Times Mirror* poll listed the following group as potential challengers to the incumbent: Reverend Jesse Jackson (22%); New York governor Mario Cuomo (17%); former president Jimmy Carter (13%); Congressman Richard Gephardt of Missouri (10%); US senator Bill Bradley of New Jersey (8%); US senator Al Gore of Tennessee (7%); and undecided (23%).

But perhaps it was Bush who did the most to hurt his own reelection bid. During his acceptance speech at the 1988 Republican National Convention, he uttered his famous Reaganesque line, "Read my lips—no new taxes!"

He hadn't made the mistake that Walter Mondale had during his convention address of 1984 when he confirmed that he would raise taxes. But in October 1990, Bush succumbed to the Democrats' Senate and House majorities by backing off from his pledge and increasing tax rates. The conservative wing of the Republican Party, especially the Reagan devotees, were furious!

Meanwhile, in the Middle East, things were heating up. Like almost every president since World War II, Bush had to deal with a tyrant who wanted to control the oil rich region from the rest of the world. In his case, that individual was Iraqi president Saddam Hussein who had been in power for eleven years but, like most, yearned to become a bigger player on the world stage.

On August 2, 1990, Hussein took a page out of the book of other dictators by attacking a small, defenseless land, in this case it was his neighbor, the country of Kuwait. He moved about one hundred thousand Iraqi troops into the tiny nation, and in January 1991 the United States countered by sending thousands of troops to the Middle East including thirty-two destroyers.

Operation Desert Storm, a United Nations mission led by US generals Colin Powell and Norman Schwarzkopf, was a brief but powerful display of American force. On February 28, 1991, Iraq officially surrendered and immediately retreated from Kuwait.

The six week Persian Gulf War resulted in propelling the president's approval rating to an apparently insurmountable 89 percent, the highest number ever registered.

The prevailing view for potential candidates was to wait until 1996 because Bush would be unbeatable in 1992. That resulted in none of the major prospects listed in that 1990 poll joining the campaign.

Instead, many lesser known political figures entered the race. Among those was Bill Clinton, the relatively obscure governor of Arkansas. He had become somewhat of a political joke in 1988 with his elongated convention nomination speech for Michael Dukakis, that was only scheduled for fifteen minutes per policy, before endorsing the Democratic nominee. Instead, he extended it to an uninspiring thirty-three minute declaration, interrupted by boos and chants. The speech was so poorly received that the audience cheered when he said, "In conclusion . . . "

The next day, the press skewered him like a roasted razorback pig over an Arkansas campfire, but the governor countered the attacks by making the rounds on television talk shows and laughing at himself. Over time, his reputation rebounded and on October 3, 1991, Clinton announced that he was a candidate for president. The proclamation violated his pledge from the 1990 gubernatorial campaign to serve a full four-year term rather than run for the White House as only 5 percent of registered Democrats favored him in August 1991.

Even though the party's field was relatively shallow, Clinton was in trouble early on. Like so many politicians, he had a weakness for women with whom he wasn't married. On May 8, 1991, during the governor's Quality Management Conference at the Excelsior Hotel in Little Rock, employee Paula Jones alleged that the then-governor had sexually harassed her. There were also rumors going back as far as 1983 that he and former Miss America Elizabeth Ward Gracen had also been romantically linked.

After much discussion among the candidate and his campaign staff, it was decided that they needed to get out in front of all the innuendoes that were circulating. He did so, along with his wife Hillary, on one of America's high profile stages. On Sunday, January 26, 1992, the couple appeared on the CBS news magazine show *60 Minutes* although it wasn't just any episode. A larger than usual audience was expected to tune in that week as it would immediately follow the broadcast of the Super Bowl.

The couple fielded questions from reporter Steve Kroft while, in true Clinton fashion, never admitting to anything but also never denying it. In the end, the strategy succeeded as forty million viewers sat in judgment of the candidate. It was the second largest audience ever for a television interview. But the sideshow didn't end that evening.

It was followed the next day by a New York press conference where Little Rock news reporter Gennifer Flowers alleged that she had an ongoing twelve-year affair with Clinton. The accuser became the newest overnight celebrity, but the tales of Bill Clinton's female conquests were already wearing thin on the public of whom many considered the matters to be private.

In 1992, Bush and Clinton cruised to easy nominations. However, on February 20, they were joined in the race by Texas businessman H. Ross Perot who announced his intention to run as an independent if his supporters could get his name on the ballot in all fifty states.

Perot, a 1953 graduate of the Naval Academy, made his initial fortune with the creation of Electronic Data Systems (EDS), a pioneer in technology equipment and computer services management. They became the IT department for many companies as well as the first to service banks and provide early support for both Medicaid and Medicare in his home state of Texas. Over the years his empire grew, and with it, Perot became a billionaire in 1984 when General Motors Corp. bought EDS for nearly $2.6 billion.

The affable Texan was a straight shooter who had never run for public office.

In early 1992, it was revealed that Clinton had used family and political connections to avoid serving in the military during the Vietnam War. Ironically, when his draft lottery number was drawn on December 1, 1969, the college student received a high number (311), meaning that those whose birthdays had been drawn as numbers 1 to 310 would have to be drafted before him, making it unlikely that he would ever have to serve. In fact, the highest number drafted that year was 195.

Also in 1969, Clinton had written a letter to Colonel Eugene Holmes, the commander of the ROTC unit at the University of Arkansas, "Because of my opposition to the draft and the war, I am in great sympathy with those who are not willing to fight, kill and maybe die for their country."

When the letter was made public during the campaign, the words didn't sit well with many voters especially veterans. It appeared even worse since Bush and Perot had both served and the incumbent president had been a decorated war hero. It was at that point that Clinton's team decided to shift gears and make a bigger play for the youth vote.

Past campaign directors used a similar strategy that had paid off twenty-four years earlier for another candidate. Back then, Richard Nixon made an appearance on the popular comedy television program *Rowan & Martin's Laugh-In*, which turned out to be a smart move. Audiences reacted positively to viewing the candidate in a nonpolitical format.

History repeated on June 3, 1992, one day after Clinton's victory in the California primary when he appeared on *The Arsenio Hall* Show wearing sunglasses and toting his saxophone where he played his rendition of Elvis Presley's "Heartbreak Hotel."

The crowd went wild. "It's good to see a Democrat blowing something other than the election," Hall deadpanned, but it was during the interview segments that the candidate began to make some inroads with the college-aged voters.

But the polls told a different story as on June 11, 1992, a Gallup Poll had Perot in the lead with 39 percent, 31 percent for Bush, and 25 percent for Clinton.

The Democratic National Convention was held July 13–16 in New York City where US senator Al Gore of Tennessee was confirmed as Clinton's running mate.

To have two young, white southern males on the same ticket during that era was unusual although it was also the beginning of the postconvention bounce in the polls, which would see Clinton catapult from last to first in the race.

One day later, Perot quit his independent bid for the White House saying that a three-way race would not result in a majority winner in the electoral college and would put the election into the House of Representatives.

The billionaire declined to endorse either Bush or Clinton but did leave the door open for a possible return. He concluded, "If all the volunteers call me and say, 'Look, we need to get together and figure out what to do,' certainly I owe it to them to get together with them any time they want to."

As July turned to August, Clinton had surged to a 51 percent to 39 percent lead. In turn, after the Republican Convention, Bush could only manage a meager bounce to 42 percent while Clinton held steady at 51 percent. The news was even worse for the president as he finished July with a job approval rating of only 29 percent.

Clinton used a prevailing campaign theme as he constantly repeated that the United States was suffering through, "the worst economic performance since the Great Depression!"

In reality, the US unemployment rate in 1992 was only around 7.5 percent as compared to 24.75 percent in 1933. But that didn't matter in the opinion of many Americans because Bush had broken his word when he raised taxes.

However, on October 1, Perot announced that he was back in the race. The decision was timely as the finishing touches were being put on the upcoming debates: October 11 in St. Louis, Missouri; October 15 in Richmond, Virginia; and October 19 in Lansing, Michigan. Since Perot supporters had managed to get his name on the ballots of all fifty states, it was decided to include the billionaire in the forum.

The debates were symbolic of everything that went wrong for the Bush team as polls showed him finishing last in each encounter. But it was the second contest held in Richmond that caught him in an embarrassing moment.

During the discussion, a camera showed President Bush checking his watch. The gesture gave viewers the distinct impression that the Republican nominee would rather have been elsewhere. A few years later, the former candidate reflected, "Yeah, oh God, do I remember. I took a huge hit. That's another thing I don't like [about] debates, you look at your watch and they say that he shouldn't have any business running for president. He's bored. He's out of this thing, he's not with it and we need change. They took a little incident like that to show that I was, you know, out of it. They made a huge thing out of that."

In Gallup's final preelection poll, Clinton had 49 percent; Bush 37 percent, and Perot 14 percent. It was an early confirmation of the final outcome.

Table 21.1　The Election of 1992

Presidential candidate	Party	Home state	Popular vote Count	Percentage	Electoral vote
William Jefferson Clinton	Democratic	Arkansas	44,909,806	43.01%	370
George Herbert Walker Bush (Incumbent)	Republican	Texas	39,104,550	37.45%	168
Henry Ross Perot	Independent	Texas	19,743,821	18.91%	0
Andre Verne Marrou	Libertarian	Alaska	290,087	0.28%	0
Bo Gritz	Populist	Nevada	106,152	0.10%	0
Lenora Fulani	New Alliance Party	New York	73,622	0.07%	0
Howard Phillips	US Taxpayers Party	Virginia	43,369	0.04%	0
Other			152,516	0.13%	
Total			104,423,923	100%	538
Needed to win					270

Vice President Elect, Albert Gore Jr., US Senator (D-TN)

The numbers told the true story of the election of 1992. In March 1991, President Bush—leader of the free world during the fall of the Berlin Wall and winner of the Gulf War—seemed invincible. His approval rating stood at 89 percent in the Gallup polls. Yet he won only 37.7 percent, the lowest share of the popular vote of any incumbent president since William Howard Taft in 1912.

Against most predictions, 19 percent of the vote went to Ross Perot, the best result for a third party candidate since Theodore Roosevelt in 1916. Governor Clinton became the sixteenth winner of a presidential election with under 50 percent of the popular vote. His 43.2 percent of the people's majority equated into 370 electoral college votes in thirty-two states. The result for Clinton was not a landslide as his share of the popular ballot was similar to Mondale's in 1984 and Carter's in 1980, and less than Dukakis's in 1988. However, Democrats controlled both houses of Congress, and almost two-thirds of the governorships and state legislative chambers.

THE AFTERMATH

While some White House rivals such as Herbert Hoover and Franklin Roosevelt truly had no use for one another, that was not the case with Clinton and Bush. Although the campaign of 1992 was filled with its share of political squabbling, the two men grew closer over the years. After both were out of office, they teamed up to serve on humanitarian missions to help victims of the Indonesian tsunami (2004) and Hurricane Katrina (2005).

Clinton and Bush weren't the only presidential buddies. The 1976 White House opponents Gerald Ford and Jimmy Carter became very close friends in their later years. In 2006, Carter delivered one of the eulogies at Ford's funeral.

In the presidential campaign of 1992, billionaire businessman Ross Perot ran as a third party candidate against George H. W. Bush and Bill Clinton capturing 19 percent of the vote. Over the years, campaigns have become increasingly expensive. So much so that in 1992, Perot spent $65.4 million of his own money to help finance his run. That was more than the combined net worth of both of his opponents.

It wasn't the first time that a candidate paid the freight on their presidential aspirations as George Washington (1788 and 1792) and businessman Donald Trump (2016) along with Michael Bloomberg (2020) picked up large portions of their own election tabs. Each man was among the country's wealthiest during his era.

In the 1980s and early 1990s, US senator John Heinz of Pennsylvania was a rising star in the Republican Party. He was being mentioned as the party's potential presidential candidate for 1996 but was killed in an airplane accident in April 1991. Following his death, his widow Teresa met and, in 1995, married her deceased husband's senatorial colleague John Kerry of Massachusetts. In 2004, Senator Kerry became the Democratic Party's nominee for president. However, he lost the election and for the second time, Teresa Heinz-Kerry failed to become the nation's First Lady.

The election of 1992 wasn't the last campaign for only George H. W. Bush, it was the final run for another candidate. Republican Harold Stassen had served as governor of Minnesota from 1939–1943. He became remembered as the "Grand Old Party's Grand Old Loser" having run and lost for president ten times between 1948 and 1992.

In his swan song, Stassen failed to garner at least 1 percent of the popular vote. He died in 2001 at the age of ninety-three.

In 1998, ex-president George H. W. Bush gave a speech in Tokyo on behalf of Global Crossing, a telecommunication and computer networking company. He was to be paid $80,000 but elected to be compensated in Global Crossing stock rather than cash. In 1999 and 2000, the onetime commander in chief sold those shares for more than $4.5 million.

In the presidential election of 1992, Governor Bill Clinton of Arkansas defeated the incumbent George H. W. Bush. In 2016, two of the contenders for the nation's highest office were former First Lady Hillary Rodham Clinton and former Florida governor Jeb Bush, the ex-president's son.

Bill Clinton had a difficult time getting the job of attorney general filled in his administration after being elected in 1992. His first nominee was Zoe Baird, a lawyer for the Justice Department. She withdrew her name from consideration for the position when it was learned that she had hired illegal immigrants to serve as her chauffeur and nanny and neglected to pay their social security taxes.

History repeated as the next candidate under consideration was US district judge Kimba Wood. It was later discovered that she had also hired an illegal alien as a nanny. This was during a time when it was legal to do so, prior to the enactment of the Immigration Reform and Control Act of 1986 making the hiring of undocumented workers unlawful, but Clinton feared that it might cause controversy. It was also later revealed that Wood had once trained as a Playboy bunny in 1966.

That led to former Miami-Dade County (FL) state attorney Janet Reno becoming the first female US attorney general. The fact that she was childless and unmarried may have worked in her favor.

On November 25, 1993, America's true version of the odd couple was married. On that day James Carvelle, a liberal Cajun from Louisiana, took Mary Matalin, a conservative from Chicago, as his wife.

But the most noteworthy aspect of the union was that during the election of 1992, Carville was the campaign manager for Bill Clinton while Matalin served as the deputy manager of H. W. Bush.

"If you're as ugly as I am, you can't just date anyone," he quipped. "You've got to expand the playing field. And, I think I did pretty good."

President Bush took a great deal of heat for reneging on his "no new taxes" pledge from 1988. But his successor also changed his tune when it came to government revenue.

During the presidential campaign of 1992, candidate Bill Clinton stated, "I want to make it very clear that this middle-class tax cut, in my view, is central to any attempt we're going to make to have a short-term economic strategy."

A year later, he raised taxes.

THE FOLLOWING ELECTION

In 1996, the roles had reversed from 1992 when many of the top Democrats refused to run because of George Bush's high approval ratings. Now Republicans sat on the sideline believing that Clinton was a strong candidate.

But there was one prospect that had the incumbent's campaign staff losing sleep. Colin Powell was a fifty-eight-year-old African American, retired four-star general who was one of the top officers during *Operation Desert Storm*. In the fall of 1995, he had just concluded a triumphant promotional tour for his hugely successful memoir, *My American Journey*. Large, adoring crowds had greeted him across the country, and his immense popularity seemed to know no limits.

A Powell candidacy would have been Clinton's worst nightmare becoming a reality. A war hero who graduated from West Point with no political baggage or scandals was not who the incumbent's reelection team wanted as their next opponent.

In September, a Gallup Poll measured the favorability ratings for Powell to be higher than for any other potential candidate in the 1996 race. "Running as a Republican in a two-way race against Bill Clinton," the poll said, "Powell handily beats the sitting president, 54% to 39%."

Everything that could go wrong for Clinton most certainly would if Powell were to join the race. He would assuredly lose the African American majority from 1992, which had helped push him over the top in several states. There would be comparisons between Clinton, an alleged draft dodger, and Powell, a career soldier and Vietnam veteran, which was the last thing that the president needed.

The United States had a long line of winning generals from its history who went on to the White House and Clinton didn't want to be evicted by America's newest hero. His team's polling showed that, other than Powell, they should have no problem defeating anyone else from the GOP field and returning to Pennsylvania Avenue for another four years. However, there was nothing for the Democrats to do but sit, wait, and hope.

On November 8, 1995, almost a year to the day before the next election, the incumbent got his answer. At a press conference held in Alexandria, Virginia, the former battlefield commander announced he would not be a candidate. One of the key reasons behind the decision was his wife's concern for his personal safety.

At that point, the election was essentially over as Clinton coasted to an easy victory a year later. He defeated US senator Robert Dole of Kansas, 379–159 in the electoral college. But his team's fear had not been without foundation as a *Voter News Service* poll released a surprising set of results the day after the 1996 election.

The survey included Powell as the Republican nominee, in place of Dole, and the results were astonishing. Using a sampling of 3,697 registered voters (that's about three times the norm), Powell won the election with 50 percent. Clinton was far behind at 38 percent and third party candidate Ross Perot had 9 percent. It proved that the president's apprehensions had been well grounded.

"In one generation," Powell said, "we have moved from denying a black man service at a lunch counter to elevating one to the highest military office in the nation and to being a serious contender for the presidency."

With obvious feeling, he added, "This is a magnificent country, and I am proud to be one of its sons."

22

The Election of 2000

George W. Bush (Republican) vs. Al Gore (Democrat)

"Rarely is the question asked: Is our children learning?"

—Republican candidate George W. Bush at a campaign stop
in Florence, South Carolina, January 11, 2000

In its history, the United States has had a few dynasties. They are nothing compared to older civilizations such as the United Kingdom and China, and most of the more prominent in America have come in business rather than politics, but there have been exceptions.

John Adams became the nation's second president and his son John Quincy later fulfilled the office after capturing the election of 1824. They became the first father and son to hold the country's highest position. In later years, John Quincy's offspring Charles became a prominent leader of the Republican Party.

In 1960, it appeared that the Adams regime would be eclipsed by another Massachusetts family, the Kennedys. Some of its older members had been involved in Boston politics until 1938 when Joe Kennedy Sr. became ambassador to the United Kingdom. It was then that he began putting together a plan where his oldest son would become the first Irish Catholic president.

That dream became a reality in 1960 when his second child John Fitzgerald was elected to the nation's highest office. He appeared to be the first of the family that would make it to the White House as many of the clan with bright futures were already involved in public service. But a series of tragedies and accidents have limited JFK as the only family member to serve as president.

However, when it comes to political power and longevity, the Bushes have made their own mark. It began in 1918 when businessman Samuel Bush of Columbus,

Ohio, was appointed the chief of the Ordnance, Small Arms, and Ammunition Section of the War Industries Board with national responsibility for government assistance to munitions companies during World War I. His son, Prescott Bush, was a US senator for Connecticut from 1952–1963.

Prescott's oldest son was George Herbert Walker Bush, the forty-first president of the United States (1989–1993), who also served as vice president; a US congressman; and director of the CIA. In 1945, he married Barbara Pierce, the fourth cousin, four times removed to Franklin Pierce, the nation's fourteenth president.

Two of their sons were elected governors: George W. in Texas in 1995 and Jeb in Florida in 1999. Jeb Bush's son, George P., was elected commissioner of the Texas General Land Office in 2015.

Since Bill Clinton was completing his second term, it meant that both parties would be searching for new candidates in 2000. Democratic voters who wanted more of what they had in the White House had an opportunity as the sitting vice president Al Gore announced on June 16, 1999, that he would be a candidate for the top job. He had patiently bided his time through Clinton's trials and tribulations including his impeachment and now hoped that any negativity from his former running mate wouldn't spill over onto his own campaign.

Twenty-four years earlier in his first run for Congress, Gore won an overwhelming 94 percent of the vote. His dominance was such that he ran unopposed for his next two House terms. In 1990, when he ran for his second term in the Senate, Gore became the first statewide candidate in Tennessee's history to take all ninety-five counties.

He didn't come from a long lineage of major political power brokers like others had, but there was some history hanging from his family tree. His father, Al Gore Sr. was a US senator for Tennessee from 1953–1971 and was an outspoken proponent of segregation. His son was able to avoid any sins of the father and in 2000 easily cruised to the Democratic nomination.

On the other side, many of the top Republicans were busy saying "no thanks," to the opportunity of running for the big seat in the Oval Office. Among that contingent were Newt Gingrich, former Speaker of the United States House; Jack Kemp, former HUD director and New York congressman; former president George H. W. Bush; Senator Fred Thompson of Tennessee; and Governor Tommy Thompson of Wisconsin.

But there was another Bush who did have an interest in going to Washington, George W. had worked on both of his father's presidential campaigns alongside master strategist Lee Atwater, which gave him the opportunity to learn the inner workings of a candidature. However, the future appeared murky back in 1976, as he was starting his career in the oil business, when the thirty year old Bush was arrested for driving under the influence near his parents' home in Kennebunkport, Maine. He pleaded guilty, paid a $150 fine, and his driving privileges were temporarily suspended in that state.

Four years earlier, in late 1972, Bush took his then-sixteen-year-old brother Marvin out drinking. On the way home, he ran his car over a neighbor's garbage cans.

He later challenged his dad (the future president) to a fist fight, during an argument about his drunk driving.

His turning point came in 1986 when Bush quit drinking after a visit with evangelist Billy Graham and eight years later was elected governor of Texas. He returned to Texas where he defeated the incumbent in 1994 to become the state's governor. Bush won reelection in 1998 with a record 69 percent of the vote becoming the first governor in Texas history to be elected to two consecutive four-year terms.

Senator John McCain of Arizona made a primary run for the GOP but, in the end, Bush easily garnered the nomination. It meant that the candidates of the two major parties for the election of 2000 each had ties to the previous two administrations. It also meant the run of World War II veterans as presidential candidates had come to end with the arrival of the two "baby boomers."

Bush selected former secretary of defense Dick Cheney as his running mate. He had been serving as the head of the campaign's vice presidential search committee. Among the requirements for the candidates (it is said that there were eleven) was to fill out a detailed, eighty-three-questionnaire delving into their backgrounds. But none was ever interviewed as Cheney submitted his own name to Bush who made the final decision. He also never filled out his own query.

In October, Bush and Gore took part in three debates and then charged for the finish line. Interestingly, between the first and third forums, the viewership dropped by about ten million. Gallup's first poll in September had Gore holding a 47 percent to 44 percent, which remained steady through a final survey taken the week prior to the election with Gore holding a 48.2 percent to 48.1 percent advantage. However, no one could have predicted the cavalcade of events that would take place on election day.

Around 7:50 p.m. (eastern time) on November 7, the television networks, who were each trying to be the first to call a winner, declared Gore to be the victor in Florida over Bush before the polls had closed. The Sunshine State was considered to be an important battleground where neither candidate was expected to win by a large margin. However, two hours later, at 9:54 p.m., the networks retracted their claim. Then at 2:17 a.m., several outlets announced that Bush had won Florida, which would have given him the presidency. But that changed at 3:58 a.m. when the networks rescinded their latest declaration.

"We don't just have egg on our face," NBC anchorman Tom Brokaw stated, "we have an omelet."

NBC had been first to declare a winner in Florida on Tuesday, saying Gore had won at 7:50 p.m. Its rivals quickly followed suit, basing their information largely on polling data provided by *Voter News Service (VNS)*, a consortium created by The Associated Press (AP), ABC, CBS, CNN, Fox, and NBC.

"Let's get one thing straight right from the get-go: We would rather be last in reporting returns than be wrong," said anchor Dan Rather of CBS at the outset of coverage. "If we say somebody's carried the state, you can take that to the bank!"

But something went wrong at the election's depository.

When the networks took back the Bush projection at around 4:00 a.m., ABC anchor Peter Jennings confessed on the air that "we're not absolutely sure quite what to do next."

It made for gripping television and created a ratings bonanza as many Americans stayed awake through the night to watch the real-life political drama. Between 2:00 a.m. and 3:00 a.m. (eastern), Nielsen Media Research reported that 22 percent of American homes with TVs had their sets on. The audience for ABC, CBS, and NBC was 225 percent higher than usual at that hour.

Bush supporters in Austin and Gore's backers in Nashville held vigils in the streets, watching big-screens and cheering at the network projections, only to see their coverage close without declaring a final winner.

The comedy of errors triggered a chain of events that had never been seen in an American presidential contest, and over the next month the drama continued to play itself out in courtrooms and television studios across the nation:

November 8: In the early hours, Bush's lead in Florida, where its twenty-five electoral votes were the decisive margin, hinged on just a few hundred individual ballots. Gore called the Texas governor with a concession, but an hour later called again to retract it.

November 9: An incomplete count put Bush's lead at 1,784 votes. Because of the narrow difference, a mandatory machine recount was ordered in all sixty-seven counties.

November 10: The machine recount was completed in all but one county leaving Bush's lead at 327. Democrats then requested a manual recount in Miami-Dade, Broward, Palm Beach, and Volusia counties, where ballots were in dispute. The supervisor of elections in Palm Beach County confirmed that 19,120 votes in that area had been disqualified but did not explain why.

November 11: Palm Beach County announced that it would manually recount all 462,657 ballots cast there. Bush sued in US District Court in Miami to bar the action.

November 12: Volusia County began its recount. Democrats said they would sue the elections supervisor in Seminole County because GOP workers were permitted to correct errors on thousands of applications for absentee ballots of Republicans.

November 13: A federal court refused to stop the manual recounts as Florida election officials announced plans to certify statewide results without counting overseas absentee ballots. The Gore campaign sued to extend the deadline as Florida's secretary of state, Republican Katherine Harris, said she would not extend the deadline of 5:00 p.m. on November 14 for certifying election results.

November 14: With a full machine recount and Volusia County's hand count complete, Bush had a lead of three hundred votes on this deadline day. A state judge upheld the target date but said further recounts could be considered later.

Harris announced that she gave counties until 2:00 p.m. on November 15 to submit written justification for additional time.

November 15: Broward County's canvassing board decided to begin a manual recount of all 587,928 ballots cast there. Harris said that she would not accept results of any hand recounts when it came time to certify the Florida vote on November 18. Miami-Dade had not yet decided on a recount.

November 16: The Florida Supreme Court permitted manual recounts in Palm Beach and Broward counties but left it to a state judge to decide whether Harris must include those votes in the final tally. Hand counts began in Palm Beach County, continued in Broward County, and were considered by Miami-Dade. Gore's legal team filed an emergency motion in state court to prevent Harris from certifying the results until the manual recounts have been completed.

November 17: Judge Terry P. Lewis of the Leon County Circuit Court permitted Harris to certify the election results and declare a winner without hand recounts. But the state Supreme Court placed a hold on that decision until it could consider a Gore appeal. Miami-Dade decided to conduct a recount.

November 18: After the overseas absentee ballots were counted, Bush's lead increased to 930 votes.

November 20: Lawyers for Bush and Gore argued before the Florida Supreme Court on whether hand counts were to be included in the final tally.

November 21: The Florida justices ruled unanimously that hand counts in the three counties must be included and set 5:00 p.m. on November 26 as the earliest time for certification.

November 22: Bush's lawyers appealed to the US Supreme Court arguing that the state court effectively rewrote state election statutes after the vote. Miami-Dade canceled its manual recount saying it didn't not have enough time to complete it by the mandated November 26.

November 23: The state Supreme Court refused Gore's request to require the counting to continue in Miami-Dade.

November 26: Harris declared Bush the winner in Florida by 537 votes.

November 27: Gore sued to contest the election in Florida. The case was assigned to Leon County.

November 28: Judge N. Sanders Sauls of the Leon County Circuit Court rejected Gore's request for an immediate hand recount of disputed ballots from Miami-Dade and Palm Beach counties, saying a hearing was needed first.

November 29: Gore appealed to the Florida Supreme Court asking for the immediate recount of 14,000 disputed ballots. Meanwhile, in an unorthodox ruling, Leon County judge N. Saunders Sauls ordered the questionable ballots, booths, and voting machines to be brought to his courtroom for the upcoming trial.

November 30: The Florida State Legislature attempted to challenge state law in order to name its own presidential electors.

December 1: The US Supreme Court heard arguments on Bush's appeal, which argued that the Florida Supreme Court improperly extended the November

14 deadline for certification. Local Democrats filed suit accusing the Martin County canvassing board of mishandling absentee ballot applications.

December 3: Bush's running mate, Dick Cheney, in televised interviews, urged Gore to concede. He replied that he had given little thought to concession.

December 4: The US Supreme Court ordered the Florida Supreme Court to clarify its ruling on the extended certification date. Sauls rejected Gore's contest.

December 6: Florida's legislative leaders called for a special session to appoint electors pledged to Bush. Gore appealed Sauls's ruling to the Florida Supreme Court.

December 7: The Florida Supreme Court heard arguments on Gore's contest.

December 8: The Florida justices, on a 4–3 vote, ordered an immediate manual recount of all ballots in the state where no vote for president was machine-recorded effecting perhaps as many as forty-five thousand ballots.

December 9: On Bush's appeal, the US Supreme Court halted the manual count pending a hearing.

December 10: Lawyers filed briefs with the US Supreme Court. The Bush team said the manual vote recount violated the US Constitution's guarantee of equal protection, as the Gore team argued that the issue was the importance of counting every vote.

December 11: The US Supreme Court heard arguments.

December 12: The Florida House of Representatives voted to appoint electors for Bush. The US Supreme Court overturned the Florida Supreme Court, ruling 5–4 that there may be no further counting of Florida's disputed presidential votes thus removing the final obstacle for Bush to claim victory.

In his dissent, Justice John Paul Stevens wrote, "Although we may never know with complete certainty the identity of the winner of this year's presidential election, the identity of the loser is perfectly clear. It is the Nation's confidence in the judges as an impartial guardian of the rule of law."

December 13: Gore conceded and Bush, as president-elect, called for reconciliation.

Table 22.1   The Election of 2000

Presidential candidate	Party	Home state	Popular vote Count	Percentage	Electoral vote
George Walker Bush	Republican	Texas	50,456,002	47.87%	271
Albert Arnold Gore Jr.	Democratic	Tennessee	50,999,897	48.38%	266
Ralph Nader	Green	Connecticut	2,882,955	2.74%	0
Pat Buchanan	Reform	Virginia	448,895	0.43%	0
Harry Browne	Libertarian	Tennessee	384,431	0.36%	0
Howard Phillips	Constitution	Virginia	98,020	0.09%	0
John Hagelin	Natural Law	Iowa	83,714	0.08%	0
Other			51,186	0.05%	
(abstention)	—	—	—	—	1
Total			105,421,423	100%	538

Vice President Elect, Richard B. "Dick" Cheney, former Secretary of Defense (R-WY)

While most like to focus on the problems with the vote count in Florida, there was another factor in Al Gore losing the election. When he was defeated in Tennessee, it was the first time that a presidential candidate had failed to win his home state since George McGovern lost his native South Dakota in 1972. Even in the 1984 race, Walter Mondale won just one state, but it was his home turf of Minnesota.

The state race wasn't exactly a nail-biter as George W. Bush won the land of the Volunteers with a 51 percent to 47 percent margin of nearly twenty thousand popular votes. Tennessee's eleven electors would have put Gore at 271 and thereby made him the next president of the United States. Ironically, it was his first-ever defeat on his home soil.

In Florida, Bush won the twenty-five electoral ballots by a margin of only 537 votes out of almost six million cast. But perhaps the Texan anticipated a problem as his campaign raised $13.82 million for recount activities while Gore collected just $3.46 million.

Thousands of potential presidential votes were lost in Florida's most error-prone counties because of confusing ballot designs, inconsistent counting methods, or election officials simply never checking ballots that were rejected by machines.

An examination of 15,596 discarded ballots, examined in a joint project by journalists from *the Orlando Sentinel, the South Florida Sun-Sentinel,* and the *Chicago Tribune,* were identified by elections officials as "overvotes" or "undervotes," meaning counting machines either detected multiple votes for president or no votes at all.

Many ballots were rejected because voters selected Bush or Gore, then also wrote in the candidate's name. Counting machines read those ballots as double votes, and canvassing boards in nine of the fifteen counties either never looked at the ballots or decided not to count them. The review found 962 cases where such a vote for Bush or Gore was not counted. In the other six counties, those votes were counted:

- Some voters used pens instead of pencils on their ballot or made marks that were outside the ovals they were supposed to fill in. Counting machines detected no votes on those ballots, and canvassing boards never examined them. The review found 275 with easily discernible votes that were thrown out.
- When voters tried to erase mistakes on their ballots, counting machines often detected those votes anyway. The review found 239 ballots rejected because machines detected the erased vote and read the ballot as a double vote.
- Some voters made no mistakes on their ballots but they were thrown out anyway because of apparent errors by counting machines. That happened with fourteen absentee ballots in Charlotte County.
- A ballot design that for the first time in Florida listed presidential candidates in two columns may have confused thousands of voters into believing there were two separate races. More than four thousand ballots—representing one-third of all the rejected ballots in those counties—were thrown out because voters selected a candidate in both of the two columns.

- Hundreds of voters cast "anybody but" ballots, 781 casting votes for everyone in the first column but Bush and 197 for everyone but Gore—a 3–1 margin that might have cost Gore up to 584 votes on Election Day. These votes weren't included in the 1,700 clear votes the study identified.
- The ballots examined by the *Sentinel* were discarded for many reasons. But in almost all cases it was because of mistakes made by the voters. Some simply failed to follow instructions. Others took the instructions too literally. While many seemed confused by unnecessarily complicated instructions or the ballot design.

From October 7, 1999 to February 14, 2000, New York City businessman Donald Trump campaigned as a candidate for the Reform Party.

THE AFTERMATH

For television, the key story of that election night were the safeguards that were put into place for future contests in order to prevent a repeat of the debacle of 2000. One of those was for networks not to project a winner until the polls in that state had closed.

For eight years, Bill Clinton and Al Gore put on a public persona of a happy-go-lucky pair of southerners who enjoyed working together to solve the nation's problems. But like other executive branch duos, there were problems hidden from the public.

Sometime between December 12, 2000 and Christmas Day, the two men held a stormy meeting at the White House to air their differences. Gore blamed Clinton's behavior and the impeachment as the main components for his defeat. The two, whose relationship had been difficult since the Lewinsky affair, had their showdown alone inside the mansion, which lasted for more than an hour. A source told the *Washington Post* that the tone of the conversation was "very, very blunt."

One senior Democrat said the tension between the two men, openly friendly at events such as the party convention in Los Angeles "was far worse than anyone knew." Behind the scenes, Clinton had been critical of Gore's campaign organization.

Before he became president, George W. Bush was twice elected governor of Texas. But his political record wasn't all winners as he had lost his first election when he ran for Congress in 1978.

That wasn't the first time that a member of the Bush family was defeated in their initial attempt to gain public office. In 1964, George W.'s father lost his first campaign. It was for a US Senate seat.

His brother Jeb was beaten in his first run for governor of Florida in 1994 before winning back-to-back elections.

George W. Bush and his dad were each elected president so it was no surprise that they inked major book deals after leaving office. But the Bush women have also made their mark in the literary world. Former First Ladies Barbara and Laura Bush each wrote best sellers as did ex-First Daughter Jenna Bush.

At one time, Laura Bush was a school librarian.

As almost everyone knows, John Adams and George H. W. Bush had sons who also served as president. But there are a few other similarities that were repeated between the second and forty-first presidents.

The sons shared their father's first names, were also Ivy League graduates, lost the popular vote but not the electoral contest, and succeeded two-term southern presidents (Monroe and Clinton). Both the Adams and Bush families are descendants of the Mayflower Pilgrims.

THE FOLLOWING ELECTION

On September 8, 2004, the CBS news program *60 Minutes* was scheduled to air an expose on George W. Bush's tour of duty with the National Guard in 1972–1973. The lead-in to the piece, which was produced by Mary Mapes and presented by anchor Dan Rather, said that it would present "documentation" critical of Bush's performance and hints that he received preferential treatment.

The fact that his opponent Senator John Kerry's (D-MA) war record from Vietnam had been put into question made the saga even more compelling. The program garnered big headlines, but as the weeks wore on, it was discovered that CBS had failed to authenticate the documents and experts concluded that they were forgeries. Mapes was fired immediately and Rather's contract was not renewed when it ran out in 2006.

Kerry's apparent big break had turned into a basket of false hope.

On November 2, 2004, the public headed to the polls with the hope that the current election wouldn't turn into a long, drawn-out escapade that had to be decided by the Supreme Court as it had in 2000. Based on the exit polling in various swing states, it appeared for much of the evening that Kerry would become the forty-third president of the United States.

An election exit poll is a survey of voters taken immediately after they have left their polling stations. Unlike an opinion poll, which asks for whom the voter plans to vote, an exit poll seeks to know for whom the voter actually cast their ballot.

Going into the election, a *USA Today/Gallup* Florida preelection poll showed that among likely voters, the challenger had a slight edge over Bush, 50 percent to 47 percent. It was the Sunshine State that had been in the center of the election 2000 controversy, but on the evening of the 2004 vote, reporters at each of the major networks were briefed by pollsters at 7:54 p.m. (eastern) that Kerry had an insurmountable lead and would win in a rout. They predicted that he would capture at least 309 electoral votes to Bush's 174, with 55 too close to call. Against those numbers, the statistical likelihood of Bush winning was less than 1 in 450,000.

However, by 2:00 a.m., there had been a drastic change as the president had built an edge of 121,012 votes in Florida.

But the news wasn't all good for the incumbent. The Republican Party had targeted Pennsylvania during the campaign, and its twenty-one electoral votes, as one of the "blue" states that it could turn "red" as Bush had visited there more than any other state. He had a 50 percent to 46 percent polling edge among likely voters in the Keystone State and appeared to have another positive on the map as he also held a 52 percent to 44 percent advantage in Wisconsin.

But in two stunning upsets, Kerry captured both states by 2.5 percent in Pennsylvania and a narrow .38 percent margin in Wisconsin, which temporarily kept him in the race.

However, Ohio had yet to declare a winner and no Republican had ever been elected president without winning the Buckeye State even though in its final pre-election poll, the survey had Kerry leading 50 percent to 46 percent. Based on exit polls, CNN had predicted that Kerry would defeat Bush in Ohio by a margin of 4.2 percentage points, but in the final tally Bush kept the streak in-tact with a 2 percent victory.

As the results from the south, the southwest, the Midwest, and Rocky Mountain regions rolled in, the final chapter was written. Bush had earned a hard fought 286–251 electoral victory. Had Kerry been able to win either Ohio or Florida, he could've begun making plans to redecorate the Oval Office.

In the end, the usually reliable exit polls had dashed the hopes of the Democratic challenger.

23

The Election of 2008

Barack Obama (Democrat) vs.
John McCain (Republican)

"I've now been in fifty-seven states. One left to go."

—Barack Obama on the campaign trail, May 9, 2008, in Beaverton, Oregon

One of the best things that can happen to a candidate during an election year is when a national crisis takes place. This allows all the entrants an opportunity to tell the voters how the incumbent mishandled events and possibly explain how they would deal with it. Such was the case in 2008.

A major economic recession struck that fall as candidates were crisscrossing the country trying to sway voters in their direction. But this setback wasn't just a blip on the stock market computer screens. The International Monetary Fund (IMF) concluded that it was the most severe economic and financial meltdown since the Great Depression and, by the time it was over, became regarded as the second worst downturn of all time.

While President Bush and his team searched for a way to dig the country out of its financial quagmire, the campaign, which for some had begun two years earlier, was heading into its final weeks. From its beginning, the search for the next commander in chief had taken its fair share of scrutiny.

Heading into the election of 2008, the Democrats and Republicans had one major objective in common, they were both looking for the person who would assume the leadership role of their respective parties. For the GOP, Bush was going to be term-limited out of office so a new face would be needed atop their ranks. One year before the election, on November 21, 2007, a *Zogby* Poll showed that among Republicans, former New York City mayor Rudy Giuliani had expanded his national lead over his second-place rival Fred Thompson, a former US senator and Hollywood actor, as many voters had just begun to focus on the race for the White House.

Giuliani had gained worldwide attention for his handling of his city's crisis during the 9/11 attacks and its recovery. A hard-liner against terrorism, he had originally gained fame as a prosecutor in the 1980s putting away members of some of New York's most notorious crime families.

In that poll, Giuliani had widened his lead over Thompson to fourteen points, 29 percent to 15 percent, compared to the previous month's 28 percent to 20 percent margin. Former Arkansas governor Mike Huckabee jumped over former Massachusetts governor Mitt Romney into third place. Huckabee had 11 percent, with Romney and Arizona senator John McCain at 9 percent.

On the Democratic side, US senator Hillary Rodham Clinton of New York led Senate colleague Barack Obama of Illinois 38 percent to 27 percent in the new poll representing a ten-point fall from October. The drop followed a month of attacks on the former First Lady from her rivals and a heavily criticized performance in a late-October party debate. Former senator John Edwards of North Carolina was in third place, climbing four points to 13 percent. All other Democratic contenders scored in low single digits, including New Mexico governor Bill Richardson at 4 percent. In a *CBS News* poll of January 2007, 40 percent of Democratic voters surveyed said that they didn't know much about Senator Obama.

But just eight years earlier, as an Illinois state senator, it appeared that any opportunity for the eager candidate to move into the national spotlight might be over before it began. He was born in Hawaii in 1961 and graduated from Columbia University and Harvard Law School. Obama was the first African American to serve as president of the school's prestigious *Law Review*. That was followed by a move to Chicago where he worked as a community organizer and taught classes at the University of Chicago Law School. His father, who died in 1982, was a native of Kenya.

In 1996, he entered the political arena by running for the state senate from Illinois' 13th District. But Obama wasn't the first choice among local Democratic party leaders who wanted someone with name recognition and sought out Jesse Jackson Jr. as their candidate. However, the son of the well-known civil rights spokesman and former presidential candidate, decided to pursue a seat in the US House of Representatives, which provided an opening for the eager law schoolteacher who was waiting in the wings.

Jackson won his race capturing an impressive 76 percent of the vote on his way to his new job in the nation's capital. Meanwhile, luck was on the side of Obama as there were problems with incumbent Alice Palmer's paperwork, which meant that the newcomer would run unopposed in the Democratic primary. A few months after Jackson's resounding victory, Obama took the District 13 state seat by a staggering 82 percent.

In 1998, he was easily reelected and then two years later decided to make his own run for the US House in another district. But his opponent in the 1st District wasn't a newcomer to the rigors of hardball politics. Bobby Rush was a longtime and well-known figure in Chicago. He was the cofounder of the Illinois chapter of the Black Panther Party; a former city alderman; and had already been elected by landslide margins to four terms in Congress. He was also the incumbent for that district.

When Obama challenged Rush, the political veteran easily disposed of the thirty-eight-year-old state official in the primary election, 61 percent to 30 percent. He went on to win another term and, as of 2020, continued to work from his familiar congressional seat in the nation's capital. In an interview a few years after that initial encounter, Rush reflected on his former opponent, "He was blinded by his ambition. Obama believes in Obama. And, frankly, that has its good side but it also has its negative side."

The loss was a bitter pill to swallow for the former Ivy Leaguer who said, "Less than halfway into the campaign, I knew in my bones that I was going to lose. Each morning from that point forward I awoke with a vague sense of dread, realizing that I would have to spend the day smiling and shaking hands and pretending that everything was going according to plan."

When that objective crumbled, some believed that any possibility of Barack Obama ascending to the national level of the political scene might also be gone. In 2002, he was reelected unopposed to his state Senate seat where it was beginning to appear that he might remain for the rest of his career. However, that possibility was altered with one decision.

On April 15, 2003, incumbent Republican US senator Peter Fitzgerald announced that he would not be seeking reelection in 2004. The move was unusual because in 1998 he spent $13 million of his own money to help finance his campaign and was departing the Senate after serving just one term while gaining a reputation of trending away from the standard party line.

With Fitzgerald out of the picture, wealthy businessman Jack Ryan captured the GOP. nomination while Obama became the Democrats' choice. In May 2004, a *Chicago Sun Times* poll had Obama leading the race, 48 percent-40 percent. With more than six months to go before the election, the Republican appeared to be in striking distance.

That was until the facts of his 1999 divorce from his wife, actress Jeri Ryan, was made public during the campaign. It was a messy split and when it was over, both parties asked the Los Angeles District Court to seal the file for the protection of their five year old son. The request was granted but five years later the *Chicago Tribune* and local television station *WLS-TV* petitioned the court to release the documents. On June 22, 2004, the files were made available to the public.

As the details of the divorce had Jack Ryan's aspiring political career going down like the *Hindenburg*, Barack Obama was making his big move for the US Senate. On the evening of July 27, the Illinois legislator gave the keynote address at the Democratic National Convention being held in Boston. Even though the speech was slated for just eight minutes, Obama took advantage of the free television exposure and stretched his remarks to more than double the time. The following day, he received glowing reports in the media to the point where he had replaced the party's presidential nominee John Kerry as the star of the convention.

Two days after the speech, amid scandal from the released divorce documents and the positive publicity from Obama's prime time national television appearance, Ryan withdrew from the race. Former United Nations ambassador Alan Keyes was tabbed as the GOP's substitute candidate but he was unable to curb Obama's momentum and lost in a landslide, 70 percent to 27 percent.

Once he was sworn into the Senate on January 4, 2005, Obama's political ambitions accelerated to the fast track. On Sunday, October 22, 2006, he mentioned that he was considering running for president during a segment of the television program, *Meet the Press*. By January 2007, he revealed that he had formed an exploratory committee and on February 10, the junior senator made the formal announcement of his intention to run for the White House. At the time, he had served just slightly more than one-third of his only term in Congress and had gone from a little known Illinois state senator to presidential candidate in a matter of months.

Most of the action for the nomination on the Democratic side featured a battle between Obama, Hillary Clinton, and former North Carolina senator John Edwards who left the race in January 2008 and eventually endorsed Obama. Clinton had the advantage of having her husband, the former president as her chief fundraiser, and he didn't mince words when it came to her opponent. "Obama doesn't know how to be president," Bill Clinton told friends and political advisers in 2007. "He doesn't know how the world works."

However, in every election that she and her husband had won during their careers, they had both been dependent on support from African American voters who had always backed them. But that lifeline wasn't available in 2008 as most of the black vote went for Obama.

On June 7, with her backing dwindling and the campaign deep in debt, the New York senator withdrew from the race and supported Obama. In return, over the next few years the nominee helped retire Clinton's estimated $22 million campaign debt. He also selected Joe Biden, the longtime US senator from Delaware as his running mate.

While Giuliani was the toast of the Republicans in November 2007, his time as the top choice didn't last long as three months later, in January, his numbers dropped, and he was out of the race. In the opening weeks of 2008, others joined the one-time New York mayor on the sidelines while the McCain campaign surged past the other contenders. On March 4, 2008, the former POW from the Vietnam conflict had secured his party's nomination.

McCain's story was well-known as the one-time military pilot was shot down in 1967 and held by the Viet Cong as a captive for five and a half years as he was constantly tortured. Following his release in 1973, the former naval captain was elected to the US Senate from Arizona in 1987 after serving five years in the House. He had run for the Republican presidential nomination in 2000 but lost to George W. Bush.

McCain bypassed several better known candidates and raised more than a few eyebrows with his choice of the forty-four-year-old governor of Alaska Sarah Palin as his vice presidential running mate. She became the first women to ever be tabbed for the position by the Republicans. However, Obama won in an electoral landslide 365–173. The turnout of 131,304,731 for the presidency was the most in history and accounted for 61.6 percent of eligible voters.

Table 23.1   The Election of 2008

Presidential candidate	Party	Home state	Popular vote Count	Percentage	Electoral vote
Barack Hussein Obama II	Democratic	Illinois	69,498,516	52.93%	365
John Sidney McCain	Republican	Arizona	59,948,323	45.65%	173
Ralph Nader	Independent	Connecticut	739,034	0.56%	0
Bob Barr	Libertarian	Georgia	523,715	0.40%	0
Chuck Baldwin	Constitution	Florida	199,750	0.15%	0
Cynthia McKinney	Green	Georgia	161,797	0.12%	0
Alan Keyes	America's Independent Party	New York	47,941	0.04%	0
Other			242,685	0.18%	—
Total			131,313,820	100%	538
Needed to win					270

Vice President Elect, Joseph R. "Joe" Biden, former US Senator (D-DE)

Two of the presidential candidates in 2008 were Democrat Hillary Clinton and Republican Fred Thompson. The duo had served in the United States Senate together from 2001 to 2003 but that wasn't the first time that their paths had crossed.

More than thirty years earlier, in 1973, Thompson was appointed as counsel to assist the Republicans on the Senate Watergate Committee, a special body convened by the US Senate to investigate the Watergate scandal. Thompson is sometimes credited for supplying Republican senator Howard Baker's famous question, "What did the President [Richard Nixon] know, and when did he know it?"

During 1974, Clinton was a member of the impeachment inquiry staff advising the House Committee on the judiciary during Watergate. She helped research procedures of impeachment and the historical grounds and standards. Both were unsuccessful in securing the nominations of their respective parties in 2008.

The collapse of the country's fourth largest investment bank, Lehman Brothers, took place on September 15, 2008. On that day, Republican candidate John McCain declared that "the fundamentals of our economy are strong." With a mere seven weeks until Election Day, it was obviously the wrong thing to say the wrong time.

THE AFTERMATH

When Obama won the presidency in 2008, he continued a pattern from the three chief executives who had preceded him. George H. W. Bush, Bill Clinton, and George W. Bush along with Obama had each lost elections before reaching the nation's highest office.

In 1970, George H. W. Bush, who was a US congressman at the time, ran for the US Senate seat from Texas but was soundly defeated by fellow congressman Lloyd Bentsen. His son George W. ran for the House of Representatives from Texas' 19th District in 1978 but lost by 6 percent of the vote. In 1980, just two years after being elected the nation's youngest governor, Clinton was defeated in his reelection bid in Arkansas. With Obama's loss for the congressional seat in 2000, he became the latest president who had experienced the agony of defeat but, in every case, it was the last political election lost by each man before gaining the White House.

In 2008, former Massachusetts governor and successful businessman Mitt Romney was a Republican candidate for president. In 1968, his father George Romney, a former governor (Michigan) and successful businessman, was a Republican candidate for president. Neither of them won their party's nomination but Mitt became the GOP's top pick four years later.

Barack Obama's father was born in Kenya, but he isn't the first US president with a parent born outside the country. Six other chief executives had at least one foreign-born parent. Andrew Jackson (1829–1837) is the only president born of two immigrants, both Irish. Those with one immigrant parent include Thomas Jefferson (1801–1809) and Woodrow Wilson (1913–1921)), whose mothers were born in England; James Buchanan (1857–1861) and Chester Arthur (1881–1885), both of whom had Irish fathers; and Herbert Hoover (1929–1933) whose mother was Canadian.

Obama was the first president of a foreign-born parent to be elected in eighty years. He was also the first to have a parent who was born in Africa.

24

The Election of 2012

Barack Obama, Incumbent (Democrat) vs. Mitt Romney (Republican)

"We are not going back to a set of policies that say you're on your own and that's essentially the theory of the other side. You know, George Romney."

—From a campaign speech given by President Obama at the New Amsterdam Theater in New York City's Times Square on June 5, 2012. He was referring to his opponent Mitt Romney but mistakenly called him "George," Mitt's father who had run for the office in 1968.

It is said that in an election the incumbent always has the advantage, but in 2012 it appeared that Barack Obama was destined to join the short list of one term presidents. To sum it up, his first stint in the Oval Office hadn't gone well:

- The national debt increased by almost $6 trillion, which was the most for any president in a single term.
- Unemployment grew from 6.8 percent to 7.8 percent and in October 2009 it hit a staggering 10.2 percent. The worst in twenty-six years.
- His signature program, the Affordable Care Act (*Obamacare*), which was created to provide health insurance at reasonable rates to all Americans, was unpopular with a large portion of the public.
- Just two months before the election, a US ambassador and two former Navy SEALS were murdered in Benghazi, Libya. That action touched off accusations against the White House and the State Department of ignoring a situation that had become out of control.
- The price of gasoline had doubled since he had taken office.
- In 2009, Obama signed the $825 billion stimulus bill into law. A large part of it was earmarked for repair of the nation's infrastructure but after three years

the program that was expected to create thousands of jobs was rampant with broken promises and massive debt forcing the president to concede, "Shovel-ready (jobs) was not as shovel-ready as we expected."

• There had been a 122 percent increase in food stamp spending to $89 billion along with a ten million person increase in the number of individuals receiving welfare to 107 million, which worked out to more than one-third of the US population.

With all of those factors going against him, it appeared that the incumbent had no chance of retaining office. Although, unbelievably, he won!

In 2012, the candidates for president were the sitting president Obama (D) and the former governor of Massachusetts Mitt Romney (R). One of the campaign's major issues was the *Affordable Care Act*, which was passed by Congress and signed into law in 2010. It gave the government more control over the type and cost of health insurance. However, the challenger had a difficult time arguing against the measure as his state had adopted a similar program in 2006 which was recognized as "*Romneycare.*"

When it was over, the campaign analysts went to work trying to figure out why Obama was victorious with so many factors against him, which broke down to two crucial reasons. First, his campaign team headed by David Axelrod simply outworked their opponents. They got out the vote in key demographic areas that they had targeted and captured important swing states like Ohio, Virginia, and Florida. But there was another critical item for Obama's reelection. While the pundits filled the airways with chatter and speculation, Mother Nature was preparing to cast the most decisive vote of the race.

On October 22, tropical storm Sandy started to brew off the coast of Nicaragua. It began with meager winds of about forty miles per hour. Two days later, it had become a full-fledged Category 1 hurricane crossing the Caribbean as its gusts had doubled to eighty miles per hour. The storm struck many islands including Haiti, where residents were still trying to recover from a massive earthquake that had leveled much of the country two years earlier. As the hurricane passed, more than fifty people died on the impoverished island due to flooding and mudslides.

Hurricane Sandy moved from Jamaica to Cuba on October 26 with winds reaching 110 miles per hour. There was further destruction as it crossed the Bahamas on its trek toward the United States. By the twenty-eighth, powerful waves were crashing onto North Carolina's Outer Banks, washing out portions of the state's Highway 12, and continuing on a northward path.

At 8:00 p.m. on October 29, one week prior to the election, Sandy's center came ashore near Atlantic City, New Jersey. The storm was no longer considered a hurricane but was still producing strong winds and powerful tides. To make matters worse, the surge was intensified by the full moon. This effect takes place when the sun, earth, and moon are grouped in a straight line, intensifying their gravitational effects on the planet.

President Barack Obama (center) and FEMA Administrator Craig Fugate (right) greet New Jersey Governor Chris Christie (left) on the tarmac of the Atlantic City (NJ) International Airport on October 31, 2012, where they were going to inspect damage caused by Hurricane Sandy. The photo set off a fury among members of the Republican Party. Credit: Official White House Photo by Chuck Kennedy

It was this force of nature that punished the Jersey Shore and its neighbor New York City. Subway tunnels were flooded in addition to streets in Lower Manhattan and Brooklyn. Numerous other areas in the tri-state region were pummeled as Sandy completed its trail of ruin. Among the locations was the community of Hempstead, New York, where Obama and Romney had held one of their debates on October 16.

Meanwhile, in the media, the week-long weather event had pushed the selection of the nation's next commander in chief to the back burner. Potential voters were more concerned about contributing goods and money for hurricane relief as opposed to listening to another political speech. Due to the storm, both campaigns pulled back their appearances and early voting was disrupted at some of the precincts.

On October 29, both camps chose to suspend their campaigns in the wake of the situation with the storm. It was just the break that Obama needed as, on that day Romney was up 5 points, 51 percent to 46 percent among likely voters in *Gallup's Daily Tracking Poll.*

With time running down to the election and a temporary truce, Romney literally disappeared from the national stage. Such was not the case for President Obama who, as the nation's leader, was expected to visit the storm damaged areas and was followed by a swarm of media as he toured the ravaged sites. The Obama campaign didn't have to follow any preconceived plan, they simply sent the candidate to places where the devastation was the worst. It had been proven by his predecessors in previous disasters that those types of images tended to stick in the minds of the public.

It was as if they were following the advice of Obama's former chief of staff, Rahm Emanuel, who once stated, "You never want a serious crisis to go to waste." As election day neared and Obama continued to be seen with hurricane victims, the daily poll numbers were shifting away from the challenger.

The biggest impact came on October 31 when a photo of New Jersey governor Chris Christie (R) greeting Obama on the tarmac at the Atlantic City airport with a warm handshake and a smile went viral. Many of the GOP faithful were upset with Christie who was also vice chairman of the Republican Governors Association and one of the party's most high-profile office holders.

The governor took the president on a tour of New Jersey's hardest hit areas, which received widespread news coverage. When he was asked later about the assistance that the state received from Washington, DC, Christie remarked, "The federal government's response has been great. . . . The president has been outstanding in this and so have the folks at FEMA [the Federal Emergency Management Agency]."

The comments didn't set well with many inside the Republican Party who believed that the Garden State's top official had given the opposition an unofficial, but pronounced, endorsement. "So all this other noise, I think, is coming from know-nothing, disgruntled Romney staffers who, you know, don't like the fact that I said nice things about the president of the United States," stated Christie, who was never shy about sharing his opinion on any matter. "Well, that's too bad for them."

On Sunday, November 4, just forty-eight hours before the election and with the campaign back in full swing, Romney made an attempt at damage control from *Sandy's* press coverage as he asked Christie to attend his last major rally, which was being held in eastern Pennsylvania, just a few minutes away from Trenton (New Jersey's state capital). But in a surprising response, the governor turned down the invitation citing that he did not want to risk his state's opportunity for additional federal disaster money.

Nonetheless, the challenger's outlook appeared solid as the rally in Bucks County drew thirty thousand spectators. Additionally, in the final *Gallup Poll* taken the day before the election, Romney clung to a 50 percent to 49 percent lead over Obama, whose approval rating was at 50 percent.

In the United States, whether it's sports or politics, many times the evaluation doesn't center around how the victor won but how the defeated lost. Such was the case with the election of 2012. Little was made of the fact that Romney had lost four key states (New Hampshire, Florida, Ohio, and Virginia) by a combined total of only 333,908 popular votes. Had the contest gone the other way in those four states, the sixty-four electoral votes that they provided would have been the margin of victory for the GOP candidate.

Perhaps more important was the lack of success by Team Romney as about three million Republicans who voted in 2008 didn't participate in 2012. That year the spotlight was on just ten states: Colorado, Florida, Iowa, Nevada, New Hampshire, North Carolina, Pennsylvania, Ohio, Virginia, and Wisconsin.

Sometimes the numbers don't tell the entire story. As an example, despite losing the popular vote 51 percent to 48 percent—this contest was much closer than the final tally indicated. The final electoral college count gave President Obama a wide 332 to 206 margin over the challenger. A total of 270 electoral votes were needed to win the presidency. But a closer look shows that the final outcome actually hinged on just those four states:

- Romney lost New Hampshire's four electoral college votes by a margin of only 40,659.
- Romney lost Florida's twenty-nine electors by just 73,858. A swing of one county could have made the difference.
- Romney lost Ohio's eighteen electoral votes by a margin of 103,481. Once again, one county could have provided victory for the other candidate.
- Romney lost Virginia's thirteen electors' ballots by only 115,910 popular ballots.
- By adding the sixty-four electoral college votes from these four key states to Romney's 206, remove them from Obama's 332, and the challenger would have defeated Obama 270 to 268. But in the real world of hardball politics, the incumbent was reelected.

However, most of the conversation centered around Hurricane Sandy and such topics as President Obama's attentiveness to the needs of those who had been affected, which had been highlighted in the media. Additional analysis was how the superstorm played havoc with voters in areas where the damage was at its worst. In the end, 233 people lost their lives in the storm that left more than $75 billion of damage in its wake.

For those who worked on the opposing campaign and wondered how much impact Sandy had on the outcome, they didn't have to wait for an answer. In exit polls taken by CBS on election night, 26 percent of those polled said Obama's response was an important factor, while 15 percent—about one in six voters—stated that it was the most important factor in their final choice.

Obama became the first president to be reelected since 1940 with an unemployment rate that was higher than 8 percent. In that year, Franklin Roosevelt won a third term even though 14.6 percent of the nation was out of work. President Obama entered the 2012 election year with a job approval rating that was dangerously low (roughly 40 percent) and an unemployment rate that was risky (more than 8 percent). Those were threatening numbers for an incumbent seeking reelection.

Obama became the first president to be reelected to the office with less votes than he was first elected since every state moved to deciding electors

Overall, voter turnout was down, from 131 million in 2008 to 122 million in 2012. Obama won 7.6 million fewer votes than he did in 2008, and Romney won 1.3 million fewer than McCain in that same election.

Although their reasons may have differed, undoubtedly both sides could only wonder what might have been if Sandy had headed into the Atlantic before striking the East Coast. That would be a question for another election cycle.

Table 24.1   The Election of 2012

Presidential candidate	Party	Home state	Popular vote Count	Percentage	Electoral vote
Barack Hussein Obama II	Democratic	Illinois	65,915,795	51.06%	332
Willard Mitt Romney	Republican	Massachusetts	60,933,504	47.20%	206
Gary Johnson	Libertarian	New Mexico	1,275,971	0.99%	0
Jill Stein	Green	Massachusetts	469,627	0.36%	0
Virgil Goode	Constitution	Virginia	122,389	0.09%	0
Roseanne Barr	Peace and Freedom	Hawaii	67,326	0.05%	0
Rocky Anderson	Justice	Utah	43,018	0.03%	0
Tom Hoefling	America's	Iowa	40,628	0.03%	0
Andre Barnett	Reform	New York	956	<0.01%	0
Other			216,196	0.19%	
Total			129,085,410	100%	538
Needed to win					270

Vice President Elect, Joe Biden, incumbent

One of the more important factors for the lack of success by Team Romney was about three million Republicans, who voted in 2008, didn't participate in 2012.

THE AFTERMATH

The election set the latest record for presidential campaign expenditures as the two candidates combined spent a total of $2.23 billion! One can expect those numbers to go up in future elections.

In May 2017, Barack and Michelle Obama signed a joint book deal for $65 million. It was the highest advance in the nation's history for a former president and spouse.

On November 6, 2018, Mitt Romney was elected to the open US Senate seat in Utah. He had interviewed with President-elect Trump for a cabinet post two years earlier but was never offered the position.

25

The Election of 2016

Hillary Rodham Clinton (Democrat) vs. Donald J. Trump (Republican)

"You ought to be ashamed of yourself."

—Donald Trump (R-NY) to his opponent Hillary Clinton (D-NY)
during their debate in St. Louis on October 9, 2016

By 2016, most television networks were carrying some type of "reality" programming. These are shows disguised to look at individuals, some famous, others not, living their daily lives without a script. However, most of them are about as real as professional wrestling matches even though they do produce big money for the broadcasting companies.

One of the most watched encounters that year was a true, no-holds-barred, daily row between two wealthy senior citizens who were Ivy League graduates that didn't bother to hide their disdain for one another. In addition to those barrages, the duo lit up the screens during three prime-time specials that fall season where they continued to verbally whiplash one another in face-to-face settings. While the viewer ratings were high, so were the pair's individual unpopularity scores.

In short, audiences loved to hate both of them.

The combatants in that year's biggest reality show were the two major presidential candidates, Democrat Hillary Rodham Clinton and Donald J. Trump, the Republican. As soon as they were established as their party's contenders, a war of words, that included accusations of misdeeds and personal insults, ensued driving their followers to take a hard stand with their support. So much so that the bad feelings on both sides didn't end on election night.

Like so many other candidates, Clinton was no stranger to the political arena but she began her quest from the other side of the fence as a teen, and during her early years of college she was a proud "*Goldwater Girl*" who donned a wild west outfit and straw cowboy hat in support of the GOP's nominee Arizona senator Barry Goldwater, the iconic conservative who converted Ronald Reagan, among others, from the left. She was just sixteen years old when he headed the 1964 Republican ticket.

However, by the time Hillary delivered the commencement address at Wellesley College some five years later, she had made a full liberal conversion stating, "Every protest, every dissent, whether it's an individual academic paper or Founder's parking lot demonstration, is unabashedly an attempt to forge an identity in this particular age."

An avowed feminist, she had shared the spotlight with her husband Bill ever since he served his first term as governor of Arkansas beginning in 1979. She was also the family's breadwinner because even though he had been elected to the state's highest office, and would subsequently be reelected three more times, his yearly salary was only $35,000. Meanwhile, Hillary was earning $92,000 annually as a senior partner at the Rose Law Firm of Little Rock, along with additional profit-sharing and retirement plans totaling between $100,001 and $250,000.

On Sunday, January 26, 1992, the Washington Redskins defeated the Buffalo Bills, 37–24, in Super Bowl XXVI. CBS, which had broadcast the game and wishing to hold as much of the audience as possible, had an in-depth interview scheduled with the Clintons as their lead story on the *60 Minutes* news program, which followed the contest. Bill had announced his candidacy three months earlier, but it was Hillary who made her national debut to many of the viewers.

Rumors of the governor's womanizing were well-known, especially in his home state, and since he had become a candidate for national office the stories were beginning to spread. Four years earlier, Team Clinton had watched fellow Democrat and presidential frontrunner Gary Hart's campaign disintegrate when he was caught romancing someone who wasn't his wife of twenty-nine years and they were determined not to make the same mistake.

When interviewer Steve Kroft broached the topic, Hillary immediately grabbed the bull by the horns and quipped, "You know, I'm not sitting here, some little woman standing by my man like Tammy Wynette. I'm sitting here because I love him, and I respect him, and I honor what he's been through and what we've been through together. And you know, if that's not enough for people, then heck—don't vote for him." Her reference was to Wynette's 1968 country music mega-hit *Stand By Your Man*.

The message was loud and clear that the marriage might be unconventional in terms of tradition but from a political standpoint, the partnership was iron clad. She realized that her own aspirations were unequivocally hitched to his wagon. When her husband won the White House, Hillary used his two terms to lay the groundwork for her own future political career.

In eight years as the nation's First Lady, she provided support for the State Children's Health Insurance Program (1997) that provided federal support to states with children whose parents could not provide health coverage for them. She helped create the Office on Violence Against Women at the Department of Justice and traveled to seventy-nine countries during that period, more than any other presidential spouse.

On November 23, 1999, with just slightly more than a year left in Bill's presidency, Hillary announced her candidacy for the upcoming Senate seat held by the retiring Daniel Patrick Moynihan, which had also been occupied in the 1960s by Robert Kennedy. Earlier that same week, Mrs. Clinton and her husband closed the sale on a $1.7 million home in Westchester County. In 1964, Kennedy also had to move, from Virginia to New York, to meet the state's residence requirements in order to run for office.

Clinton won the election with 55 percent of the vote, becoming the only woman to serve in an elected office while (and after) serving as First Lady. Following the 9/11 attacks, she supported military action in Afghanistan and voted in favor of the October 2002 Iraq War Resolution, which authorized the use of military force against the Saddam Hussein regime. Clinton was reelected in 2006 with an overwhelming 67 percent of the vote while spending $36 million on her campaign, more than any other Senate candidate that year. Among her donors to both campaigns was New York businessman Donald Trump who contributed more than $4000.

On January 21, 2007, Hillary posted a video on her website with the simple phrase, "I'm in," to announce her run to become the nation's first woman president. Less than a week earlier, her Senate colleague Barack Obama of Illinois proclaimed his intention to file the paperwork to make his candidacy official. Once again, Trump was a financial contributor to Clinton's latest campaign.

At the outset, Hillary held a 20-point lead over Obama but by February 13, 2008, the race was a dead heat in the *Real Clear Politics* poll. That month, the Clinton campaign hit a roadblock when the opposition won thirteen of twenty-three states and territories in primaries that were contested on Super Tuesday (February 5) marking the beginning of the end for the New York resident. On June 7, a disappointed Clinton pulled the plug on her campaign and endorsed Obama.

The former candidate returned to the Senate and in 2010, the Clintons' daughter, Chelsea, married business executive Marc Mezvinsky. Among the "A-List'" celebrities who were among the invited guests attending the nuptials was Donald Trump. Five years earlier, the Clintons had attended the businessman's wedding to his third wife, Melania, in 2005 at his Palm Beach estate.

Following Obama's election, the new president helped retire Clinton's campaign debt and appointed her secretary of state. She left the post in 2013 with immediate speculation that she would run for president again. The wait was short as the former cabinet member made her announcement on April 12, 2015.

Two months later, as Hillary hit the campaign trail, Trump arrived in the lobby of the sixty-eight-story New York City venue that carries his name to announce that he was the twelfth candidate to join the ever-growing Republican field. He wouldn't be the last as four more prospects would eventually complete the roster. For the real estate magnate, there was nowhere to go but up as the CNN poll had him tied for tenth place with 3 percent and at 4 percent in the *Fox News* and *Washington Post/ABC News* polls—coming in tenth and tied for ninth, respectively.

As opposed to Clinton, who was a native of Chicago, Trump was born and bred in New York. For college, he didn't stray far from home as in 1964 the freshman started out at Fordham University in the Bronx for his first two years.

But feeling that he needed an Ivy League degree to make the necessary connections in the business world, in 1966, Trump transferred to the prestigious Wharton School of Business at the University of Pennsylvania. He was not the most dedicated of students but brought a broad knowledge of his specialty—real estate—to the institution. A former classmate, Edward M. Sachs Jr. recalled, "He was a real estate expert. . . . I was very amazed with his command of the subject and his interest in it. He knew the history of high-rise developers like a textbook."

However, it wasn't all work and no play for the future leader of the free world. During his college years he once went on a blind date with actress Candice Bergen who was also attending Penn at the time. Apparently, the date had little impact on the aspiring performer, as she supported Hillary Rodham Clinton in the 2016 election.

Trump's political affiliations resemble those of someone sampling all the goods from the kitchen shelf. He has belonged to several parties and nonorganizations over the decades leading to his White House run. His long and winding road map to Washington, DC, began when he was originally a Democrat until 1987; then a Republican from 1987 to 1999; became a member of the Reform Party from 1999 to 2001; returned to the Democratic Party from 2001 to 2009; switched back to the Republican Party again from 2009 to 2011; was an independent from 2011 to 2012; and went back to the Republicans in 2012.

It wasn't the first time that a potential chief executive had changed teams as another well-known celebrity went from the Democratic Party to the Republicans before Trump arrived on the scene—Ronald Reagan.

Prior to his ascension as a contender to the world's most powerful job, for fourteen seasons Trump was the host of the highly rated reality television program *The Apprentice* on NBC. In 2015, the network announced that the show had been renewed, but shortly afterward Trump informed the world that he wouldn't be returning because he was running for president.

His role on the program had earned him Emmy Award nominations in 2004 and 2005 making him the only president to be suggested for that distinction. It was reported that during the show's run, he had earned $214 million.

Before taking on Clinton, Trump had to wade through the fifteen other candidates in the field of his party, which he did one by one. But there was one prospect for whom the campaign became personal.

In June 2015, former Florida governor Jeb Bush, the son of the forty-first president and the brother of the forty-third, entered the race as the odds-on favorite to gain the Republican nod. An *NBC/Wall Street Journal* poll taken at the time gave Bush a 5-point lead over the others in the field including Trump who checked in at eleventh place with just 1 percent of those surveyed choosing him.

However, a battle of words that had been simmering for years accelerated to a full boil that summer. It began in 2013 when Trump wrote, "We need another Bush in office about as much as we need Obama to have a third term. No more Bushes!"

He relentlessly used his well-known tag line to attack the other candidates throughout the GOP primary battle and later onto Clinton branding his opponents as "low energy."

Family members verbally retaliated with former First Lady Barbara Bush saying, "I'm sick of him." During one of the GOP debates, Jeb Bush told the moderator, "I am sick and tired of him going after my family." But the end came for the man who had hoped to follow his father and brother to the Oval Office as, clearly defeated, he dropped out of the race on February 20, 2016, having spent a record $150 million but could only secure three delegates.

There was no drama at either convention as the nominations had been wrapped up weeks earlier. Voters were turning their focus toward the upcoming debates: September 26 in Hempstead, New York; October 9 in St. Louis; and October 19 in Paradise, Nevada.

The three face-offs were like viewing scenes from a bad marriage as Americans watched the two candidates carve each other up like holiday turkeys. Polls showed that neither of them delivered a knockout punch like Jimmy Carter had in 1976 but they did give Clinton a slight edge on content. However, the ratings set television records for presidential debates proving that many viewers still enjoyed watching their candidates scrap and hurl barbs at each other.

The last nine days of the campaign were as good for Trump as they were bad for Clinton. He made thirty-two stops including six in Florida; five each in North Carolina and Pennsylvania; along with four in Michigan. The polls in each of the swing states were razor thin with the Republican appearing at his final rally at 1:00 a.m. on Election Day in Gerald Ford's hometown of Grand Rapids, Michigan.

Hillary made it to eighteen states but there had been questions about her health for weeks. She fainted while departing a ceremony in New York honoring the fifteenth anniversary of the September 11 attacks and had to be helped into a van by her Secret Service detail. Her doctor said that she was suffering from pneumonia and dehydration but Trump wasted little time making it an issue announcing at a rally where he crowed, "But here's a woman, she's supposed to fight all of these different things and she can't even make it fifteen feet to her car. Give me a break. Give me a break."

The public's dissatisfaction with both candidates was shown in the *Gallup Poll's* final tally before the election. Trump's 61 percent unfavorable score was the worst in presidential polling history while Clinton's 52 percent negative mark rated second-worst. The third worst score was Barry Goldwater's 47 percent in 1964.

The website *Real Clear Politics* tracked ten major polls in which nine of them had Clinton leading by 1 to 6 points in the final week of the campaign. The *Los Angeles Times/USC Tracking Poll* was the only one that had Trump as the leader (by 3 points).

When the precincts started closing on Election Day, it was the start of an unimaginable nightmare for Clinton and her followers.

THE ELECTION TIMELINE (ALL TIMES EASTERN)

10:00 p.m. Most of the polling places around the country had closed as voting continued in the western United States where Clinton was expected to garner large numbers. Trump held a 140–104 lead with no major surprises or upsets. At that juncture, he needed 130 electoral votes to win.

10:21 p.m. An important pick up for Trump as he captured Ohio and its eighteen critical votes. It was the first swing state to be declared for the Republicans. He had led in the polls as voters in the Buckeye State hoped to continue their streak of correctly picking every US president since 1964.

11:07 p.m. Trump won North Carolina, dealing a crucial blow to Clinton, who had showed well in polling there. The battleground state had voted Democrat in 2008 and Republican in 2012. The Clinton camp was now in serious trouble and turned its attention on claiming gains from the reliable blue state trio of Pennsylvania, Michigan, and Wisconsin.

11:30 p.m. Trump's path to the White House became a lot clearer as Clinton's became exceedingly more difficult when he won the key battleground state of Florida with its twenty-nine electoral votes. He owned a home and was a part-time resident there. It also guaranteed that there wouldn't be a repeat of the election 2000 "Florida Fiasco."

After Florida, Trump was immediately declared the winner in Utah and Iowa picking up their combined twelve electoral votes.

1:00 a.m. Trump lead 244–215 with seventy-nine electors available. He needed just twenty-six votes to seal the deal.

1:35 a.m. Trump clinched Pennsylvania (twenty votes), another key battleground state, making his lead virtually insurmountable. Clinton had long viewed the state as a key part of her "firewall" and had held a rally in Philadelphia with Barack Obama on election-eve that featured rocker Bruce Springsteen. Trump stood at 264 electoral votes with the count continuing in Wisconsin, Michigan, and Arizona, any one of which would make him the new president-elect.

2:02 a.m. Clinton's campaign manager, John Podesta, refused to concede defeat telling supporters at New York City's Javits Center, "Let's get these votes counted and let's bring this home." He added, "Several states are too close to call so we're not going to have anything more to say tonight."

2:30 a.m. In a stunning result, Trump captured Wisconsin's ten electoral votes, putting him over the 270 threshold.

2:35 a.m. Television networks reported that Hillary Clinton had called Donald Trump to concede defeat. "They had maybe a one minute conversation, very gracious very warm, he commended her for being smart and tough and running a hard fought campaign," summarized Trump's campaign manager Kellyanne Conway.

2:50 a.m. Trump and his family along with vice president elect Mike Pence took to the stage in front of his exuberant supporters at the ballroom of New York's Hilton Marriot. "Sorry to keep you waiting, complicated business," he said jokingly. "Thank you very much." He congratulated Clinton on a hard-fought campaign and pledged to be "a president for all Americans".

7:20 a.m. Trump became the first Republican candidate to win Pennsylvania, Wisconsin, and Michigan since H. W. Bush in 1988. His "rust belt strategy" had paid off.

10:30 a.m. Clinton delivered her concession speech from the New Yorker Hotel's Grand Ballroom. She said, "So now, our responsibility as citizens is to keep doing our part to build that better, stronger, fairer America we seek. And I know you will."

With the Trump victory, his campaign manager Kellyanne Conway became the first woman to run a winning presidential election. Contrastingly, her husband, George, a Washington, DC, attorney, was not a fan of the new president and never hesitated in publicly criticizing him.

Clinton received 227 electoral points and approximately 59.9 million popular votes, which was actually a slightly larger total number of popular ballots than Trump received (approx. 59.7 million). It made Clinton the first woman presidential candidate to receive any electoral ballots and the female nominee with the most popular votes cast for her in a general election.

In the presidential elections of 1824, 1876, 1888, 2000, and 2016, the candidate receiving the most popular votes didn't win the office. It was because Andrew Jackson, Samuel J. Tilden, Grover Cleveland, Al Gore, and Hillary Clinton, respectively, didn't garner enough electoral ballots to secure the victory.

Of all presidents, Trump won the most electors (304) of those who lost the popular vote.

On several occasions, Trump stated that he wasn't a politician but a businessman. He also said that he ran a self-funded campaign, but like most politicians, and some businessmen, that statement was only partially true. It is estimated that he spent $66 million from his own pocket although many citizens also donated to his effort. Included in the campaign war chest was nearly $647 million raised by the candidate and the GOP. Amazingly, in total, he spent just $285.5 million.

By comparison, Barack Obama and Mitt Romney, the 2012 White House combatants, each shelled out more than $1 billion on their respective campaign efforts. Trump wasn't the first to dig deep into his own pockets. In 1992, fellow businessman Ross Perot spent $64 million of his personal funds to run as an independent.

Table 25.1   The Election of 2016

Presidential candidate	Party	Home state	Popular vote Count	Percentage	Electoral vote
Donald Trump	Republican	New York	62,984,828	46.09%	304
Hillary Clinton	Democratic	New York	65,853,514	48.18%	227
Gary Johnson	Libertarian	New Mexico	4,489,341	3.28%	0
Jill Stein	Green	Massachusetts	1,457,218	1.07%	0
Evan McMullin	Independent	Utah	731,991	0.54%	0
Darrell Castle	Constitution	Tennessee	203,090	0.15%	0
Bernie Sanders	Independent	Vermont	111,850	0.08%	1
Gloria La Riva	Socialism and Liberation	California	74,401	0.05%	0
John Kasich	Republican	Ohio	2,684	0.00%	1
Ron Paul	Libertarian	Texas	124	0.00%	1
Colin Powell	Republican	Virginia	25	0.00%	3
Faith Spotted Eagle	Democratic	South Dakota	0	0.00%	1
Other			760,210	0.56%	—
Total			136,669,276	100%	538
Needed to win					

Vice President Elect, Mike Pence, Governor (R-IN)

THE AFTERMATH

During the presidential campaign of 2016, young voters heard Republican candidate Donald Trump constantly use the phrase, "Make America Great Again!" Many found it new and refreshing.

As the campaign progressed, the eventual nominee stated, "I've actually trademarked it. I mean, I get tremendous raves for that line. . . . I could come up with different lines. You would think they would come up with their own."

Perhaps the new president should have followed his own advice because before Trump was a household name, the slogan was already in use. It was begun by Ronald Reagan in his 1980 White House run and appeared that year on numerous placards, buttons, and posters. In 2013, two years before Trump announced his candidacy, author Hal Moroz published his book, _President Ronald Reagan: Let's Make America Great Again._

After a difficult primary season, most of the Bush family wanted nothing to do with Donald Trump. But there was one notable exception.

George P. Bush, Jeb's son, who was running for Texas land commissioner stated, "From Team Bush, it's a bitter pill to swallow, but you know what? You get back up and you help the man that won, and you make sure that we stop Hillary Clinton."

In turn for his support, Trump endorsed the younger Bush as both went on to victory.

In every presidential election year between 1952 and 2016, the Republican candidate who was leading in the polls on Christmas of the previous year went on to become the party's nominee.

On the Democratic side, it has often proven to be a fight for the nomination that goes into the spring of that year's election. That was not the case in 1964, 1980, 1996, and 2012 where an incumbent Democrat was in the White House seeking reelection.

Donald Trump (R) and Hillary Clinton (D), the presidential candidates of 2016, both claim New York as their home state. However, it should come as no surprise when a potential chief executive hails from the Empire State.

New York has had fifteen nominees for commander in chief including Martin Van Buren (D) and Thomas Dewey (R) who were each tabbed twice by their respective parties. Also, Mrs. Clinton relocated to New York in 1999 to run for the US Senate seat which she won. Prior to that, she lived in Illinois, Massachusetts (college), Connecticut (law school), Arkansas, and Washington, DC.

The tough talk between the Democrats in Congress and the newly elected Republican president had grown more bitter during the campaign. Just nineteen minutes following his swearing-in on January 20, 2017, *The Washington Post* became the first media outlet to run a story about a possible Trump impeachment.

On December 18, 2019, after an exhaustive investigation that cost taxpayers millions of dollars, the democratically controlled House of Representatives voted to impeach President Trump on two charges of obstruction of Congress and abuse of power. He became the third chief executive in American history to receive the sanction.

In the end, like his fellow impeached predecessors, Andrew Johnson and Bill Clinton, Trump was acquitted and remained in office to complete his term.

Bibliography

ARTICLES

Achenbach, Joel. 'A party that had lost its mind': In 1968, Democrats held one of history's most disastrous conventions (*Washington Post*, August 24, 2018).

Agrawal, Nina. All the times in U.S. history that members of the electoral college voted their own way (*Los Angeles Times*; December 8, 2016)

Alterman, Eric. Florida 2000 Forever (americanprogress.org; December 9, 2010).

Amadeo, Kimerly. President Ronald Reagan's Economic Policies (thebalance.com; June 29, 2019).

Anderson, Jack. Washington Merry-Go-Round (*The Chillicothe Constitution-Tribune*; December 16, 1975).

Andrews, Evan. Fidel Castro's Wild New York Visit (history.com; September 18, 2015).

Andrews, Stefan. The Famous Impromptu Flight Amelia and Eleanor Took in Their Dinner Gowns (thevintagenews.com; November 18, 2018).

Anirudh: 10 Interesting Facts About U.S. President James Madison (learnodo-newtonic.com; December 18, 2017).

Anthony, Carl Sferrzza. Our Presidents and Cigars (*Cigar Aficionado*; Autumn 1993).

Apple, Jr., R.W. Carter Wins the Democratic Nomination; Reveals Vice-Presidential Choice Today (*New York Times*; July 15, 1976).

Arbelbide, C. L. Abrupt Transition (*Prologue*ter 2000).

Arnold, Peri E. William Taft: Campaigns and Elections (millercenter.org; retrieved May 7, 2019).

Asim, Jabari. *What Obama Means: For Our Culture, Our politics, Our Future* (William Morrow Paperbacks; 2010).

Bailey, Jr., John W. "The Presidential Election of 1900 in Nebraska: McKinley Over Bryan," (Nebraska History; 1973).

Balcerski, Thomas J.: Beards, Bachelors, and Brides: The Surprisingly Spicy Politics of the Presidential Election of 1856 (common-place.org; Summer 2016).

Baskin, Robert E. Kennedy To Visit Texas Nov. 21–22 Dallas Included (*Dallas Morning News*; September 26, 1963).

Bauder, David. Networks Try To Explain Blown Call (Associated Press; November 8, 2000).

Baumgold, Julie. Nixon in New York (*Washington Post*; July 6, 1980).

Bergen, Anthony. "I Thought I Could Swing It": The Strange Life and Presidency of Silent Cal (medium.com; May 30, 2015).

Berish, Amy. FDR and Polio (Franklin D. Roosevelt Presidential Library and Museum; December 4, 2012.

Binkovitz, Leah. Who Were the Six Indian Chiefs in Teddy Roosevelt's Inaugural Parade? (Smithsonian.com; January 16, 2013).

Blasco, Erin. You asked, we answered: Which presidents have visited the museum? (american history.si.edu; January 18, 2013).

Boaz, David. The Man Who Would Not Be King (Cato Institute; February 20, 2006).

Bomboy, Scott. The story of the wildest party in White House history (constitutiondaily.com; March 4, 2013).

Boomhower, Ray E. Losing the Vote, Winning the Election (indianahistory.org; retrieved April 11, 2019).

Brands, H. W. The Real Story of Reagan's 11th Commandment (politico.com; April 5, 2017).

Braswell, Sean. Bill Clinton's Great Sax Appeal (ozy.com; June 8, 2016).

Britton, Rick. James Monroe, Bona Fide Hero of the American Revolution (*Journal of the American Revolution*; January 31, 2013).

Broder, David S. and Edsall, Thomas, B. Clinton Releases '69 Letter on his Draft Deferment (*Washington Post*; February 13, 1992).

Buchanan, Michael. October 10, 1973, Vice President Spiro Agnew Pleads No Contest To Tax Evasion (Today In Crime History; October 10, 2011).

Buell, Charles. Charles Evans Hughes (coolidgefoundation.org; retrieved May 26, 2019).

Caddell, Patrick.election surprise? The uprising of the American people (fox news; November 7, 2016).

Calamur, Krishnadev. The Last Time a U.S. President Visited Cuba (*The Atlantic*; Feb 18, 2016).

Calson, Cody K..: McClellan becomes the Army's commanding general (desertnews.com; October 29, 2014).

Camden, Jim. Electoral College wasn't done deal in 1976. Will it be in 2016? (*The Spokesman-Review*; December 17, 2016).

Cappello, Nile. Are We Ready For A Gay President? Well, We May Have Already Had One (huffingtonpost.com; June 9, 2016).

Channing, Walter. The Mental Status of Czolgosz, the Assassin of President McKinley (*American Journal of Insanity*; Ocober 1902).

Chen, Edwin. Perot Quits Presidential Race: Clinton's Goal: the Revitalizing of America: Politics: Texan cites the Democratic Party's new vigor for his exit and says he didn't want a three-way race thrown to the House. Now it's Clinton vs. Bush (*Los Angeles Times*; July 17, 1992).

Cillizza, Chris. How Mitt Romney could have won (*Washington Post*; May 31, 2013).

Clarke, Thurston. It Will Not Be Lyndon': Why JFK Wanted to Drop LBJ for Reelection (*The Daily Beast*; November 18, 2013).

Clay, Henry. Letter to Francis Preston Blair (Clay, Papers IV, 47; January 29, 1825).

Clines, Francis X. The Powell Decision: The Announcement: Powell Rules Out '96 Race; Cites Concerns for Family and his Lack of 'A Calling' (*New York Times*; November 9, 1995).

Clymer, Adam. Carter Is Edged in Poll by Reagan and Ford: Kennedy Leads Both (*New York Times*; July 1, 1979).

Cohen, Danielle. This Day in History: The 1913 Women's Suffrage Parade (archives.gov; March 3, 2016).

Cohen, Michael D. Presidential Races Can Change Significantly as Election Day Approaches (gallup.com; October 26, 2000).

Colloff, Pamela. Go Ask Alice (*Texas Monthly*; November 1998).

Colloff, Pamela and Hall, Michael. Married to the Mob (*Texas Monthly*; November 1999).

Colville, Liz and Cummings, Dennis. 1872: Susan B. Anthony Votes in Presidential Election (sweetsearch.com; July 6, 2017).

Comen, Evan. The Size of a Home the Year You Were Born (24/7 Wall St; May 25, 2016).

Condon, George E. Wilson's Wedding (theatlantic.com; November 20, 2015).

Conradt, Stacy. The Quick 10: 10 Campaign Slogans of the Past (mentalfloss.com; October 8, 2008).

Cooper, Jr., John Milton. The Pause That Depresses (*New York Times*; December2008).

Costello, William. Coasting with Ike in '56 (*The New Republic*; November 16, 1959).

Cox, Patrick. "Not Worth a Bucket of Warm Spit" (historynewsnetwork.com; June 17, 2019).

Crabtree, Steve. The Gallup Brain: Americans and the Korean War (gallup.com; February 4, 2003).

Crowley, Candy. Bush leads Gore by 327 votes in Florida recount, Associated Press reports (cnn.com; Nov.10, 2000).

Cummins, Joseph. Dirty Campaigning in the Roaring Twenties: Herbert Hoover vs. Al Smith (mentalfloss.com; October 17, 2008).

Dale, Porter H. The Calvin Coolidge Inauguration Revisited: An Eyewitness Account (ver, monthistory.org; retrieved May 24, 2019).

Dallek, Robert. Presidency: How Do Historians Evaluate the Administration of Lyndon Johnson? (History News Network; 2002).

Dalton, Bill. Death of a boy, and a presidency (*The Andover Townsman*; January 17, 2013).

Dean, John W. The Telling Tale of the Twenty-Seventh Amendment: A Sleeping Amendment Concerning Congressional Compensation Is Later Revived (supreme/findlaw.com; September 7, 2002).

Dearstyne, Bruce W. The Russians Tried Once Before to Meddle in a U.S. Presidential Election (History News Network; December 29, 2016).

De Cesar, Wayne T. and Page, Susan. Jefferson Buys Louisiana Territory, and the Nation Moves Westward (National Archives; Spring 2003, Vol. 35, No. 1).

Democratic Party. Democrats Outline their 1856 Party Platform (herb.ashp.cuny.edu; retrieved January 31, 2019).

Dichter, Steve. 1940 Republican Convention (Broadcast Pioneers of Philadelphia; July 2016).

Dickerson, John. How Truman Reinvented Campaigning (*Daily Beast*; April 13, 2017).

Doenecke, Justus. James A. Garfield: Campaigns and Elections (millercenter.org; retrieved March 27, 2019).

Donohue, Keith. Authors on the Record: Custer's Trials (*Prologue Magazine*; Winter 2015, Vol. 47, No. 4).

Dotinga, Randy. The GOP Convention Debacle That Spawned San Diego's 'Finest City' Motto (*Voice of San Diego*; July 20, 2016).

Drye, Willie. A Timeline of Hurricane Sandy's Path of Destruction (*National Geographic*; November 2, 2012).

Dugan, Andrew and Newport, Frank. Americans Rate JFK as Top Modern President (gallup.com; November 15, 2013).

Edwards, Lee. Ronald Reagan vs. Gerald Ford: The 1976 GOP Convention Battle Royal (nationalinterest.org; April 16, 2016).

Edwards, Phil. Thomas Jefferson's secret reason for sending Lewis and Clark West: to find mastodons (vox.com; April 13, 2015).

Ellis, Richard J. and Dedrick, Mark. The Presidential Candidate, Then and Now (Perspectives on Political Science, Fall 1997).

Farby, Merrill: The Law That Started the New Deal (time.com; March 9, 2016)

Fazio, John C. Confederate Complicity In the Assassination of Abraham Lincoln - Part 2 (The Cleveland Civil War Roundtable; 2008).

Fennell, Christopher. An Account of James Monroe's Land Holdings (histarch.illinois.edu; September 2, 2012).

Fenton, Ben. Gore blamed Clinton for his defeat in election (UK Telegraph; February 8, 2001).

Ferranti, Seth. How the Mafia Fueled Richard Nixon's Political Career (vice.com; November20, 2017).

Field, Marvin D. Nixon, Knight Both Lead Brown in Early Test of Voter Popularity (The California Poll; October 13, 1961).

Field, Mervin D. Nixon has strong lead over Humphrey. Wallace attracts more Democrats than Republicans. Residual support for McCarthy still a factor in Humphrey poor showing (Field Research Corp.; September 23, 1968).

Fitzgerald, Sandy. FDR Bible Goes 'Missing' at de Blasio's Swearing-In (newsmax.com; January 2, 2014).

Foote, Joe and Curran, Kevin. Ronald Reagan Radio Broadcasts (1976–1979) (Library of Congress; 2007).

Forgey, Quint. Trump vs. the Bushes: A political rivalry of its time (politico.com; December 1, 2018).

Frank, Jeffrey. How F.D.R.'s Death Changed the Vice-Presidency (*The New Yorker*; April 17, 2015).

Frankel, Max. M'Govern Wins by Big Margin on Disputed California Seats in a Major Step to Nomination (*New York Times*; July 12, 1972).

Furgurson, Ernest B. Moment of Truth: Scandal in the Election of 1884 (*American History Magazine*; April 6, 2016).

Gallup, George. The Gallup Poll and the 1950 Election (*The Public Opinion Quarterly*; Spring, 1951).

Ganzel, Bill. Bank Failures (livinghistoryfarm.org; 2003).

Gilman, D. C., Peck, H. T., Colby, F. M., Meyer, Henry Herman. (*New International Encyclopedia*; 1905).

Gimiao, Cara. Warren G. Harding Was The First Celebrity-Endorsed President (Atlas Obscura; August 31, 2015).

Glass, Andrew. Zachary Taylor's body exhumed, June 17, 1991 (politico.com; June 16, 2011).

———. George W. Bush suspended from Texas Air National Guard, Aug. 1, 1972 (politico.com; August 1, 2013).

———. Polk becomes president, Nov. 5, 1844 (politico.com; November 5, 2013).

Glass, Andrew: McCarthy nearly upsets LBJ in New Hampshire primary: March 12, 1968 (politico.com; March 12, 2016)

———. Presidential election results left in doubt, Nov. 7, 1876 (politico.com; November 6, 2016).

———. Republicans nominate Warren G. Harding, June 12, 1920 (politico.com; June 12, 2018).

———. Reagan recovers in second debate, Oct. 21, 1984 (politico.com; October 21, 2018).

———. President Wilson lands in France, Dec. 13, 1918 (politico.com; December13, 2018).

———.Truman declines to seek another term, March 29, 1952 (history.com; March 29, 2019).

Glassman, James K. and Hassett, Kevin A. Dow 36,000 (theatlantic.com; September 1999).

Gold, Matea. The campaign to impeach President Trump has begun (*Washington Post*; January 20, 2017).

Goldfeder, Jerry H. Could Terrorists Derail a Presidential Election? (*Fordham Urban Law Journal*; 2005).

Golshan, Tara. Bill Clinton's first major appearance at a convention almost destroyed his career (vox.com; July 26, 2016).

Goodman, Bonnie K. OTD in History… August 23–29 1968 violent protests rage outside the Democratic National Convention as Hubert Humphrey nominated (medium.com; August 27, 2018).

———. OTD in History… November 3, 1948, Truman retains the presidency in an election upset against Dewey (medium.com; November 5, 2018).

Gore, Leada. Senator, slave owner and quite possibly gay, Alabama's William Rufus King was country's 13th VP (al.com; July 4, 2014).

Gould, Lewis L. 1912 Republican Convention (Smithsonian.com; August 2008).

———. William McKinley: Campaigns and Elections (millercenter.org; retrieved April 20, 2019).

Graff, Henry A. Grover Cleveland: Campaigns and Elections (millercenter.org; retrieved April 4, 2019).

Green, Aimee. Presidential love affair confirmed: Portland grandson of Warren G. Harding thankful for DNA results (oregonlive.com; August 16, 2015).

Greenberg, David. Was Nixon Robbed? (slate.com; October 16, 2009).

Greene, John Robert. "Agnew, Spiro." In Purcell, L. Edward, ed. Vice Presidents: A Biographical Dictionary, Updated Edition (Facts On File, Inc.; 2001).

Greene, Leonard. Bill Clinton made insensitive 'race jab' about Obama in 2008 (*New York Post*; September 3, 2012).

Greenspan, Jesse. History of the Presidential Cabinet (history.com; January 12, 2017).

———. George H.W. Bush's Role in WWII Was Among the Most Dangerous (history.com; Februaryt 13, 2019).

Grimsley, Mark. What if FDR Had Not Run for a Third Term? (*World War II Magazine*; March 5, 2018).

Guerrieri, Vince: The Election of 1920 (ohiomagazine.com; February 2015).

Hall, Cheryl. Ross Perot, self-made billionaire, patriot and philanthropist, dies at 89 (*Dallas Morning News*; June 9, 2019).

Haltiwanger, John. President Ulysses S. Grant was once arrested for speeding on a horse-drawn carriage, proving the POTUS is not above the law (*Business Insider*; December 17, 2018).

Hamilton, Alexander. Letter to George Washington (archives.gov; September1788).

Hamill, Pete. Prohibition (pbs.org; 2011).

Henneberger, Melina and van Natta Jr., Don. Once Close to Clinton, Gore Keeps a Distance (*New York Times*; October 20, 2000).

Hartlaub, Peter. San Francisco's long history as a vibrant, weird convention town (*San Francisco Chronicle*; May 13, 2019).

Hay, Jared. Political Campaigning from 1888, Benjamin Harrison's "Front Porch" Campaign (*Indianapolis Monthly*; November 7, 2016).

Haynes, Stan M. When Baltimore was convention central (*Baltimore Sun*; June 25, 2012).

Helling, Dave. 1944 Democratic Convention: Not Just Choosing A President But A Vice President (*Kansas City Star*; July 18, 2016).

Hertzberg, Hendrik. Recession Election (*The New Yorker*; October 25, 2010).

Hirschkorn, Phil. EXCLUSIVE: America's last great convention: Mondale, Jackson & Hart dish to Salon about wild 1984 DNC (solon.com; February 15, 2015).

Hogan, Margaret A. John Quincy Adams: Foreign Affairs (millercenter.org; retrieved December 22, 2018).

Holcomb, Jesse. How the Lehman Bros. crisis impacted the 2008 presidential race (pew research.org; September 19, 2013).

Holden, Charles J. and Messitte, Zach. Spiro Agnew and the Golden Age of Corruption in Maryland Politics: An Interview with Ben Bradlee and Richard Cohen of *The Washington Post* (The Center for the Study of Democracy; Volume 2, Number 1, Fall 2006).

Hollar, Sherman. Andrew Jackson (Britannica Educational Publishing; 2012).

Hollis, Daniel W. "Cotton Ed Smith": Showman or Statesman? (jstor.org; October, 1970).

Hollis, Nicholas E. The Wormley Agreement (Washingtoniana Collection; retrieved March 20, 2018).

Holzel, David. Five Amazing Facts About Franklin Pierce (Mental Floss; November 19, 2007).

Hughes, Ken. Richard Nixon: Life After the Presidency (millercenter.org; retrieved July 31, 2019).

Jarmul, David. American History: Truman Wins the Election of 1948 (voanews.com; August 17, 2011).

Jay, Paul. Undoing New Deal: The 1944 Coup Against VP Henry Wallace (transcript) (The Real News Network; December 4, 2017).

Johnson, Brad. Exit Polls 2012: Hurricane Sandy Was A Deciding Factor For Millions Of Voters In The Election (Climate Progress: November 6, 2012).

Johnson, Ted. Ford-Carter debate flashback: When the candidates went silent for 27 minutes (*West Central Tribune*; September 25, 2016).

Jones, Jeffrey M. Gore, Bush Rally Traditional Constituent Groups (gallup.com; November 9, 2000).

———. Closeness of Election Underscored in State Poll Results Four of six showdown state races too close to call (gallup.com; November 1, 2004).

———. Gerald Ford Retrospective (gallup.com; December 29, 2006).

Kaus, Mickey. Let the Healing Begin, But Not Yet (slate.com; November 9, 2004).

Kelley, Peter. What's in a name? UW doc's is Hayes, Rutherford P. (not B.) Hayes (uwnews; August 21, 2008).

Kennedy, Robert C. "Citizen Parker" (*New York Times*; 2001).

Kennedy, Jr., Robert F. Was the 2004 Election Stolen? (*Rolling Stone*; June 1, 2006).

Kerry, John. Vietnam Veterans Against the War Statement by John Kerry to the Senate Committee of Foreign Relations (*Congressional Record*; April 23, 1971).

Killen, Patrick J. Amy Carter's concern about nuclear warfare and the strategic... (United Press; October 30, 1980).

Kilpatrick, Carroll and Oberdorfer, Don. Richard M. Nixon Becomes President With 'Sacred Commitment' to Peace (*Washington Post*; January 21, 1969).

King, Elizabeth. 4 Protests to Know About Before the Women's March on Washington (time .com; January 20, 2017).

King, Gilbert. The Ugliest, Most Contentious Presidential Election Ever (smithsonianmag .com; September 7, 2012).

———Geronimo's Appeal to Theodore Roosevelt (Smithsonian.com; November 9, 2012).

———. War and Peace of Mind for Ulysses S. Grant (Smithsonian.com; January16, 2013).

King, John. The Stalking of the President (Smithsonian.com; January 17, 2012).

King, Wayne. Georgia's Gov. Carter Enters Democratic Race, for President (*New York Times*; December 13, 1974).

Klein, Scott. "Out of the Depths": The Last Days and Strange Death of Horace Greeley (medium.com; January 10, 2016).

Klunder, Willard Carl. "Lewis Cass, Stephen Douglas, and Popular Sovereignty: The Demise of Democratic Party Unity," in *Politics and Culture of the Civil War Era* ed by Daniel J. McDonough and Kenneth W. Noe (Macmillan; 2006).

Koenig, Louis W. Presidents: A Reference History (The Gale Group, Inc.; 2002).

Kolasky, William. Senator John Sherman And the Origin of Antitrust (Antitrust, Vol. 24, No. 1; Fall 2009).

Lamb, David. Times Poll Finds Public Wants New Direction for U.S (*Los Angeles Times*; February 26, 1987).

Lampkin, Benjamin. 6 Presidential Facts About James Buchanan (mentalfloss.com; October 19, 2015).

Landry, Alysa. Herbert Hoover: Only US President to Have Lived on Indian Reservation (newsmaven.io; August 2, 2016).

Lange, Greg and Stein, Alan J. George Wallace and Ronald Reagan campaign in Seattle on October 12, 1968. (HistoryLink.org; January 1, 1999).

Langton, James. Clinton grants pardon for his drug-offending brother (telegraph.co.uk; January 21, 2001).

Leahy, Michael Patrick. 333,000 Votes in 4 Swing States Would Have Given Romney the Presidency (breitbart.com; November11, 2012).

Leidner, Gordon. How Lincoln Won the 1860 Republican Nomination (*Washington Times*; August 10, 1996).

Lepore, Jill. The Tug of War (*The New Yorker*; September 2, 2013).

———. How to Steal an Election (*The New Yorker*; June 27, 2016).

Lester, Will. 'Dewey Defeats Truman' Disaster Haunts Pollsters (*Los Angeles Times*; November 1, 1998).

Leval, Jessica. A Brief History of the Modern Presidential Debate (aei.org; September 29, 2008).

Lewis, Dan. Abraham Lincoln Created the Secret Service the Day He Was Shot (mentalfloss .com; December14, 2010).

Little, Becky. For Over 150 Years, U.S. Presidents Had No Term Limits (history.com; February 28, 2018).

LoGiurato, Brett. GALLUP: Romney Surges Back To 5-Point Lead Over Obama (*Business Insider*; October 29, 2012).

Longley, Robert. Grenada Invasion: History and Significance (thoughtco.com; December 3, 2018).

Loo, Dennis. No Paper Trail Left Behind: the Theft of the 2004 Presidential Election (project censored.org; May 2, 2010).

Lucas, Fred. Rigged Election? Past Presidential Contests Sowed Doubt and Nearly Led to Violence (dailysignal.com; October 18, 2016).

Lussier, Charles. Zachary Taylor, Louisiana's only president, was lifelong Army man with no interest in political office (theadvocate.com; December 3, 2015).

Lussier, Charles. Political odd couple James Carville, Mary Matalin say it's OK to disagree, even over Trump (theadvocate.com; February 6, 2019).

Madonna, G. Terry and Young, Michael. The First Political Poll (fandm.edu; June 18, 2002).

Magourney, Adam. With Echoes of 2000 Vote, Ohio Count Is at Issue (*New York Times*; November 3, 2004).

Maloney, Wendy. New Online: James K. Polk Papers (loc.gov; September 21, 2017).

Mancini, Mark. 12 Facts About the Election of 1800 (mentalfloss.com; July 28, 2016).

Manning, Lona: 9/16: Terrorists Bomb Wall Street (*Crime Magazine*; October 4, 2012).

Mark, David. George P. Bush urges Republicans to back Trump (cnn.com; August 8, 2016).

Markel, Dr. Howard. When a secret president ran the country (pbs.org; October 2, 2015).

———. The 'strange' death of Warren G. Harding (pbs.org; October 2, 2015).

Martin, Jonathan and Chozick, Amy. Hillary Clinton's Doctor Says Pneumonia Led to Abrupt Exit From 9/11 Event (*New York Times*; September 11, 2016).

McCarthy, Ciara and Phipps, Claire. Election results timeline: how the night unfolded (*The Guardian*; November 9, 2016).

McCarthy, Erin. Why Are Elections Held on Tuesdays? (mentalfloss.com; November 3, 2012).

McCarthy, Tom. The last-minute map: how to read each presidential candidate's final stops (*The Guardian*; November 7, 2016).

McCullough, David. "I Hardly Know Truman" (American Heritage; July/August 1992).

———. Champion of the Navy - Comments to the Naval Institute regarding John Adams role in the birth of the U.S. Navy (navalhistory.org; October 12, 2012).

McCullough, Gene. John Adams and the Camino de Santiago (americanpilgrims.com; November 2009).

McMaster, John Back. The Third Term Tradition (*The Forum*, Volume 20; September 1895–February 1896).

McNamara, Robert. Monroe Doctrine (thoughtco.com; February 1, 2019).

Melero, Julius. The 19th Century Navy in South America: The Baltimore Affair and Water Witch Incident (navalhistory.org; April 15, 2015).

Melnick, Jordan. Back in the Day: FDR Shooting Attempt at Bayfront Park (Beached Miami; February 15, 2011).

Mikkelson, David. Abraham Lincoln and Failure (snopes.com; July 12, 2000).

Millard, Candice. Destiny of the Republic: A Tale of Madness, Medicine and the Murder of a President (Anchor Books; 2020).

Miller, Neil Z. The polio vaccine: a critical assessment of its arcane history, efficacy, and long-term health-related consequences (N.Z. Miller/Medical Veritas 1; 2004).

Miller, Thomas. Case of the Late William H. Harrison, President of the United States (*The Boston Medical and Surgical Journal*; June 2, 1841).

Miner, Michael. The Real Action in '68 (chicagoreader.com; August 28, 2008).

Mitchell, Greg. Pressing Issues (gregmitchellwriter.com; August 23, 2016).

Moe, Richard. Why (and How) FDR Ran for His Third Term (History News Network; August 12, 2013).

Moore, Dorothy L. William A. Howard and the Nomination of Rutherford B. Hayes for the Presidency (Vermont History; Autumn 1970).

Moore, Jack. Educating Amy: The incredible history of a DC public school that taught a president's daughter (wtop.com; August 14, 2017).

Morgan, William G. The Origin and Development of the Congressional Nominating Caucus (Proceedings of the American Philosophical Society; 1969).

Morganthau, Tom. Why Kennedy Withdrew From 1984 Race (*Newsweek*; December12, 1982).

Munger, Sean. Earth: Blackstone Hotel, Chicago, site of the original "smoke-filled room." (seanmunger.com; June 11, 2015).

Murdock, Deroy. The Night Chris Christie Killed the Romney Campaign (National Review; February 4, 2016).

Naughton, James M. Ford Announces Candidacy for '76 'To Finish the Job' (*New York Times*; July 9, 1975).

Nasaw, Daniel. US election: 10 oddities explained (bbc.com; November 1, 2012).

Nelson, Steven. Flashback: Debate glitch took 27 minutes to fix in 1976 (*Washington Examiner*; June 27, 2019).

Newport, Frank, Jones, Jeffrey M. and Saad, Lydia. Ronald Reagan From the People's Perspective: A Gallup Poll Review (gallup.com; June 7, 2004).

———. What History Tells Us About Second and Third Debates (gallup.com; October 7, 2004).

Newport, Frank, Jones, Jeffrey M., Saad, Lydia, and Carroll Joseph. Where the Election Stands: June 2007 (gallup.com; June 27, 2007).

Nichols, Bill and Harris, John F. 50 greatest political moments: Great slogans (politico.com; April 8, 2008).

Nilsson, Jeff. 1912: A Chaotic Presidential Election (*Saturday Evening Post*; November 3, 2012).

Novak, Matt.'Speeches Must Be Short': Radio and the Birth of the Modern Presidential Campaign (psmag.com; May 3, 2017).

Nowicki, Dan. In 1974, Goldwater and Rhodes told Nixon he was doomed (*Arizona Republic*; August 2, 2014).

O'Connor, Kyrie: Vote! 7 things to know about Election Day (*Houston Chronicle*; November 7, 2016).

O'Dowd, Niall. Guess which American president personally hanged two Irishmen from the scaffold? (irishcentral.com; November 28, 2017).

Onion, Rebecca. The Art of the New Deal (slate.com; March 31, 2016).

Onuf, Peter. Thomas Jefferson: Campaigns and Elections (millercenter.org; retrieved September 28, 2018).

Pappas, Theodore N. Bright's Disease, Malaria, and Machine Politics: The Story of the Illness of President Chester A. Arthur (*The Surgery Journal*; December19, 2017).

Parton, James. The Presidential Election of 1800 (theatlantic.com; July 1873).

Paschall, Valerie. The Taft Bridge Through The Years: From 1908 Until 2008 (d.c.curbed .com; April 11, 2014).

Peterson, Dennis L. The 'Most Wholesome and Best in the American Boy' (*Scouting Magazine*; October 2000).

Phelan, Ben. What Became of the Chicago Seven? (pbs.org; October 19, 2015).

Pinheiro, John C. James K. Polk: Campaigns and Elections (millercenter.com; January10, 2019).

Priebus, Reince. The Five Biggest Failures From President Obama's Stimulus Law (*U.S. News & World Report*; February 17, 2012).

Pruitt, Sarah. That Time a Foreign Government Interfered in a U.S. Presidential Election—in 1796 (history.com; March 16, 2017).

———.The Whiskey Ring and America's First Special Prosecutor (history.com; May 18, 2017).

Purdy, Mike. Did Eisenhower's Wife Tilt the 1960 Election to JFK? (presidential history.com; November 3, 2014).

Rable, George C. McClellan Redux? The Often-Reported, Imminent Return of Little Mac (*Journal of the Abraham Lincoln Association*; Volume 38, Issue 2, Summer 2017).

Rasmussen, Frederick N. Obama's hardly the first American president to favor train travel (*The Baltimore Sun*; January 18, 2009).

———. President Harrison Made History (*The Baltimore Sun*; March 3, 2012).

Reader, Stephen. Explainer: Why Dixville Notch Votes at Midnight (wnyc.org; January 9, 2012).

Reid, T. R. Ill-Starred, Stumbling, Ever Gutsy (*Washington Post*; June 4, 1980).

Reinhart, R. J. George H. W. Bush Retrospective (gallup.com; December 1, 2018).

Rice, William. The day it rained on Herbert Hoover's presidential inauguration in 1929 (*New York Daily News*; March 5, 1929).

Richmond, Jeff. Eight Notable Presidential Campaign Aircraft That Changed The Speed Of Politics (avgeekery.com; Septmber 18, 2016).

Rodriguez, Lisa. Backstory (broadcastingandcable.com; November 12, 2000).

Roig-Franzia, Manuel. John Edwards will not be retried, Justice Department announces (*Washington Post*; June 13, 2012).

Roseberger, Homer T. Inauguration of President Buchanan A Century Ago (Records of the Columbia Historical Society, Washington, DC, Vol. 57/59;1957/1959).

Ross, Tara. This Day in History: The tragic death of Calvin Coolidge's son (taraross.com; Posted on July 5, 2017).

Rothman, Lily. The Primary Election That Put New Hampshire on the Political Map (time .com; February 9, 2016).

Roy, Roger and Damron, David. Small Florida counties wasted more than 1,700 votes (*Chicago Tribune*; January 28, 2001).

Rudin, Ken. On This Day In 1988: Bush-Dukakis Debate Dominated By 'Rape' Question (npr.com; October 13, 2009).

Saad, Linda. Late Upsets are Rare, But Have Happened (gallup.com; October27, 2008).

———. Presidential Debates Rarely Game-Changers (gallup.com; September 25, 2008).

———. Trump and Clinton Finish With Historically Poor Images (gallup.com; November 8, 2016).

———. Gallup Vault: A Pardon That Took a Decade to Forgive (gallup.com; September 7, 2017).

Sass, Erik. Pancho Villa's Troops Murder 18 Americans (mentalfloss.com; January 11, 2016).

Schmidt, John R. Emma Goldman's Hideout (*Chicago History Today*; January 7, 2013).

Schoen, John W. Here's what Clinton, Trump spent to turn out votes (cnbc.com; November 8, 2016).

Schwartz, Allan B. Medical mystery: The U.S. president who died in a San Francisco hotel (*Philadelphia Inquirer*; December 11, 2016).

———. Medical Mystery: Did abolitionists poison this president? (*Philadelphia Inquirer*; August 3, 2018).

———. Medical Mystery: In TV debate, Nixon looked nervous (*Philadelphia Inquirer*; retrieved June 12, 2019).

Scott, Janny. In 2000, a Streetwise Veteran Schooled a Bold Young Obama (*New York Times*; September 9, 2007).

Self, John W. The First Debate over the Debates: How Kennedy and Nixon Negotiated the 1960 Presidential Debates (jstor.org; June 2005).

Serratore, Angela. President Cleveland's Problem Child (Smithsonian.com; September 26, 2013).

Severson, Kim and Schwartz, John. Edwards Not Guilty on One Count; Mistrial on Five Others (*New York Times*; May 31, 2012).

Shafer, Jack. 1924: The Wildest Convention in U.S. History (politico.com; March 7, 2016).

Shaffer, Ralph E. The great GOP spat -- of 1916 (*Los Angeles Times*; October 23, 2005).

Shapell, Benjamin and Witten, Sara. The Death of McKinley and the Presidency of Roosevelt (shapell.org; September 14, 2012).

Shapp, Martin. Veep Heap of History: With Tales Like These, Why I'm Fixated on Nation's #2 (*California Magazine*; June 30, 2016).

Shaw, Benjamin. The Election of 1828: It's Always Been Ugly (weta.org; January 13, 2017).

Shear, Michael D. and Landler, Mark. Storm Roils Campaign as Obama Cancels Appearance (*New York Times*; October 29, 2012).

Shirley, Craig. How Gerald Ford beat Ronald Reagan at the last contested GOP convention (*Washington Post*; April 22, 2016).

Sidney, Hugh. When politics rode the rails (cnn.com; March 20, 2000).

Simmons, Amy V. The first televised Democratic Convention, 70 years later: An unplanned delegate remembers (*Philadelphia Sun*; August 5, 2016).

Skinner, Kiron K. 'Reagan's Path to Victory' (*New York Times*; October 31, 2004).

Smith, Hendrick. Carter Wins Nomination for a Second Term; Gets Kennedy Pledge of Support and Work (*New York Times*; August 14, 1980).

Spitzer, Kirk. No Fading Away For MacArthur Over Here (time.com; July 19, 2012).

Staff Report. Mrs. McKinley in a Critical Condition (*New York Times*; May 16, 1901).

———. Warden Mead Made A Mistake (*New York Herald*; October 30, 1901).

———. Wilson Stands Pat On Mexico; Not To Use Army (*Chicago Tribune*; January 14, 1916).

———. Harding, Coolidge take office (upi.com; March 4, 1921).

———. Coolidge and Dawes Nominated; General Named for Second Place After Lowden, Chosen, Refuses it (*New York Times*; June 13, 1924).

———. Woodrow Wilson Coached Princeton's First Football Team, Says Historian (*Harvard Crimson*; November 8, 1924).

———. The Third Term Tradition in American Politics (*SAGE Publications*; March 19, 1927).

———. Republicans - The Turn to the Future (time.com; September 3, 1956).

———. Nixon and Kennedy Agree to Hold Series of Face-to-Face Debates (*Los Angeles Times*; July 29, 1960).

———. Man Is Slabbed During Quarrel (*Walla Walla Union Bulletin*; November 7, 1960).

————. Mabel Walker Willebrandt Dies; Lawyer for U.S. in Prohibition; Won Many Liquor Battles as Assistant Attorney General Ran Prison System (*New York Times*; April 9, 1963).

————. Governor Lists Plans For Washington Visit (*Dallas Morning News*; September 25, 1963).

————. Presidency: Nixon Landslide of Historic Proportions (CQ Almanac 1972, 28th ed.; 1973).

————. Precedents to Indicting A Vice-President (*St. Petersburg Times*; September 27, 1973).

————. Amy Carter Arrested (*New York Times*; April 9, 1985).

————. It Was Bad Last Time Too: The Crédit Mobilier Scandal of 1872 (*American Heritage*; Feb/Mar 1991).

————. Spiro T. Agnew, ex-vice president, dies in Md. at 77 (*Baltimore Sun*; September 18, 1996).

————. KDKA begins to broadcast 1920 (pbs.org; 1998).

————. Payoff to the Vice President, 1971 (EyeWitness to History; 2000).

————. Gore Retracts Concession Call (*Washington Post*; November 8, 2000).

————. Election News Election 2000 Timeline (post-gazette.com; December 17, 2000).

————. Clinton's long goodbye (bbc.co.uk; January 20, 2001).

————. Warren G. Harding (U*K Independent*; January 19, 2009).

————. National Archives Celebrates the 145th Anniversary of Nevada Statehood (archives .gov; September 23, 2009).

————. Dred Scott Decision (history.com; October 27, 2009).

————. William Henry Harrison (history.com; October 29, 2009).

————. Women's Suffrage (history.com; October 29, 2009).

————. The Monroe Doctrine: Whose Doctrine Was It ? (NEH.gov; November 9, 2009).

————. Suez Crisis (history.com; November 9, 2009).

————. Lincoln arrives in Washington (history.com; November 13, 2009).

————. Lincoln removes McClellan (history.com; November 13, 2009).

————. Grant nominated for lieutenant general (history.com; November 13, 2009).

————. Germans unleash U-boats (history.com; November 16, 2009).

————. FDR Dies (history.com; November 16, 2009).

————. Republican Party founded (history.com; February 9, 2010).

————. Crédit Mobilier (history.com; April 26, 2010).

————. Nov. 15, 1969 | Anti-Vietnam War Demonstration Held (*New York Times*; November 15, 2011).

————. Washington on a proposed third term and political parties, 1799 (The Gilder Lehrman Institute of American History; 2012).

————. "If Any Outsider is Taken, I Hope it Will be Garfield": The 1880 Republican Convention (*The Garfield Observer*; August 24, 2012).

————. A Timeline of Hurricane Sandy's Path of Destruction (nationalgeographic.org; November 2, 2012).

————. The Papers of Martin Van Buren (1782-1862) (vanburenpapers.org; 2016).

————. The Troubled Elections of 1796 and 1800 (Constitutional Rights Foundation; Fall 2016).

————. A brief history of the Super Tuesday primaries (constitutioncenter.org; February 29, 2016).

————. US election: 10 US election oddities (bbc.com; November 3, 2016).

———10 Interesting Facts About US President Grover Cleveland (learnodo-newtonic.com; April 15, 2017).

———A landmark demonstration of Morse Code telegraphy (*UK Telegraph*; May 4, 2017).

———. Days of Rage: Timeline of the 1968 Democratic National Convention (abc7chicago .com; August 24, 2018).

———. March on Washington (history.com; September 19, 2018).

———. The Revolution of 1800 (digitalhistory.uh.edu; retrieved September 28, 2018).

———. An Imperfect Election (mountvernon.org; retrieved November 7, 2018).

———. John Quincy Adams (u.s.history.org; retrieved December. 20, 2018).

———. Andrew Jackson - Key Events (millercenter.org; retrieved December. .24, 2018).

———. John C. Calhoun, 7th Vice President (1825-1832) (senate.gov; retrieved January 2, 2019).

———. 1868 Grant vs. Seymour (*Harper's Weekly*; retrieved February 23, 2019).

Ulysses S. Grant - Key Events (millercenter.org; retrieved February 24, 2019).

———Grant vs. Greeley (*Harper's Weekly*; retrieved February 27, 2019).

———Hayes vs. Tilden (*Harper's Weekly*; retrieved March 5, 2019).

———. 1892 Homestead Strike (aflcio.org; retrieved April 14, 2019).

———. This Month in Climate History: May 27, 1896, St. Louis Tornado (noaa.gov; retrieved April 16, 2019).

———. History of the Cherry Blossom Trees and Festival (archive.org; retrieved May 8, 2019).

———. Lierary Digest out in 1938 (pbs.org; June 14, 2019).

———. 1932: FDR's First Presidential Campaign (roosevelthouse.hunter.cuny.edu; retrieved June 15, 2019).

———. Presidential Inaugural Weather (weather.gov; retrieved June 15, 2019).

———. Looking back at the Truman beats Dewey upset (constitutioncenter.org; retrieved June 30, 2019).

———. Gallup Presidential Election Trial-Heat Trends, 1936-2008 (gallup.com; retrieved July 5, 2019).

———. Eisenhower at Gettysburg (nps.gov; retrieved July 8, 2019).

———. 1960 Presidential Debates (cnn.com; retrieved July 10, 2019).

———. Flashback Miami (*Miami Herald*; retrieved July 29, 2019).

———. June 13, 1825: President John Quincy Adams Nearly Drowns in Tiber Creek (New England Historical Society; retrieved December 11, 2018).

———. Martin Van Buren, 8th Vice President (1833-1837) (senate.gov; retrieved December 31, 2018).

———. John C. Calhoun, 7th Vice President (1825-1832) (senate.gov; retrieved January 2, 2019).

———. Grover Cleveland used Pol-Am to avoid military service (ampoleagle.com; retrieved April 2, 2019).

———. White House Transitions Fact Sheet (whitehousehistory.org; retrieved January 6, 2019).

———. "Theodore Roosevelt, 25th Vice President (1901)" (US Senate; retrieved April 19, 2019).

———. "The Great Commoner" (The Agribusiness Council; retrieved April 19, 2019).

———. Geronimo (biography.com; retrieved April 30, 2019).

———. Teapot Dome Scandal (history.com; June 10, 2019).

————. Vietnam Statistics (uswardogs.org; retrieved October. 18, 2019).

Storer, Doug. Luck ran out with a Carnation when McKinley gave it away (*St. Petersburg Independent*; September 7, 1984).

Strauss, Robert. To understand 2016, consider 1856 (*Constitution Daily*; November 25, 2016).

Stretch, Bonnie Barrett. If Stuart Didn't Paint It, Who Did? (artnews.com; October 1, 2004).

Sullivan, Nate. Hebert Hoover: Failures & Criticisms (study.com; retrieved June 6, 2019).

Swint, Kerwin. Adams vs. Jefferson: The Birth of Negative Campaigning in the U.S. (Mental Floss; September 9, 2012).

Tawfik, Adrian. Abraham Lincoln and Election Fraud ? No Way! (democracychronicles.org; July 20, 2013).

Thackeray, Lorna. Custer's brothers and nephew rode with him to their doom (*Billings Gazette*; June 21, 2001).

Todd, Chuck and Nurray, Mark: Jeb Bush surges to lead GOP pack in new 2016 poll (MSNBC; June 22, 2015).

Torry, Jack: Nixon said no to recount in 1960 outcome (Toledo Blade; Nov.10, 2000)

Trani, Eugene P. Warren G. Harding: Campaigns and Elections (millercenter.org; retrieved May 21, 2019).

Traub, James. The Ugly Election That Birthed Modern American Politics (nationalgeographic .com; November 12, 2016).

Treese, Joel D. The Japanese Mission of 1860 (whitehousehistory.org; April 23, 2015).

Trickey, Erick. How Woodrow Wilson's War Speech to Congress Changed Him – and the Nation (Smithsonian.com; April 3, 2017).

Trickey, Erick. The Brief Period, 200 Years Ago, When American Politics Was Full of "Good Feelings" (smithsonian.com; July 17, 2017).

Trickey, Erick. When America's Most Prominent Socialist Was Jailed for Speaking Out Against World War I (Smithsonian.com; June 15, 2018).

Wall, Mike. Voting from Space: How Astronauts Do It (space.com; November 8, 2016).

Walsh, Kenneth T. Party Like It's 1976 (*U.S. News and World Report*; May 16, 2016).

Waxman, Olivia M. The True Story Behind The Front Runner: How Gary Hart's Scandal Changed Politics (time.com; November 7, 2018).

Weidinger, Patrick. 10 People Whose warnings Went Unheeded (Listverse; February 9, 2012).

Weigel, David. When Ronald Reagan Blew a Presidential Debate and Dropped Seven Points in the Polls (slate.com; October 10, 2012).

Weiner, Rachel. Chris Christie: Obama 'outstanding' in response to Hurricane Sandy (*Washington Post*; October 30, 2012).

Whipple, Chris. Ted Kennedy: The Day the Presidency Was Lost (abc news; August 31, 2009).

Whiteman, Tom. White Mountain Chronicles: Grover Cleveland and his ties to Tamworth (*Conway Daily Sun*; July 13, 2018).

Whitney, Gleaves. "Modern Campaigning Origins" (Ask Gleaves; 2004).

Wilford, John Noble. How Epidemics Helped Shape the Modern Metropolis (*New York Times*; April 15, 2008).

Willis, Ann. Barack Obama calls Mitt Romney 'George' in latest election gaffe (*UK Telegraph*; June 5, 2012).

Wilson, Charles Morrow. Lamplight Inauguration (*American Heritage*; December 1963).

Wilson, Gaye. "Jefferson's Big Deal: The Louisiana Purchase"" (*Monticello Newsletter*, 14; Spring 2003).

Wilson, Sara. The McKinley Assassination (shapnell.org; September 6, 2012).

Witcover, Jules. Lincoln's vice-presidential switch changed history (*Chicago Tribune*; November 16, 2014).

Woolley, John and Peters, Gerhard. 1876 (The American Presidency Project; 1999).

Yockelson, Mitchell. The United States Armed Forces and the Mexican Punitive Expedition: Part 1 (*Prologue Magazine*; Fall 1997, Vol. 29, No. 3).

Young, Patrick. President Grant's Atonement to America's Jews For His "Infamous Order" Expelling Them (*Long Island Winds*; October 12, 2016).

Zapesochny, Robert. James Polk: The Last President Who Kept His Promises (spectator.com; September 21, 2016).

Zeitz, Josh. The Death of the Three-Time Candidate (politico.com; February 8, 2015).

Zezima, Katie. How Teddy Roosevelt helped save football (*Washington Post*; May 29, 2014).

Zimmerman, Dwight Jon. MacArthur For President (defensemedianetwork.com; September 18, 2013).

BOOKS

Abbott, W.W. *The Papers of George Washington* (University of Virginia Press; 1987).

Ackerman, Kenneth D. *Dark Horse: The Surprise Election and Political Murder of President James A. Garfield* (Viral History Press; 2011).

Adams, John. *The Portable John Adams* (Penguin Classics; 2004).

Alego, Matthew. *The President Is a Sick Man* (Chicago Review Press; 2012).

Bailey, Ronald H. *The Bloodiest Day: The Battle of Antietam* (Time-Life Books; 1984).

Beal, Richard. *Highway 17: The Road to Santa Cruz* (Pacific Group; 1990).

Bendat, Jim. *Democracy's Big Day: The Inauguration of Our President, 1789-2013* (iUniverse; 2012).

Bimber, Bruce. *Information and American Democracy: Technology in the Evolution of Political Power* (Cambridge University Press; 2009).

Bishop, Jim. *The Day Lincon was Sho*t (Harper Perennial; 2013).

Blumenthal, Karen. *Hillary Rodham Clinton: A Woman Living History* (Square Fish; 2017).

Bly, Nellie. *The Kennedy Men: Three Generations of Sex, Scandal, and Secrets* (Kensington; 1996).

Boller, Paul F. *Franklin D. Roosevelt. Presidential Anecdotes* (Oxford UP; 1981).

———. *Presidential Diversions: Presidents at Play from George Washington to George W. Bush* (Harcourt; 2007).

Bonner, Kit and Carolyn. *USS Iowa at War* (Zenith Press; 2007).

Borneman, Walter R. *Polk: The Man Who Transformed the Presidency and America* (Random House Books; 2008).

Borzo, Henry. *Imperialism in the Election of 1900 in the United States* (luc.edu: 1947).

Bourland, Gary. *The Worst President--The Story of James Buchanan* (iUniverse; 2015).

Campbell, Ballard C. *Disasters, Accidents, and Crises in American History: A Reference Guide to the Nation's Most Catastrophic Events* (Facts On File; 2008).

Carols, Robert A. *The Path To Power* (Alfred A. Knopf; 1982).

Chace, James. *1912: Wilson, Roosevelt, Taft & Debs-- the Election that Changed the Country* (Simon & Schuster; 2005).

Chernow, Ron. *Grant* (Penguin Press; 2017).

Collins, Gail. *William Henry Harrison: The American Presidents Series: The 9th President,1841* (Times Books; 2012).

Cook, Blanche Wiesen. E*leanor Roosevelt, Vol. 2: 1933–1938* (Viking; 1999).

Crapol, Edward P. *John Tyler, the Accidental President* (The University of North Carolina Press; 2012).

Davis, Michael A. *Politics as Usual: Franklin Roosevelt, Thomas Dewey and the Wartime Presidential Campaign of 1944* (University of Arkansas; December 2005).

Edwards, Lee. *Goldwater: the man who made a revolution* (Regnery Publishing; 1995).

Eisenhower, John S. D. *Zachary Taylor. The American Presidents series* (Times Books Macmillan; 2008).

Elliot, Michael A. *Custerology: The Enduring Legacy of the Indian Wars and George Armstrong Custer* (University of Chicago Press; 2007).

Fitrakis, Bob, Wasserman, Harvey, and Rosenfeld, Steve. *Did George W. Bush Steal America's 2004 Election?: Essential Documents* (CICJ Books; 2005).

Frémont, John C., Mary Lee Spence, Donald Jackson, eds. *The Expeditions of John Charles Frémont The Bear Flag Revolt and the Court-Martial* (Univeristy of Illinois; 1973).

Frum, David. *How We Got Here: The '70s* (Basic Books; 2000).

Geraghty, Timothy J. *Peacekeepers at War: Beirut 1983 – The Marine Commander Tells His Story* (Potomac Books; 2009).

Gin, Willie. *Minorities and Reconstructive Coalitions: The Catholic Question* (Taylor & Francis; 2017).

Gienapp, William E. *The Origins of the Republican Party 1852-1856* (Oxford UP; 1987).

Goldman, Robert Morris and Andrew. *The National Party Chairmen and Committees: Factionalism at the Top* (Routledge; 1990).

Goldzwig, Steven R. *Truman's Whistle Stop Campaign* (Texas A&M University Press; 2008).

Greenberg, David. *Calvin Coolidge* (Times Books; 2006).

Gunther, John. *Roosevelt in Retrospect* (Harper & Brothers; 1950).

Hamilton, Neil A. *Presidents: A Biographical Dictionary* (Checkmark Books; 2010).

Hayes, Rutherford B. *The Diary and Letters of Rutherford B. Hayes, Nineteenth President of the United States* (Ohio State Archeological and Historical Society; 1922).

Heidenrich, Chris. *Frederick: Local and National Crossroads* (Arcadia Publishing; 2003).

Hendricks, Nancy. *America's First Ladies: A Historical Encyclopedia and Primary Document Collection of the Remarkable Women of the White House* (ABC-CLIO; 2015).

Hersh, Seymour. *The Dark Side of Camelot* (Little, Brown; 1997).

Hirschfeld, Fritz. *George Washington and Slavery: A Documentary Portrayal* (University of Missouri; 1997).

Holt, Michael F. *By One Vote: The Disputed Presidential Election of 1876* (American Presidential Elections) (University Press of Kansas; 2008).

Holzer, Harold. *The President Is Shot! The Assassination of Abraham Lincoln* (Calkins Creek; 2004).

Hoogenboom, Ari. *Rutherford B. Hayes: Warrior and President* (University Press of Kansas; 1995).

Ingersoll, Charles Jared. *Historical Sketch of the Second War Between the United States of America, and Great Britain, Declared by Act of Congress, the 18th of June, 1812, and Concluded by Peace, the 15th of February, 1815* (HardPress Publishing; 2014).

Ireland, John Robert MD. *The Republic* (Nabu Press; 2012).

Johns, A. Wesley. *The Man Who Shot McKinley* (A. S. Barnes;1970).

Kessler, Ronald. *The Sins of the Father* (Warner Books; 1996).

Key, V. O. *Southern Politics in State and Nation* (University of Tennessee Press; 1984).

Kimball, Warren. *Forged in War: Roosevelt, Churchill and the Second World War* (William Morrow & Co., 1997).

Krug, Larry L. *The 1924 Coolidge-Dawes Lincoln Tour* (Schiffer Publishing; 2007).

Levin, Mark. *Unfreedom of the Press* (Threshold Editions; 2019).

Lincoln, Evelyn. *My Twelve Years with John F. Kennedy* (Bantam; 1966).

Madison, James. *The Federalist No. 51* (Independent Journal; 1788).

Mahoney, Richard D. *Sons & Brothers: The Days of Jack and Bobby Kennedy* (Arcade Publishing; 1999).

Manners, William. *TR and Will: A Friendship that Split the Republican Party* (Harcourt, Brace & World, Inc.; 1969).

Martin, Gilbert. *Churchill: A Life* (Holt Paperbacks; 1992).

Martin, John Bartlow. *A Voice for the Underdog* (Indiana University Press; 2015).

Matthews, Jefferey J. "To Defeat a Maverick: the Goldwater Candidacy Revisited, 1963-1964" (*Presidential Studies Quarterly*; Vol. 27, No. 4, Fall, 1997).

May, Gary. *John Tyler* (Times Books; 2008).

McCullough, David. *John Adams* (Simon & Schuster; 2008).

McPherson, James B. *Tried by War: Abraham Lincoln as Commander in Chief* (Penguin Books; 2009).

Mofford, Juliet Haines. *Andover Massachusetts, Historical Selections from Four Centuries* (MVPP; 2004).

Moore, Chieko; Hale, Hester Anne: Benjamin Harrison. *Centennial President* (Nova Publishers; 2006).

Moroz, Harold R. *Born Again: The Year and Events that Changed America Forever! Election 2000 and September 11th* (iUniverse; 2002).

Morris, Jr., Roy. *Fraud of the Century: Rutherford B. Hayes, Samuel Tilden, and the Stolen Election of 1876* (Simon & Schuster; 2004).

Nevins, Allan. *Grover Cleveland: A Study in Courage* (Dodd, Mead & Company; 1933).

Newton, Michael. *Age of Assassins: A History of Conspiracy and Political Violence, 1865-1981* (Faber & Faber; 2012).

Nixon, Richard: *RN: The Memoirs of Richard Nixon* (Simon & Schuster; 1978).

Obama, Barack. *The Audacity of Hope* (2008; Vintage).

O'Brien, Cormac. *Secret Lives of the First Ladies* (Quirk Books; 2009).

O'Brien, Michael. *The Story of the Sun: New York, 1833-1918* (Palala Press; 2016).

O'Reilly, Bill. *Killing England* (Henry Holt and Co.; 2017).

Paglen, Trevor. *Blank Spots on the Map: The Dark Geography of the Pentagon's Secret World* (Berkley; 2010).

Parson, Lynn Hudson. *John Quincy Adams* (Rowman & Littlefield Publishers; 1999).

Pinskar, Matthew. *Lincoln's Sanctuary: Abraham Lincoln and the Soldiers'Home* (Oxford University Press; 2005).

Reitano, Joanne. *The Tariff Question in the Gilded Age: The Great Debate of 1888.* (The Pennsylvania State University; 1994).

Remini, Robert V. *Andrew Jackson: The Course of American Empire, 1767-1821*, Volume 1 (Johns Hopkins University Press; 1998).

Rice, Jo. *The Guinness Book of 500 Number One Hits* (Guinness Superlatives Ltd.; 1982).

Robinson, Edgar Eugene. *The Presidential Vote 1896-1932* (Stanford University Press; 1947).

Ross, Irwin. *The Loneliest Campaign* (New American Library; 1968).

Schumacher, Michael. *The Contest: The 1968 Election and the War for America's Soul* (University of Minnesota Press; 2018).

Shales, Amity. *Coolidge* (HarperCollins; 2013).

Sherman, John. *Recollections of Forty Years in the House, Senate and Cabinet An Autobiography* (The Werner Company; 1895).

Sherman, William T. *Sherman's Memoirs* (D. Appleton; 1889).

Smith, Jean Edward. *FDR* (Random House; 2007).

Staff Report. United States. Louisiana Purchase Exposition Commission: Final Report of the Louisiana Purchase Exposition Commission, 1906 (Echo Library; 2008).

———. *Presidential Elections, 1789-2008* (CQ Press; 2010).

———. *The Columbia Electronic Encyclopedia*, 6th ed. (Columbia University Press; 2012).

Starr, Kevin. *Golden Dreams: California in an Age of Abundance, 1950-1963* (Oxford University Press; 2011).

Stringer, Joshua. *The Greatest American Comeback: Harry S. Truman and the 1948 Election* (ir .uiowa.edu; Fall 2017).

Thurston, Clark. *The Last Campaign* (Henry Hill & Co.; 2008).

Ward, Artemus. *Deciding to Leave: The Politics of Retirement from the United States Supreme* (SUNY Press; 2003).

Wead, Doug. *All the Presidents' Children: Triumph and Tragedy in the Lives of America's First Families* (Atria Books; 2004).

Weston, Mark. *The Runner-Up Presidency* (Rowman & Littlefield; 2016).

White, Theodore H. *The Making of the President 1964* (Athenaeum Publishers; 1965).

Winkler, Allan M. *Franklin D. Roosevelt and the Making of Modern America* (Longman; 2006).

Witcover, Jules. Party of the People (Random House; 2003).

Withers, Bob. *The President Travels by Train– Politics and Pullmans* (TLC PUBLISHING; 1996).

Zirbel, Craig I. *The Final Chapter on the Assassination of John F. Kennedy Collectors Edition* (The Final Chapter LLC; 2010).

COLLECTIONS

Papers of John F. Kennedy. Pre-Presidential Papers. Senate Files. Series 12. Speeches and the Press. Box 905, Folder: Al Smith dinner, New York City, 22 October 1959.

The Eleanor Roosevelt Papers Project at George Washington University.

General Assembly: Report of the Special Committee on the Problem of Hungary (United Nations, 1957).

VIDEO

George Washington (CBS; 1984).

WEBSITES

blueandgraytrail.com
constitutionfacts.com
deadpresidents.tumblr.com/
doctorzebra.com
dyslexiahelp.umich.edu
fdrlibrary.com
history.house.gov
jfklibrary.org
loc.gov
millercenter.org
Monticello.com
montpelier.org
mountvernon.org
nih.com
presidentialcampaignselectionsreference.wordpress.com
presidentprofiles.com
RangeVoting.org
rogerjnorton.com
SwiftVets.com
thehermitage.com
tugofwar.co.uk
ushistory.org
ustornadoes.com
weather.gov
whitehousehistory.org

About the Author

For thirty-one years, **Mike Henry** taught American history to students from elementary school to college. His technique of using the events of the past to show how they impact our lives in the present made him a popular classroom instructor and guest speaker. After the inception of *No Child Left Behind*, he averaged a success rate of more than 80 percent on mandated testing where the majority of his students were at or below the poverty level.

Mike is a two-time award winner of Who's Who Among America's Classroom Teachers. Following his retirement, he wrote *Black History: More Than Just A Month*, which was published in 2012. The book has become popular among those wanting to learn more and for educators of African American history.

What They Didn't Teach You in Your American History Class was released in 2014 and nominated for the James Harvey Robinson Prize. Its sequel, *What They Didn't Teach You in Your American History Class: The Second Encounter* debuted in 2016. These works are for those who are interested in learning about the fascinating backstories that are not included in most history texts.

In 2015, Mike introduced his American History for Kids series. The first volume *Tell Me About the Presidents* was nominated for the Grateful American Book Prize. All his works are published by Rowman & Littlefield.

The follow-up effort is titled *Christmas with the Presidents*. It tells how our nation's leaders spent their holiday seasons ranging from the simple to the elaborate and even heroic. The book is a fun read for children and their parents

The writer's latest work is *That Tuesday in November*. As always, Mike's new book is filled with backstories of little known events of the people and events that are connected to the nation's most impactful presidential elections.

"True education begins with reading," said the author. "Once that takes place, learning can happen with any subject matter."

Mike and his wife, Pamela, who is also a retired educator and coeditor of his books, reside near Dallas, Texas.

www.ingramcontent.com/pod-product-compliance
Lightning Source LLC
Chambersburg PA
CBHW021815270326
41932CB00007B/190